Praise for *Can You Hear Me Now?*

"Fierce, unapologetic energy . . . r
Chavannes's] book. Whether she's reflecting on her childhood as a
Caribbean immigrant growing up in a cold, foreign country, or as
a Black woman in government, Caesar-Chavannes refuses to back
down from addressing difficult issues or calling out problematic
people. Even more so, she understands the importance of aligning
purpose with accountability and action."

—*The Tyee*

"I can hear you, C3. I found myself tearing up in parts and chuckling
in others—I heard your passionate voice, felt your determination and
smiled at your undeniable wit, all reverberating throughout the pages
of this book. Yours is an important journey. Thank you for telling it.
You are as inspiring as you are authentic."

—Jody Wilson-Raybould, Canadian MP,
and author of *Indian in the Cabinet*

"Celina's memoir is the perfect mix of coming-of-age story, radical
authenticity and #BlackGirlMagic. Never has a former Canadian
politician stripped down and shown up in such an honest way. If
you can't hear Celina by the time you've finished this book you need
to get your hearing checked."

—Tracy Moore, host of *Cityline*

"Though you can learn from lost voices, you can learn more from
those who have found their voices. Celina found hers."

—Tanya Tagaq, Polaris Prize–winning singer
and artist, and author of *Split Tooth*

"*Can You Hear Me Now?* took me on a roller coaster of emotions that pale in comparison to all the tragedies and triumphs that Celina has endured. As a Black mother, a Black woman in Canadian society, I have never resonated with a story more. Like Celina, I have often been the chocolate chip in the cookie, but you do not need to be of a certain race or gender to hear Celina loud and clear—which she absolutely deserves at long last."

—Tanya Hayles, founder of Black Moms Connection and anti-Black racism consultant

"Celina tells her story with the kind of whole-hearted and bare-faced honesty you don't see in the 'typical' autobiography. Which makes sense, because for Celina there's no such thing as 'typical.' And that's what makes her book so refreshing, and delightfully fun and inspiring. Facing her failures (and her critics), Celina takes ownership of her journey—from self-made successful entrepreneur to social justice trailblazer."

—Kirstine Stewart, author of *Our Turn*, and Head of Shaping the Future of Media at the World Economic Forum

"Folks looking to learn about the power of raising your voice can go right from the source, thanks to Caesar-Chavannes' new book, *Can You Hear Me Now? . . .* Inspiring."

—*The Peterborough Examiner*

"Like her public service, Caesar-Chavannes' memoir is a work of authenticity."

—*The McGill Tribune*

"Caesar-Chavannes writes in a direct, conversational style. The fast-paced memoir is a fresh read, timely and speaks to the issues of racism and sexism that confront us right now."

—*New Hamburg Independent*

CAN YOU HEAR ME NOW?

**How I Found My Voice and Learned
to Live with Passion and Purpose**

Celina Caesar-Chavannes

VINTAGE CANADA

Published by Vintage Canada, a division of Penguin Random House Canada Limited, Toronto, in 2022. Originally published in Canada in hardcover by Random House Canada, a division of Penguin Random House Canada Limited, Toronto, in 2021. Distributed in Canada and the United States of America by Penguin Random House Canada Limited, Toronto.

Vintage Canada and colophon are registered trademarks.

www.penguinrandomhouse.ca

LIBRARY AND ARCHIVES CANADA CATALOGUING IN PUBLICATION

Title: Can you hear me now? : how I found my voice and learned to live with passion and
    purpose / Celina Caesar-Chavannes.
Names: Caesar-Chavannes, Celina, 1974- author.
Identifiers: Canadiana 20200252577 | ISBN 9780735279612 (softcover)
Subjects: LCSH: Caesar-Chavannes, Celina, 1974- | LCSH: Businesspeople—Canada—
    Biography. | LCSH: Politicians—Canada—Biography. | LCSH: Leadership. |
    LCGFT: Autobiographies.
Classification: LCC HC112.5.C24 A3 2022 | DDC 338.092—dc23

Cover: Talia Abramson, based on a design by Leah Springate
Cover photo and concept: Candice Rayne Chavannes
Text design: Leah Springate

Printed in the United States of America

2 4 6 8 9 7 5 3 1

Penguin
Random House
VINTAGE CANADA

To my mother, O'Dessa Caesar.
The iron that sharpened me

To my children, Desiray, Candice and Vidal John.
The inspiration and hope in my voice

To my husband, Vidal Alexander Chavannes.
The rock that steadies my disruption

CONTENTS

INTRODUCTION

EVERY TIME I WAKE up on my own, and not to the annoying sound of my alarm, I am amazed. I am not a morning person. Pre-noon daylight has an irritating hue I cannot stand, especially during the winter, when the sun shines sharpest and brightest on the coldest days.

On the morning of Thursday, March 21, 2019, I opened my eyes to that aggravating light shining through the window of my twenty-sixth-floor condo in Ottawa, and wondered if I'd slept through the alarm. I could have checked the time on my phone, but that required energy I did not have. I blinked, and tiny black particles of day-old mascara fell into my eyes. I rubbed them, which only made the situation worse. I sighed. Here I was, conscious before I had to be, dealing with 24-hour mascara dust and the same incredible headache I'd gone to bed with the night before.

The headache was from the stress generated the previous day over revealing my new-found freedom from the Canadian political party system. The day—the first in my career as an Independent member of Parliament and not as a part of the Liberal caucus—had been long and hard. I felt like an empty tube of toothpaste someone had tried to squeeze one last time.

And then my cell phone began to buzz, message after message reminding me of the previous day's events and promising a difficult time ahead. I ignored them, rolled out of bed and went over to look out the window. The neighbouring rooftops had no signs of snow and neither did the streets. That was a good thing: any hint of white on the rooftops or the roadways completely threw off my shoe game, forcing me to wear an oversized pair of Sorels I'd inherited from my eldest daughter, who no longer wanted to be seen in them. Today, I could wear a pair of heeled boots. My moment of fashion satisfaction was interrupted by more buzzing from the phone. For heaven's sake! It didn't stop. Remember the days when in order to communicate with someone, you had to find a piece of paper, locate a pen or pencil, write the letter, find an envelope, figure out the address, paste on a stamp and walk to the mailbox? I longed for those days.

But there was no getting away from it: everyone I knew—and lots of people I didn't—had strong opinions about my decision to leave the Liberals after several tense weeks of confrontation with Prime Minister Justin Trudeau. And with social media and my public presence as an MP, all of them knew how to reach me to express those opinions directly. What they didn't know was that it wasn't just my issues with the prime minister that had brought me to this point.

I'd been swept out of my quiet life—running a business and raising my family in Whitby, Ontario—by the tornado of an election, and dropped in Ottawa. An Oz, for sure, but in shades of grey. Unlike many of my colleagues, I had never dreamed about being a politician, had never even taken a political science course or been interested in more than the headlines, and had never done the school trip to our nation's capital. The first time I entered the House of Commons was when I started my job as a member of Parliament. I thought business and research were my things, and that philanthropy was the way I'd give back to society. I had zero political aspirations.

But then Jim Flaherty, the finance minister in Stephen Harper's Conservative government, died suddenly on April 10, 2014, just after he had stepped down to spend more time with his family. A by-election was called in his riding, which was my riding. I found myself running (more on how that came about later). I lost that contest to the former mayor of Whitby: not surprising given that the mayor had name recognition in the community and I did not; that I was a Black woman running in a constituency that was 70 percent white and had never voted in a Black candidate; and that hardly anyone could remember the last time Whitby had voted Liberal.

But I didn't lose by much, and I really don't like to lose—a powerful motivator. When the next general election came around, in 2015, I ran again. This time I found even more support on the doorsteps of my riding. People—and not only Liberals—were looking for a fresh perspective on politics and found it in me: not only a Black woman from an immigrant background who had built her own company from scratch and had the business acumen Conservative voters believed they could trust, but also a person who embodied the values of diversity and inclusion that the times demanded, and that Trudeau's Liberal Party was featuring in its campaign.

This time I won. A fairy tale, right?

So why walk away from the party only four years after that victory to sit as an Independent? That was what all the people buzzing my phone wanted to know: my constituents, who liked the way I'd been representing the riding, and were disappointed that I wasn't a Liberal anymore; Black leaders, who thought now that I had a seat at the table I should learn how to compromise in order to keep it, and that I was letting the community down by not playing the game; other politicians who didn't want to lose an ally; and party functionaries who wanted to berate me for what they saw as me piling on against a leader who was already in hot water over the SNC-Lavalin affair and the way he had treated two female ministers who stood up to him. The feminist PM with a female problem.

I had my own point to make and different battles to fight. Something unexpected had happened to me in Ottawa. I would say that I had arrived on Parliament Hill ready to play for the Liberal team. I had encountered many cynical voters who predicted that as soon as I faced my first challenge as an MP, I would become just another politician. I promised them that I would not. I'd spoken with others who believed in me, but who thought that the old elite ways were so entrenched I had no hope of changing anything. I'd also met voters who wanted me to live up to our campaign promise that we would do politics differently, who hoped I would remain the authentic Celina they'd voted for, who wanted me to challenge the old ways in which our country was run. I promised them that I would strive to bend the status quo, that I would bring change. There were a lot of promises to keep, and I'd intended to keep every one.

During my first months as a politician I was so fresh to it all it was like I was up at 30,000 feet staring down at the whole strange landscape, at the same time as I was struggling to take a few steps on the ground towards the aims I felt I was elected to achieve. It seemed to me that most of the people here were not interested in doing politics differently; they just said they were. Was I naïve? Perhaps. But I could also see what wasn't working in Ottawa even on the human resources level: we MPs were like a bunch of CEOs suddenly being ordered around by junior staffers empowered by the PMO and the ministers' offices to manage us. In effect, that layer of staff—Keith Beardsley, an advisor to Stephen Harper, had nicknamed them the "boys in short pants" (though some of them were women)—were bossing around members of Parliament and making profound decisions about policy that affected our country with no regard to what MPs could actually contribute. Some prime ministers are brilliant caucus leaders, building consensus on the issues where they want to make change; others lead by fear. Our leader always said that he wanted to engage with all caucus members, but even in the last year of his first term, there were some that had never met with him. In my opinion he was hiding behind the impenetrable shield of his principal secretaries, each of them smart people, but none of them responsible to a constituency themselves. To some degree, he was engaging more with international media than he was with his own caucus on critical issues.

But this isn't about the failings of one prime minister. This is about how going into politics made me understand the true meaning of the phrase "we have to do politics differently." Before I got to Ottawa I was well aware of the colour of my skin, and my gender, and the obstacles both raised, but I treated it all like a set of problems I could solve by basically outsmarting or outplaying those around me. Mostly I'd found that I could cut my cloth to whatever the circumstances required; witness my success in business and the fact that I was elected in the first place.

But I'd been running so hard for my whole life, I'd never taken time to truly reflect on what I was put on earth for. I was a wife, a mother of three, a successful business owner, but the first time I had ever lived alone, with time to think, was after I moved to Ottawa. This twenty-sixth-floor condo was the first place where I could close the door and be beholden only to myself. And what that led to, combined with what I was encountering in my work as an MP— having taken on responsibility for changing our public life so that it would apply to and represent everyone—was an awakening that was as powerful as it was painful.

It's not just politics we have to do differently, I realized. We have to do everything differently. If people like me keep trying to fit into spaces like the House of Commons, which run according to a narrative of power and privilege designed to exclude us, how can we expect those spaces to change? We need politics to be different, but the powers-that-be keep fiddling round the edges, not attacking the structure itself, which was designed to reinforce the status quo. We want our communities to be friendly and welcoming to all, but fear causes us to put up bigger fences. We want diversity, but we don't want inclusion, which requires us to move out of our comfort zones towards equity. We want to check the right boxes, but we're scared to do the work that would mean that change becomes real.

In Ottawa, I stood out so starkly I started to crack. Still, I had every opportunity to play it safe—I had the respect of most of my Liberal colleagues, and even of members across the aisle, one of whom told me early on that I should enjoy my freedom while I could because it wouldn't be long before I became a minister. Yet I chose to speak up about mental health, including my own, and about racism and equity. Paradoxically, rather than losing myself, I found my voice, my authentic self, in the House of Commons and in the give and take of serving my riding as an MP. So when I realized that the party I belonged to said they valued my unique voice and perspective, but did not want to actually listen to me, what was I supposed to do? What's the point of finding your voice, if it is muzzled because the simple truth of your message makes others uncomfortable?

Most importantly, I realized that my political journey did not start in 2014, when I first decided to put my name on a ballot. It started when a skinny little two-year-old girl from the island of Grenada in the Caribbean ended up in Canada. Although this journey felt like a roller coaster, electoral politics was only a small part of it—a scary part, sure, but I had been through scarier stuff and survived.

In Ottawa, I found the courage to stand up for myself and others, and, because of what I'd learned in the years before I got there, I realized that it was desperately important to maintain that integrity and my authentic self—so hard to do in a place that was not designed for me. It became clear to me that it was absolutely imperative that I resist the temptation to settle down and shut up, and abandon my new-found sense of purpose. In those four years in Ottawa, I found parts of me I thought were permanently lost or buried too deep to ever see the light again. I used my time in Ottawa to speak up for people who were not often heard in the House of Commons, which was a good thing, but I could not see how my efforts inside that place would lead to the kind of change we need.

Yes, I'd spent a whole day crying over my decision to walk away—I hate to let people down, and I knew that so many I respected would believe I had done just that. But I could not see how to reconcile the demands of party politics with the awakening I'd undergone. I had to leave. Sometimes the most powerful action you can take is to refuse to remain a part of the machine that is keeping you down. For a bold Black woman to keep hammering away on the political machine from the inside only enabled the people running it to say, "Yes, we can hear you hammering! Don't worry, we'll take all your concerns into account in the fullness of time."

That did not sit well with me. After all, we were supposed to be doing government differently. That is what I signed up for—to be bold, transformative and deliberate. We are running out of time to make important and necessary changes, not only in politics, but in every aspect of ourselves as human beings. I didn't know that before I got to Ottawa. But I know it now.

one

BOLD AT BIRTH

BEING BORN A GIRL, in any part of the world, has its challenges. Being born a girl of colour or a Black girl comes with an extra set of obstacles. Whether it is lack of access to education, sexualization, subjugation, trauma and violence, we face barriers no young person needs to face. I was no exception.

I was born on Monday, June 24, 1974, in the little island nation of Grenada in the Caribbean.

My first heartbreak came at six months old, when my parents and older brother, Roger, left me behind when they emigrated to Canada. I would not see them again until I was almost two years old.

It was not uncommon for Caribbean children to be left "back home" while their parents travelled abroad in search of a better life. My mom and dad didn't intend to leave me, but their visas, along with the one for my brother, came through first, and they couldn't wait for me. I was only a baby, after all, and surely I wouldn't miss them all that much—I probably wouldn't even remember. But I can't help thinking about how my relationship with my parents would have been different if I'd been on the plane with them. I think about my own children, and what it would have been like if I hadn't been there to see their first steps, soothe their cries or change their diapers.

The pain of such a rift would not fall only on the child or the parents, but on them all.

Something was lost in my relationship with my parents during those first couple of years and I have felt that loss for most of my life. But I had the blessing of staying with my paternal grandparents and my aunt Bernadette; that they loved me was a fact I never doubted. I would later come to model myself after Veronica Caesar, my grandmother. I didn't call her by any sweet name like Nana or even the more formal Grandmother—terms that should be reserved for women who smile at the whimsical things their grandchildren do, give them extra-squishy hugs or sneak them candy before dinner, because spoiling a child is more important than spoiling her dinner. I called my grandmother Mrs. Caesar. And Mrs. Caesar did not do any of those things. She was a fierce and formidable woman who was a pillar in her community and in her family. If she loved you, you knew it. If she didn't, you did not want to know it.

The Caesars were farmers, growing nutmeg, fruit and vegetables, and raising pigs and chickens, not only to feed their family of twelve children but to make a living. My father tells stories of Mrs. Caesar negotiating with the owners of the new resort hotels that were being built in Grenada in the sixties to guarantee they bought their local produce from her and paid her top dollar for it too. My father's job as a young man was to drive her around and to deliver the produce. It was a job he loved. He had the use of the truck and his mother paid him in cash, which meant he could take my mom, a country girl from farther up in the hills, on dates.

Mrs. Caesar was an entrepreneur you did not want to mess around with; the size of her success was reflected in the home the family built. The Caesar compound was surrounded by a pink concrete wall that contained a two-storey house with multiple bedrooms, a main living room, dining room and sitting area. To the side of it was a separate building that housed the kitchen with an eat-in breakfast area, all very modern for the Grenada of the period. The walled yard was big enough to hold a chicken coop and a pigpen, and enough territory to make for epic games of hide-and-seek. Mrs. Caesar was unapologetic and unafraid; a wife, mother, grandmother, businesswoman, community leader and friend. She was everything I wanted to be when I grew up.

When it was time for me to leave for Toronto, where my parents had settled, my grandfather travelled with me to New York City, where my aunt was getting married. He handed me over to my parents, who met us at the wedding; I can only imagine how strange that whole situation must have been. There was no way I would have remembered them.

According to my Canadian immigration identification record, they brought me into Canada via Lewiston, New York, on January 4, 1976. I stare at that word "January" and wonder what my toddler self made of a grey Toronto winter, having lived for all my days in a tropical paradise surrounded by a pink wall.

My first Canadian home was an apartment on Martin Grove Road in Rexdale, an area just north of the city of Toronto. I have vague memories of using a plastic place mat from our dining room table as a makeshift toboggan and sliding down the snow-covered hills nearby. So I must have found some excitement in the snow.

Most of the people in the building were immigrants, but I didn't really register that at the time. I just remember the place felt dim, dark and small after the bright world I was used to. My initial portal into the big country of Canada was underwhelming and unfriendly. Surely I didn't belong here. It strikes me now that when I first walked into the Parliament buildings almost forty years later, I felt the same sense of dislocation as I had as a little child in Rexdale—a grey unbelonging.

My parents, who were working long and hard at their jobs, soon had enough money to move us to a townhouse complex on Silverstone Drive, still in Rexdale, but with a courtyard where the neighbourhood children played. It was there I learned that a Caribbean family's unwritten rules were very different from the rules for the other families around us. First, we rarely ate out, despite having a KFC around the corner. Second, other than a few good friends and family, we had few visitors. If the doorbell rang, my brother and I were told never to answer it. Third, we were to call every person old enough to be our parents Mr. or Mrs. So-and-So; close family friends were "Aunty" or "Uncle." You were never to address an elder by their first name. Ever. It was forbidden. I am still afraid to do it as an adult. Fourth, family parties usually lasted all night, and sometimes got messy. Finally, our house was not governed by Canadian laws. Which meant that inside our walls corporal punishment was completely acceptable and handed out on a regular basis. In my opinion, I got my unfair share.

All these rules felt even more stark since I had been taken from the only people I knew and delivered to a foreign place where I was under the thumb of a stern mother, who expected me to behave like a proper little Caribbean girl.

I wanted to please her, but I also wanted to fit into the complex's courtyard culture. A neighbour boy named Robert and my brother, Roger, were the cool kids, though Robert was the troublemaker of the two. Whether it was swinging a bat in a courtyard baseball game and knocking the catcher, Roger, out cold, or kissing me during a game of kissing tag (my father witnessed the whole thing from our kitchen window and my butt paid for that kiss later), Robert was the guy whom trouble followed. I wanted to be just like him.

When my brother was teasing me one day, I responded by telling him that he "sucked the bag"—yep, a Robert phrase. Roger never swore, and he could not tell on me to my parents fast enough. My backside paid the price. Yet a simple beating could not stop me. The rule about ladies needing to act like ladies was so stuffy and boring. I loved swearing. Saying bad words gave me power over those around me. Nobody in my house swore as well as I did; by the time I started kindergarten I knew all the words. I'd seen how Robert's cursing and wayward ways made him stand out. He was never the catcher, standing behind someone else in the game. He was always the centre of attention. I had gone from being the centre of attention with my aunt and grandparents in Grenada, to being the little sister, the one who had been left behind, an afterthought, and that was not cool. Swearing, kissing the boys and acting out was a way to get my parents' attention, and it seemed like I did not care whether that attention came in the form of a whipping.

A precocious child, I would often be caught standing at the top of the stairs, fully naked, belting out a Rod Stewart song: "If you want my body and you think I'm sexy, come on sugar let me know." Let me tell you, if that is your theme song at four or five years old, it is going to get worse before it gets better. It did not matter the situation, I felt the gravitational pull of standing out and being different, which never suited my parents' vision of me as a young girl, who was to be seen, just enough, and heard, just a little. That just wasn't me. It wasn't bold enough.

"Who left this toy on the floor in the middle of the basement hall?"

My mother was asking the question, and I was certain the perpetrator was me, but I could not think fast enough to ward off trouble. I kept my distance, hoping a clever response would come to me. It didn't. My mother pulled me towards her, and as she did I slipped on the mess made by the leak from the now-warm Snoopy Sno-cone Machine, which had spread over the floor. Face planted onto the floor, I noticed that the red liquid leaving my body was mixing with the water from the icemaker, and I did not like it.

I felt myself being lifted. The large hand that covered the path by which the liquid was escaping from my forehead partially covered my eyes too, so I was only able to see some of the red drops adding colour to the linoleum tile. I was carried towards the sink and a tap whooshed on, and more red, mixed with even more water, swirled down the drain.

Darkness.

I woke to cold air hitting my skin and the night sky pierced by street lights flashing by. I was going somewhere. Where?

Darkness.

"It's okay, little girl, we are going to fix you up in no time," someone said as he spread a white sheet over my face, leaving a gap for my forehead. I did not recognize the voice or see who the person was before my face was covered. My eyes darted up to try to see through the small opening. The room was very bright, and I was very scared.

"That fall down the stairs left you with a nasty gash," the voice said.

What? I did not fall down the stairs. Who was this person and what was he talking about? I was about to come up with an elaborate story about why the Snoopy toy had been left lying around, but it seems someone else had told a story about why I had leaked red all over the floor and down the drain. I knew better than to speak up and correct this person, who sounded like an adult, so I stayed quiet.

"I am going to put a needle into your forehead to freeze the area and then we are going to stitch it up. You won't feel a thing."

I saw the needle descend towards my face, felt the point enter my forehead and started screaming and I did not stop until it was dark again.

The scar on my forehead, in the shape of a backwards seven, never went away. Neither did my questions about the story of the stairs.

Why didn't anyone ask *me* what happened? Clearly, I was there. But no one ever did ask and the story that I had fallen down the stairs stuck. Eventually I did not even try to correct it. The lie was the truth, and there was no point in challenging it. Still, I was smart enough to note that it was not true to myself, at least every time the subject came up. I was also smart enough to learn how lies could rewrite bad stuff, and that was all I needed to know.

If stories were to be told, it seemed to me, then Black people were the best at doing it. The good, bad and ugly of our history have been captured and transformed by the griots of generations past and the great orators of our present. As an observant child, I watched and listened to everything. I paid attention to words, even ones that I did not understand, especially ones I knew were not true. I studied how bodies moved and hands swayed. I felt like I spent most of my childhood silently watching the story of the lives around me unfold. And although I knew the stories I overheard were not intended for my eyes or ears, I could make myself invisible so as not to miss anything. If stories were being told, and more importantly changed, I wanted to know why.

It took me a long time to understand the story about who was rich and who was poor and what was meant by those terms in this new country. For me, coming from Grenada to Canada had meant more of an adjustment to temperature and the loss of a carefree life than anything measured in dollars and cents. I did not know if my parents had much money, but I did know that they did not like how they were earning it.

I remember my father sitting at the small kitchen table of our Silverstone townhouse with his head in his hands. It was almost as if I was watching from the ceiling, because I never would have got close enough to overhear that particular "adult" conversation. But

I remember the terrible strain on my father's face one night after he got home. Whatever had happened at work that day was so unsettling to him it had followed him home like a haunt. I was scared, but I did not know what about the situation made me feel that way. I understood that he did not like the job he was doing and that the way someone had spoken to him, the words they used, had bothered him terribly and made him look grey and emaciated.

I did not want whatever was happening to him to happen to me. I did not want someone else to use words that made me feel small or inferior. It would be years before I understood that the "haunt" around my dad was racism, and that it was a part of the Canadian experience for Black people. Was racism one of the reasons why the story about my fall was changed at the hospital? What would have happened if the truth were told? Would the haunt have taken me away?

That evening after my dad came home looking so grim, I watched my parents come up with a plan to start a trucking company so that they did not have to work where the haunt was. It was as if the spirit of Mrs. Caesar had been transported to my new life in Canada, and I was happy for it. The haunt did not destroy us; we changed the story to make it better. That is the complexity of the immigrant experience. Some of the stories that need to come to light in order to save us stay hidden. Others are revealed. I kept track of them all, for a long time unsure as to which was which.

When one day, in kindergarten, I decided to walk home from school by myself, I am sure my parents felt that they should have left me in Grenada forever. When they asked me later why I did it, I told them that I had studied the bus route and decided that the bus driver should be dropping me at home first, instead of leaving me for last. I hated being last. I figured it would be much faster if I walked home from school straight along John Garland Boulevard. I remember being surprised when I got to Finch Avenue West, because I did not recall Finch being so busy and wide. Still, I managed to make it safely across.

As I came up the path to the townhouse complex, I was shocked to see a crowd gathered outside my door. Sure, the walk had taken a lot longer than I imagined, and yes, taking the bus was probably faster, but what was all the commotion? My butt was praying louder than I was, hoping that the fuss was not related to me. The glares of my parents eliminated that hope. My backside needed to learn to pray better or find another person to be attached to.

To my parents, I may have been trouble, but at least I was smart. Definitely smarter than Roger, who avoided swearing or any form of real rebellion, but could not bring home the grades his little sister could. This sounds mean to my ears now, but at the time I felt I was in a struggle for survival and if I could do something that Roger couldn't, that was my competitive advantage. He wouldn't swear so I would; he didn't do well in school so I would always be at the top of my class. Also, every time I showed off my smartness, my mother (who, I understood much later, had had big academic dreams for herself) would shower me with praise.

In elementary school, I was top of my class in every subject. By third grade, we had moved to a semi-detached five-split house on Abell Drive in Brampton. My dad's trucking company must have been doing well. I loved that house, so much so that I live in a five-split now. The neighbourhood was full of children, and my best friend, Beverly, lived right across the road. There were afternoon dodgeball games, bike rides and walks to Bruce Beer Park, which was right behind our house.

My maternal grandmother, Ena Ella Wilson, who we called Gramsie, had come from Grenada to live with us and help take care of my little brother, Ryan. Although she was stern, she seemed to have a special soft spot for each of her grandchildren; when I got in trouble and suffered the consequences, she would tend to my wounds with all sorts of homemade remedies and special concoctions. Every one of her bush teas and healing creams worked; I wish now that I'd been clever enough to write down the recipes for some of them. As a child I dismissed a lot of her knowledge because she had no formal education. But she was our griot and her stories recalled our history. I wish that I hadn't taken her wisdom for granted.

The walk to school was terrible in the winters. I truly hated the cold (and have never gotten used to it). But the challenge of the cold did not compare with the challenge of my first true academic nemesis, a boy named Alex, who briefly ascended to the apex of our teacher's Pyramid of Champions when he beat me in the speed round of times tables. When I saw that I'd been bumped to the spot below his, right beside the third-place person, I went home bawling as if I had lost my favourite toy. Although I cannot fully remember what my mother said after I explained the situation, I am sure it was something like, "Well, if you want Alex to beat you, you will let him beat you." I truly hated that passive-aggressive shit. Why couldn't she say something like, "It's okay, dear. You will come first next time for sure." Or, "That boy has nothing on you." A hug would have been acceptable too.

But no, I got one of my mother's first lessons in independence. Only you can control what happens to you. If Alex came first, only you made that happen. Alex beating me was an opportunity to do things differently—to fight for what I wanted. She never said those last words out loud, and at the time I'm sure I didn't understand what she was trying to teach me. But by third grade my tough mother had given me enough life lessons to hand Alex's ass to him at least twice before lunch recess.

She was hard on me. And I feared her, while she feared for me. I believe now that she treated me the way she thought the world would eventually treat me, in order to prepare me for it. In her mind, maybe she was trying to protect me. In that moment, though, I was furious. I was tired of her beatings and life lessons, and mocked her in my head: "Well, if you want AAAAlllleeexxx to beat you . . ." I knew better than to mock my mother out loud or to cry or stomp away in a huff. Any or all of those reactions would have had me swiftly at the tail end of a belt, and I was more interested in beating Alex than getting a beating from my mother.

For the rest of the term, I redoubled my studies of the times tables, and every other subject, in order to be better and faster than the other children. There was no way that Alex (or anyone else, including my brothers) would ever beat me again. And for all of grade school no one ever did. I am not sure that I was ever obsessed with learning for its own sake, but I was obsessed with placing first in my classes. If academic excellence was the only thing that made my parents proud of me, I was going to do what I had to do to achieve it.

But I also couldn't stop getting into trouble. I was constantly rebellious, though I only acted on it when I was out of earshot of my mother and I was truly frightened when I was caught. I was obviously still pissed that I had been left behind, and I also thought it was unfair that I was held to different standards of behaviour than my brothers, not only by my parents, but by society. Boys got to play by different rules. I did not really know why I was the way I was, and my parents weren't bringing me to any therapy sessions so I could find out. All I know is, I had as much of an affinity for times tables as I had for time outs, and I explored both with vigour.

In sixth grade, my friend Heather and I came up with a plan to go to the Becker's convenience store across the road from our school and steal some candy. I do not understand why I thought this was a good idea. I was the dumbest smart kid I knew. It did not take long for me to get caught with candy in my pocket and no money to pay for it. The owner called the school and the administration called my parents. I knew a beating was coming when my parents got home.

To my surprise, they walked in carrying bags of candy bars. They only bought us candy on the rarest of occasions, so I thought this was great. Maybe they had finally caught on to the Canadian way of disciplining children.

Soon they called me to the dining room where they had placed the bags of candy on the table. My mother asked me if I thought we could not afford candy and if I thought stealing it was okay. I responded no, clearly and audibly, to both questions because I knew she hated it when I mumbled. There was no belt in sight, and I was not going to risk aggravating her so that she got it out.

Next she asked me if I liked candy. Still clueless to her intentions, I eagerly answered yes.

All right, she said, you go ahead and eat every single candy bar on the table. For clarification, she and my father had brought home as many as ten bags of Halloween-sized Snickers bars. Twenty to thirty candy bars times ten bags equals a lot of candy. Suddenly, I wanted a beating instead. Were these people crazy? If this was Canadian discipline, I did not want it.

I ate candy until I almost threw up. My mother sat and watched, making sure I swallowed. When I tried to pretend a bag was empty, scrunching it so it looked like all the bars were gone, she reached out and carefully flattened the bag. Eff! How did she know? Then she ever so graciously picked out the one or two bars I'd left in the bag and placed them in front of me. "You forgot some," she said in the kindest of voices. I am sure the Devil's mother was not so terrible. I have never eaten a Snickers bar since. My children have never eaten a Snickers bar either. There are some lessons you only need to learn once.

Then there are the lessons you wish you never had to learn.

I was in Grade 6 at the time. I won't say his name, but he was much older of course.

When I felt him press his body against me from behind, I was scared. What was going to happen? His arms reached around to the front of my pants, he undid them and they fell to my feet, followed by my underwear. I was scared to turn around or to say anything. He had told me to meet him, and I had come, so it was my fault that this was happening. I had never seen a penis, but when that hard, warm thing pressed against my backside, I knew what it was. I waited for something more to happen, but he just stood there with his warmth against my body, until he heard a noise and hurried away. I did the same. When he told me to meet him again, I did. I was trapped by my fear that by agreeing to meet him the first time I was just as guilty as he was. When I went back the second time, he did the same thing. Again, and again, for months. I told no one, and only escaped when we moved away.

By the time I started Grade 7, we were living in our second home in Brampton, a fully detached house with a two-car garage in the newly developing N section of the city (don't ask me why it was "N"— something about it being a planned community, rather than one that grew organically). I had my own room, plenty of backyard space, and a library full of volumes of the *Encyclopaedia Britannica*. The winding staircase made the entrance hall appear majestic and although the wall of mirrors that followed its curve from the first to the second floor seems tacky to me now, it felt unique in the late 1980s.

Materially we were going up in the world, as my parents' transportation company thrived. I remember my father coming home with what he said was the "first cellular phone ever made." I believed it because I had never seen one before. He could make a phone call from his car! How revolutionary! The case was the size of a small briefcase, but so what. Our family was rich enough to afford phones you could drive around with and that was all that mattered.

The neighbourhood children here were not like the old gang on Silverstone Drive. No one ran around playing kissing tag or baseball in the middle of the street. Every now and again, back on Silverstone, a neighbour's house would be roped off with yellow police tape and blood would be seen on the door or walkway. I doubted that would happen here in the N section. We were a long way from Abell Drive, too, where the neighbourhood children played hide-and-seek until dusk because all Black kids in my neighbourhood had the same rule—our parents wanted us indoors before the street lights came on. No children "played" on our new street. We were either too grown for such childish things or too well off to bother.

In any case, I was all for it. The N section was awesome, as far as I was concerned, and before long I made friends with other children, hanging out in their rooms, playing Nintendo or watching music videos. I was also relieved to see other students of colour in my split seventh and eighth grade class at St. Marguerite Bourgeoys, especially a good-looking boy named Garvin. Nobody had been able to eclipse the appeal of Robert, the rebel of Silverstone Drive, but Garvin came close. He wore Polo and Ralph Lauren and every now and again a Club Monaco ensemble. Even though we could afford it, my parents were not about to buy me brand-name clothing when they could get the same thing for a quarter of the cost at BiWay or Bargain Harold's.

I was nowhere as cool as Garvin. I was physically awkward, and wore frosted lipstick, which was completely inappropriate for my dark skin. Also my mother made me clothing she couldn't find at the bargain outlets, tending to frills, puffy sleeves and polka dots in red, yellow and green, which made me stand out more than my dark skin did. It did not matter. I decided I would be brave enough to approach Garvin in a sophisticated manner. Since clearly he was not the "run up to him and kiss him in the middle of the court" kind of guy, I decided to write him a letter to express my feelings and solicit a favourable response. "Dear Abby," I wrote. Not sure why I started a love letter to a boy that way. "Dear Abby, I am in love with Garvin"—I forget the rest.

Much to my chagrin, not only did the letter fall into the wrong hands, it got passed around the class (including the Grade 8 side). I was mocked mercilessly for months afterward. As far as I was concerned, all "couth" had disappeared from the N section of Brampton—these juveniles couldn't even appreciate a well-written love letter to Abby. Worse, Garvin was one of the children mocking me. I could not let him get away with it, but I did not want our chance at friendship to be ruined by my stupid letter or the resulting cruel middle-school antics. One night I decided I had to call Garvin to straighten out the matter. Clearly, he did not mean to mock me. It was just that since he was a cool kid, he had to follow the unwritten protocol of his rank. If I could get him to talk to me, one on one, it could all be sorted, and we could begin our courtship.

The phone rang and rang. I was patient and let it. Garvin would certainly answer. He had to know it was me who was calling.

His mother picked up. "Hello," I said. "How are you? Is Garvin there?" Garvin's mother said yes he was, and she didn't know why he hadn't answered the phone. My heart sank. I did. My true love was not any form of love at all. I proceeded to tell his mother the whole story. I took responsibility for my own actions, but said that I thought that Garvin had acted inappropriately as well.

When I spoke to Garvin about this years later, he told me that the conversation he had with his mother after I hung up was one he would never forget. She reprimanded him sternly: "This young lady comes from a good family," she said, and "your behaviour reflects on our whole household and how you were raised." She told him he not only had to apologize to me, but to fix the whole situation.

Her attitude is not unfamiliar to me. Most immigrant families, and especially those who came from the Caribbean, did not want their business in the streets, and they regarded their children as a reflection of that business. If you behaved badly it cast a shadow on your entire household and upbringing. The gamble they had taken to leave everything behind for a chance to make their lives and those of their families better was not about to be undermined by children acting the fool. Garvin was not the only one acting the fool, of course. But there are things you understand as a child and things you don't. With my hot temper and tendency to cuss people out when I felt attacked, I've needed to learn the lesson of reconciliation again and again, along with the lesson of accepting my share of the responsibility for the breakdown of an important relationship. And those lessons all began in the mess around a childhood crush.

Going home to Grenada every summer was an oasis in my life. It was security and steadiness. There I was still the centre of attention. It was sunny and lush and I was a beloved treasure to my grandparents. My parents would come for a little while, but work would never let them stay, and I admit I loved being away from my mother and hated going home, as much as I had become a Canadian girl and liked being petted by my relatives for my nice clothes and northern sophistication.

I've said how much I admired my grandmother Mrs. Caesar, but my grandfather Doril was the person who loved me the most. When we got to my grandparents' home on summer break, Mrs. Caesar remained stoic, standing in the yard, giving my brothers and me dignified hellos. But my grandfather clapped and laughed with delight as the car filled with his grandchildren and their suitcases pulled up. He always wore the same knee-length denim shorts, tan-coloured shirt and cap, and as he clapped, he would also wave us to come close for a hug. We always knew what came next. When we got near, he would plant his unshaven face right into our necks and give us tickles. We squealed with joy.

I always felt like he gave me extra tickles and the tightest of hugs. When we walked with him to the shop up the road, he purchased any treat we asked for. By that time, the Caesar farm operation had been reduced to picking and selling nutmeg and mace. Although I rarely went with him to the lands they owned in the mountains to pick the nutmeg, I loved sitting with him under the front veranda to peel the mace from the nutmeg and put it out in the sun to dry. We would spend hours chatting as we worked, or staying quiet—it didn't matter. It was our time to be together. I loved him in a way that I loved nobody else, not even my parents. I always promised him that I would return to Grenada one day when I was grown up to take care of him.

I particularly loved summers on the island because I was effortlessly with my own. In grade school I stood out not only for my smarts—despite all my shenanigans I maintained a straight-A average—but also because of the colour of my skin. I was one of only a few Black kids in my Catholic grade schools, and so I was exceptional in a way that was an unspoken burden. I didn't know how much of a burden I was carrying until I could feel myself relax, sitting with my grandpa helping him husk nutmeg. I didn't know it could be any different, until I hit high school, and met a peer group that was Black like me, and proud of it.

two

BOLD OR BAD—OR BOTH

WHEN I ENTERED THE CAFETERIA on my first day of high school at St. Thomas Aquinas, I recognized the usual cliques I had known in elementary school: the jocks and the cool kids, the popular girls and the nerds. But I also noticed a large new group: Black teenagers, all sitting together in the front four rows of tables on the right side of the room. These kids were not huddled in the back as if they were afraid to be there. Not at all. They were right up front, laughing loud and speaking in a fake/not-so-fake Jamaican patois. Though most of them were older than me, I went right up to them, taking the chance to establish my dominance in new territory. It felt like I was coming home. With these friends I laughed loud, just like they did, wore my hair in the latest styles I saw in Black women's magazines, and out-swore them all, finally able to show off a little of my identity as a young Black woman in the world.

I was smart enough not to talk about any of my new crowd at home, but my parents must have felt the excitement radiating out of me, because they quickly established high-school ground rules: I had to be home by 4:30 p.m. every afternoon without fail or there would be trouble. The school was in the section of town where the streets started with G and, with my house in N, it took an hour and two buses to get home. To make it by 4:30 I had to leave immediately after the bell rang. I had to ask permission for each extracurricular activity I wanted to do weeks in advance, which gave my parents lots of time to use the threat of revoking their permission if I misbehaved. My patience for my parents' control was wearing thin, especially now that I could be hanging out with these cool older kids.

In Grade 9, I obeyed the rules. By Grade 10, though, I was dying to gain a little freedom. I'd also grown even more resentful that my brothers had no such rules to follow, and that even if they had, neither of my parents would have come down on them as hard as they did on me if they broke them. I decided that while I would keep up my grades, I'd have a little fun while doing it. If I missed my 4:30 curfew it would have led to physical punishment, and I did not want that. So I started to skip class instead, first heading to the local mall and, eventually, to hang-outs in neighbouring towns where I wouldn't be spotted by gossipy Brampton housewives who might tattle on me to my mother. If I could not beat my parents, I would deceive them.

There was one more thing I had to counter if I wanted to pull off my bid for freedom: the school calling my parents to tell them I had skipped class. I learned how to craft well-written excuse letters asking for permission to leave school over my father's forged signature. (I did not dare forge my mother's.) No one in the office suspected that the nice, honour-roll student would be so deceptive, and so I got away with it.

I found myself also starting to push back against authority at school, maybe because I could not do it openly at home. I wasn't always so smart about it. Maybe even insufferable. For instance, when I received 99 percent in my religion class, I went to my teacher to protest the single missing percentage point. He was the sweetest man ever, the personification of a nice Catholic school religion teacher; he could have played Jesus in a made-for-television movie. I marched up the steps to his portable and knocked on the door, glancing through the wire-reinforced window. When my teacher waved me in, I swung open the door and immediately started demanding an explanation for the docked point, shaking my report card at him defiantly. I wanted to see every test and assignment, I insisted, so I could show him where he'd made his mistake.

My teacher looked me up and down and quietly told me to leave his classroom or he would dock me 10 percent for my insolence. Yikes! That did not go as expected.

On my way back out the door, I begged him not to tell my parents. His natural sweetness returned and he told me not to worry, he wouldn't tell.

It was a rare setback for the new incarnation of me as a "bad gyal" with a growing rep for speaking up to teachers and skipping school. I mostly loved the new me. I'm not being big-headed when I say I was one of the prettiest and smartest girls in school; I had more than enough friends and male admirers to confirm that for me. I had also discovered that the mouthier I grew the more people wanted to hang around me; the more belligerent I was, the larger the crowd.

So, when on Halloween Day in Grade 10, some Black girls found "Ni**ers Get Out" written in one of the stalls in the girls' washroom, they came to me to deal with the situation. As I marched into the washroom to see the graffiti for myself, a crowd of girls and boys followed. When I saw those words, I got so angry it didn't seem to matter anymore which white girl had written them— somebody was going to pay.

Because it was Halloween, I was not in my school uniform, but wearing a black turtleneck and a pair of wide-legged jeans that one of the school artists had painted designs on, along with my red, gold and green necklace and earrings. The school administration tried to ban us from wearing such colours, arguing that expressing pride in our Black heritage this way caused as much grief as the skinheads expressing their nihilism and white pride by wearing Doc Martens. Give me a break. I wore those colours proudly in tribute to my heroes in history (and to gain popularity with my friends).

I don't know who found the suspected culprit, but soon a white girl wearing a football player costume was brought to the bathroom to stand impromptu trial. After very little questioning, we all concluded she really had written the horrible message. We dropped her to the floor, kicking and punching her. After the punishment was delivered, I threatened her: if she told anyone what had happened, we would beat her up some more.

As I headed for homeroom—all of this had happened before first period—my followers patted me on the back, giving me props for my handling of the incident. My satisfaction lasted about ten minutes—until I heard a PA announcement, asking me to come to the office. I headed out of my classroom, turned right down the first hallway and left towards the office, my stomach sinking with every step. This could not be good.

It wasn't. My victim was lying on a stretcher in the hall, surrounded by ambulance attendants and police officers. I ducked past them and into the office, where the principal told me that the girl had a suspected punctured lung and that the police wanted to speak to me about what had happened. I was terrified. The whole situation had gotten way out of control and I had allowed it to happen. I was not even sure that the girl was actually the culprit, but when the herd around me started to chant for justice, I complied. When the police came in, they asked me if I wanted my parents present. NO, I said firmly. If I had the option of keeping them out of the situation, I was going to take it.

Some of the other Black girls had been called down too, and after the cops talked to me they asked me to wait, and began interviewing them, one by one. While I was sitting there wondering what would happen next, my father walked in carrying the cane he had been using because of a recent knee injury. The other Black girls looked at me as if to ask, "Is your father going to beat you with that thing? Is he going to beat us?"

Holy shit, I thought. My mother had sent my father. He rarely attended school meetings or functions; for him to show up meant that I was in more trouble than a whipping would fix. He paid no attention to me or the line-up of delinquent girls sitting with me, but headed straight for the principal and the police officers, furious that they thought they had the right to speak to a minor without parental consent. Go, Dad!

At last, the officers asked me to go down to the police station to make a statement. My father immediately found me a lawyer: no way was he going to leave me undefended. On the drive to the station, he didn't speak to me. I did not mind. I was not afraid of him and preferred the silence to a lecture.

It turned out that the girl had not suffered broken ribs or a punctured lung, but I still was charged with assault and went to court at least ten times before the case against me was dismissed. My mother took the opportunity to repeat the words Garvin's mother had told him, but with more fury, along with a few slaps, every time we left for another hearing. She did not leave Grenada to sit in a courthouse with a daughter who was too dumb to be smart about her actions.

I was mentally slapping myself too. What was wrong with me? It seemed to me like suddenly I was breaking all the rules at once, as if to determine which would land me in serious trouble, regular trouble or not-so-serious trouble.

When I thought about what had happened, it made me feel sick. I had been out of control and it was only luck that the girl hadn't been seriously hurt. I had no desire to hurt anyone. Why would I want to do that when I knew how bad it felt to be hurt? But I was oscillating between being the good girl who maintained good grades and the bad girl who stood out in the crowd in increasingly dangerous ways, all because she wanted to defy her mother. If leadership was a lesson I was to learn, I was going about it ass-backwards. The bad girl side was starting to dominate and I needed to reverse the trend before it was too late. But maybe it was already too late, given how intoxicating I found the feeling of freedom and power my alter ego possessed. It was like being drawn to fire. I knew it would eventually burn me, but I wanted to feel the heat.

Trying to find a path forward, I pushed hard academically. I took courses in the summer to fast-track through high school and complete five years of credits in four. Maybe in the back of my head I was also thinking that the sooner I could finish high school, the sooner I could escape my parents' house and go to university. On some level, I still felt I had to pay attention to my parents' guidance: I had bought into my mother's dream that I would be a doctor. Around Grade 11, she gave me a copy of Ben Carson's memoir, *Gifted Hands*, describing how he had risen from nothing to become a renowned paediatric neurosurgeon. I read that book cover to cover and told my mother that I was going to be a paediatric neurosurgeon just like him. If Ben Carson was the first to separate twins joined at the head, then I would be the first to separate conjoined twins wherever they had not been separated before. I still loved the attention my mother paid me when I came first in everything, and she loved the fact that I was now aiming so high.

As part of the accelerated plan, in Grade 11 I took Grade 11 math in the first semester and Grade 12 calculus in the second semester. If I wanted to be a neurosurgeon, I reasoned, I needed to be prepared with all three math courses—calculus, trigonometry and algebra—as well as chemistry, physics and biology. I could have looked into the university requirements for getting into medical school, and figured out I didn't have to push on all those fronts, but it didn't even occur to me. Since I was the first person in my family to think about going to university, I did not know what I did not know, and investigating the requirements was something I did not think to do.

Also, my mother forbade me to consult a school guidance counsellor after one of them tried to stream my older brother into basic-level courses, telling him that a job in the trades was a "good fit" for him. My mother was furious, insisting that Roger was perfectly capable of taking general or even some advanced-level courses and applying to college (which he eventually did). Back then, it was not uncommon for some counsellors to encourage Black students into taking courses that offered them few options upon graduation. My mother was not having it, and so I talked about my options with no one but her.

Back to Grade 11 math. It was known in those days as one of the hardest subjects in high school, but it was a breeze for me. I aced it. As a result, I was under the impression that my Grade 12 calculus course would be a total walk in the park. Though I was the only Grade 11 student in my calculus class, which might have given me pause for thought, I started skipping class.

I was deeply into exploring the new-found world of boyfriends. Secret boyfriends, because my mother would have killed me if she'd found out her supposedly innocent, devoutly Catholic, sixteen-year-old was being loose, exploring her sexuality and losing her virginity. I had to watch it because she was often a step ahead of me.

One time I'd gotten permission to go to the movies with girlfriends, not letting on that the plan was to meet my boyfriend at the time, who was going as well. My mother showed up at the theatre, bought a ticket and sat in the back row. I found out that night that one actually could not die from embarrassment, but it sure felt like it.

But this time I outsmarted myself. I thought I'd gone to enough classes that I had a handle on the material, but my final mark was 69 percent. I had never had a mark that low. For the first time in my life, I opened my report card and knew exactly how Roger felt when he would make me hide my report card until after the weekend, so he wouldn't get grounded after he showed his. My stomach turned. I was certainly going to get the pulp beaten out of me when my mother saw that mark.

This time it was me asking my brother not to show our parents his report card until after the weekend, while I tried to figure out what to do. Wow, how the mighty had fallen. Roger may have wanted to rat me out, but he knew full well that he needed the insulation of the weekend too. He spent Friday night and Saturday with friends, going to the clubs, while I took the time to figure out how to doctor my report card so that the "6" looked like an "8" and my 69 percent turned into an 89 percent. I showed it to my parents on Monday after school, when Roger was not around, and I lived to breathe another day.

I could lie to my mother, but lying to myself was unacceptable. I took the course again the following year and scored above 80 percent.

That calculus mark, and resorting to subterfuge to hide it, was not the first clue that my personal spotlight had started to dim. By the time I reached Grade 12, maintaining good grades—with the promise of the different life they provided—seemed like the only escape from the beatings I still got if I stayed out past curfew, was caught skipping class or committing some other nonsense my parents thought I could or should do better. It was also an escape from the pain that I had been carrying from a very young age. Fear of my mother caused me to cheat and change my marks, but there were many other hurts that also silenced me.

I had both witnessed and been subject to many atrocities—ones many young Caribbean girls and women experience—and the only way I felt able to survive was to file each painful moment away in my brain and promise that my adult self would take corrective action.

Many sleepless nights I would look out of the window at the stars and talk to the universe. I longed to become an adult who people respected and who could not be hit or taken advantage of. I vowed that my adult self would be strong and confident and would never beat or hurt a child. Actually, I amended that vow, figuring that having children was too much to risk. I could not hit my children if I did not have them, and I never wanted another child to know how it felt when dried plasma tore away from a wound as she got out of her clothes to have a shower after a beating, or the excruciating pain from the spray of water hitting the newly reopened wound.

Not having children would also spare them the sickening feeling I'd had when I was sexually assaulted and was too afraid to tell. If I'd told, I might have been blamed, and I couldn't risk being victimized twice. Scared silent.

I needed to have a back-up plan in case I did have children, though, so I promised myself that corporal punishment would never be a part of my home. I would make sure that my children felt safe and comfortable enough with me to tell me anything.

Things weren't only happening to me. I remember eavesdropping on an adult conversation at a large gathering and hearing that a young girl I knew was being sexually assaulted. I was afraid for her, but I said nothing. I did not know how to get her out of trouble without getting myself in trouble for meddling in adult affairs. I promised myself that when I was grown up, I would find her and apologize for not being able to help her. In 2017, I called her and did just that. We spent hours crying together. While the culprit continued to live as if nothing had happened, she was sent away, and I had missed her tremendously.

Once someone caught me and another girl kissing—I might have been eleven or twelve—and threatened to tell. Not only did I feel ashamed, but the thought of others finding out that I was "weird" was too much to bear. Better not to have the feelings. I resolved to stay as straight as a pin, but I made myself another promise: if I did have children, I would never make them feel ashamed of who they were or who they loved.

The pressure in my soul was daunting. I couldn't be the young woman I was becoming—no longer innocent, desperately trying to carve out a space for herself—while being contained in the box my parents had built for me where the walls seemed to close tighter every year.

Did they think that a 4:30 curfew would prevent me from having sex? Did they think that taking the bus home right after school kept me from voyaging into the dark and troubled places they were trying to protect me from? Did they think that their only girl, the first in the family aiming to go to university, would be protected from the dangers of the world because they put some arbitrary rules in place? I was beginning to think my parents were more naïve than I was. And sometime in early Grade 12 I decided I did not care how often or how hard I was beaten. I was no longer going to abide by the rules.

But how would I find real freedom? I lived at home, dependent on them for every article of clothing, every bit of food, the car they let me drive on the occasions I was allowed to go out. If I was going to make some kind of break for it, I needed a way to support myself.

I decided to approach a guy a couple of years older than me, who was a known drug dealer, and pitch him the idea of getting me involved in selling. I needed money and I could see how much those people made. I figured for sure that he would take me on. Everyone in his crew liked me, and I knew I had the smarts to turn his petty drug ring into something big. I felt I had to decide whether I was going to use my powers for good or for evil; I was so pissed off and distressed with everything, I was finding the goody two shoes bit completely unamusing and unadventurous.

To my surprise, the guy said no. He told me, "This is not for you. You are one of the smartest girls—never mind that—the smartest *people* in school. You need to do something better. I heard you are applying to university. Do that. You are not allowed to do this."

At the time it felt like another door closing. Now I thank him. He knew me better than I knew myself.

Here I am going to pause for a moment to admit, before my story disappears totally into wounds and recriminations, that there is no simple way to describe my relationship with my mother. I still wanted to please her. I still wanted her to think the best of me even as I was vowing to rebel.

She didn't just give me misery, and I gave her as much lip as she gave me licks. I never saw her take crap from anyone, and now, all grown up, I don't take any crap either. I got that from her.

She punished me in ways that I would never punish a child, but she was also the first to teach me who I was as a Black person. She gave me not only Ben Carson's book, but other books about Black history and identity. She was the one who forced me to participate in spelling bees, and other community programs. I was a competitive swimmer and involved with the Grenada Association. She was proud of me when I stood up for the Black community in smart ways (as opposed to taking out my anger on the white girl in the football costume). She taught me how to stand up for my community, and to be unafraid and unapologetic about my place (and space) in the world.

On April 29, 1992, the verdict at the Rodney King trial came down in Los Angeles. As I watched the news, I was both shaken by the violence of the riots that followed the verdict, and inspired by the actions of the community to collectively oppose the acquittal of the four white police officers who had viciously beaten a Black man.

On Monday, May 4, 1992, I got to school early in order to meet with the principal to ask if I could host a demonstration at the school that day. He was new to the school, but I had heard rumours that he had been arrested himself in the past for peacefully demonstrating; I figured he could not say no, and I was correct.

But in order for me to miss school for the day, he needed my parent's consent.

Well, there goes that plan! I thought as he made the call. There was only a slim chance that my mother would say yes, given that in her eyes, my one job was to go to school and do well.

"Good luck with the protest!" the principal said as he hung up the phone, giving me the thumbs up.

"She said yes?" I was shocked.

He nodded.

I didn't wait. I prepared my Bristol board posters in the front foyer of the school, writing "No Justice No Peace" and "Honk for Justice" in great big letters, and headed out the front doors to start my one-person protest. That is correct. For most of the day, I was the only person holding up one sign and then the other, as a handful of gracious passers-by honked in support. The crowds of Black youth that followed me when I was acting the fool were scarce when it came to doing something productive.

When students and parents did stop to ask me what my protest was all about, I took the time to explain what had happened to Rodney King. When they objected that the incident had happened in the United States, and that things were not that bad in Canada, I reminded them that a twenty-two-year-old man named Raymond Lawrence had been recently killed in the west end of Toronto by a white undercover police officer. I also reminded them that here in Brampton, earlier in the year, two police officers had been acquitted by an all-white jury of the 1988 shooting and killing of a seventeen-year-old Black youth, Michael Wade Lawson.

I stood there for most of the day, until I heard that Dudley Laws, a Black lawyer who was an icon in the community, and the Black Action Defence Committee were calling for people to come to a protest in downtown Toronto that night. I phoned my mother and asked if I could go. To my surprise, again she said yes. Her only warning was that if I saw that anything violent was about to happen, I should get out of there fast. She had been watching the riots in Los Angeles unfold and did not want me to get caught in any similar melee. Of all the days for her to be in a giving mood, this was the one that I would most appreciate.

I caught the bus to Toronto. By the time I got there the demonstrators had already left the US consulate, where they had gathered in support of justice for Rodney King and all Black people suffering and dying at the hands of police, and moved on to Nathan Phillips Square at Toronto City Hall. I moved through the crowd until I got close enough to lay eyes on Dudley Laws. I felt proud to be a part of something bigger than myself, something that could mean change for Black communities in Canada. As the crowd headed away from the square and up Yonge Street, I followed, exhilarated to be chanting "No Justice, No Peace" in solidarity with all these people in the street.

Then I heard the sound of smashing glass and frantically looked around. People were breaking the windows of the stores beside me, and up ahead was a line of police. My mother's warning sounded in my head and I bolted down the stairs of the first subway entrance I saw and pulled on the doors. They were locked. I banged, and a transit officer came and explained they were locked because of the protest. I started to cry, pleading with the man to open the doors and let me through—that my mother would kill me if I didn't get out of there right away. I'd never heard as sweet a sound as that latch clicking and the door opening. I thanked the officer profusely. My heart did not stop beating hard all the way home.

Just as I was finishing Grade 12, my grandfather Doril passed away at the age of eighty. It was devastating. Until that moment, on May 25, 1992, I didn't believe my grandparents would ever die.

Miracles happened every day, I told myself, and as we flew to Grenada, I was sure that I would find him alive. But when all the family members who had travelled from Canada and the United States arrived at the La Qua Brothers funeral home, the attendant pulled a gurney carrying my grandfather's body, covered by a white sheet, into the main room. When he pulled the sheet back, I felt such pain it was like every bone in my body had broken. As I softly touched his face, I noticed how discoloured it was; he had died of a massive heart attack. My knees went weak as I bent over to kiss his forehead. He was the one person I knew who loved me without a doubt and now he was gone.

On the day of the funeral, as the casket was being lowered into the ground, I sobbed like I never had before. I would never be able to keep my promise to return home to take care of him. If I had already become a doctor, I could have saved him from the heart attack that killed him. The day he died, he'd complained about a stomach ache, thinking he had gas pains. Still, in the evening, he had walked up the road to the shop for his rum, as usual. When he came home, he lay down and never woke up.

As I stood at the graveside, I saw the funeral directors passing shovels so the family members could drop scoops of soil on top of the casket. As the first shovelful of dirt fell into the six-foot hole and landed, it made such a terrible noise. I screamed. That terrible noise meant that his death was final. My tears would not stop coming and the noise did not stop until everything went dark.

When I came to, I was in my grandfather's room, lying on the bed he'd died in. I was comfortable there. I had no fear and I felt his love. Still, I promised myself that I would never allow anyone's death to affect me the way my grandfather's had. The pain was too much to bear.

The goalpost I kept in front of me as we flew home to Canada after my grandfather's funeral was that soon I'd be graduating from high school, and moving away from home to go to university. My marks were such that I could be accepted by McGill, Queen's and McMaster University, universities that had good medical programs, and were far enough away from home that I'd have to live in residence.

Then my mother put her foot down. Even though we could easily afford it, there was no way she was going to allow her unmarried daughter to sleep away from home. Yes, I would be going to university as planned, but to one that was commuting distance from Brampton; all the rules that governed my existence would still apply.

WTF (I yelled in my head). *What did she know about university? Why did she have the final say?*

I hated everything about the prospect of going to the University of Toronto or York University—the only options acceptable to my mother. York didn't even have a medical program and the University of Toronto wasn't far enough away! I needed to escape. University was supposed to be my chance to get away from my parents' rules and my mother's heavy hand, maybe even to find out who I really was.

But I didn't have the internal strength to win this fight. Not yet. So I applied to U of T, McMaster and Queen's and got accepted into all three. Even though it felt like swallowing a poison pill—and not the kind used to prevent a hostile takeover, but a literal one that would end my life—I agreed that I would go to the University of Toronto. My mother's demand that I live at home was the final straw. I was furious and may have even started to hate her. The beatings I endured bruised and tore my skin, but her decision not to allow me to go away to school broke my heart. If my grandfather's death foreshadowed the darkness to come, this decision pushed me into it.

three

LIES, ALL LIES

I ENTERED THE UNIVERSITY of Toronto in September 1992, in search of a bachelor of science, my first step, I thought, on the way to medical school. However, finding that bachelor would turn out to be one of the most challenging things I've ever done.

My first class was Biology 150, held in Convocation Hall. I got to the university early that morning so I could find my classroom and get comfortable. It was a beautiful fall day, the air warm enough to make me feel confident, but crisp enough to make me question why my mother made me come to this intimidating university. I studied the campus map, which showed me that Convocation Hall was a large building on the southwest end of King's College Circle, at the centre of the grand campus. So not that hard to find.

I pulled the large door open, walked inside the spacious entrance-way and looked for the classrooms. They were nowhere to be found. I went outside, reviewed the map, went inside and looked around again. No luck. I went outside again and finally a passer-by noticed I looked lost and asked if I needed help. When I told her I was looking for Convocation Hall, she smirked and pointed: I was, indeed, standing right in front of it.

By the time I got myself sorted, the only seat I could find was in the large theatre's third balcony. Why was my course being held here and not in a classroom? I could barely see what was happening on the stage. And why so many people?

The professor's voice came loud and clear over the sound system. "Look to the person on your left. Now look to the person on your right," he demanded. We all did as we were told. I graciously said hello and shook hands with my fellow first years. This was good, I thought. We would likely be study partners or, even, friends.

The uneasy feeling in my stomach was starting to go away when the professor delivered the punchline: "Two out of three of you will be gone by the end of the year." I felt light-headed. The people on either side of me looked as if they were here to stay. I was the one who seemed out of place, the darkest person out of the three of us. Someone should have stuck a fork in me, because I instantly figured that I was done. I had gone from being the centre of attention in a high school full of Black students, to sitting out of sight at the back of the class, a smart girl in a sea of equally smart people. Nobody would care about my African-coloured necklaces or hoop earrings here. This was a race to academic dominance and I was literally starting at the back of the pack.

I had been able to ace my grades in high school, but here I just felt lost. I had to be home in Brampton at night, so I couldn't go to any of the campus social events or hang out in residence, making friends, which would have made the place more welcoming. The U of T campus in the early nineties felt largely white and Asian to me; I only saw a few Black students, and it was not like I could just go up to them and say, "Hey, I'm here too." I didn't have the confidence to do that. I knew I was smart, but my brain kept telling me I didn't belong here. When I was between classes, I wandered the campus aimlessly. I did not even want to be here.

I wanted to be at McMaster or Queen's. I wanted to be anywhere but Toronto.

My insecurity and distraction made me do dumb things. For instance, during my first chemistry lab, we were supposed to make a powdered detergent like Tide. When I read the instructions the night before, I couldn't quite grasp them, even though they were written in plain English. Still I went to the dingy old basement lab in the chemistry building on campus at the right time and started to prepare the ingredients as instructed. I weighed, heated, measured and poured perfectly. I made exactly what I was supposed to make . . . until I didn't. I looked at the white substance I'd created and it still did not click that I was making a powdered soap. I was convinced it was supposed to be a liquid. So I added water to the mixture and handed it to the teaching assistant.

"Did you add water to this?" he asked with a very perplexed look on his face. I did not need to respond to know that I was going to fail the lab.

It was a large, cold campus with old, dirty spaces that made me feel isolated and afraid. But no matter how much I didn't like the place, I couldn't quit. The only thing I had to aim at in life was a medical degree. I didn't know any other path. I didn't even consider becoming a lawyer, an engineer, a pharmacist, a history major. I didn't realize those options existed. I'm astonished now to think back on how narrow my tunnel vision was. As far as I was concerned, sticking with it was my only shot at becoming the only thing I had ever dreamed about—a neurosurgeon. For a girl who got straight As, I was dumb about the world.

Every day I longed to go back to high school, to my friends and the comfort of knowing who I was. Here my smart girl identity was a faded memory of someone I once knew. The person who took her place was deeply confused and lost.

Soon, instead of going to class, I was spending my days with one troubled boyfriend or another. The badder the better. Not going to school, earning an illegal income and not really caring about me seemed to be my prerequisites. I did not care if they cheated on me, because I was cheating on them. During the evenings and weekends I would lie to my parents in order to get out of the house. I drank too much and partied too hard. I often woke up the next morning wondering how I survived the night. When I had to write an exam, I had to cram. I took amphetamines so I could stay up and read the entire textbook the night before. Of course the inevitable happened. I barely passed first year, and was put on academic probation. This time, I did not worry about my parents' reaction. I simply doctored my transcript, changing my bad grades to good ones, and showed my parents the forgery.

To say it all made me feel bad is an understatement. I felt pretty much like I was dying every day. Over the summers, I recuperated with trips to see relatives in Grenada, which always restored me. I also had a steady job at a pharmacy in a Brampton grocery store, where I was relied upon and liked by everyone. My colleagues there were like a second family; among them I could pretend that all was well with the world. No matter how bad my day was, walking into that pharmacy made me feel better.

At the beginning of second year, I vowed to do things differently, but I was on a downward spiral, hunting for anything and anyone who could help me escape reality, even if only temporarily. I spent even more time with boyfriends than in class. By the end of the second year, my marks were so bad I was kicked out of the university. I was also pregnant.

That particular boyfriend and I had been dating on and off since high school; he was the one constant that reminded me of the girl I once was. I knew the relationship was toxic and that I should focus on school, but still I turned to him. He was my new version of fire, and though I got burned again and again, I kept coming back. However, as familiar as he was, I knew I did not want a family with him. And, while I could forge my marks to fool my parents and plead with the university to let me back in, I could not hide a pregnancy. I made the decision to have an abortion.

Even though I sat in the clinic waiting room for the same reason that everyone else was there, I felt ashamed to be there. I was part of a Catholic family who went to church every Sunday and always sat near the front. My parents gave generously to the church and we volunteered regularly. My father and I were called upon to read scripture at Sunday mass; he also sang in the choir. I was not only ashamed, I was damned.

The only thing I wanted more desperately than to leave that clinic was to have my mother with me. It was weird, but I needed to have her there. I wanted to tell her that I was in really big trouble. That I was in over my head and drowning. But I was a coward who was afraid to own my mistakes. Though I felt she was the only one who could help me out of the situation, there was too much pain and fear between us. I just couldn't tell her the truth. I kept my head bowed the entire time, so nobody would see me or, even worse, recognize me. I wished desperately for the kind of mother who would speak to me honestly and show me the options. A mother who would tell me to go on birth control to prevent this sort of mess from happening in the first place. But that was not my mother, and I would not risk giving her the chance to be there for me for fear that she wouldn't be. The only people who knew about the abortion were my boyfriend and my best friend.

The next time I was asked to sign up for a church rally for life, I ducked out of it. Lightning was bound to strike me as a hypocrite and sinner, and might kill the people on either side of me too.

—

You'd think I wouldn't have doubted my abilities so much, when it turned out that once again I was able to persuade the university to let me back in. But I was not really thinking. The proof? I just couldn't crawl out of the same bad habits that had led to academic disaster.

Towards the end of the second semester that year, I received a message from the Registrar's Office that I needed to meet with a counsellor named Sally Walker. I remember every detail of that walk through the curved corridors of New College on my way to the appointment. I was fucking up big time, and hoped desperately that this person would be able to tell me how to fix everything.

Sally, a slim woman with big curly red hair, met me in reception. She smiled at me and led me to her office, chatting all the way. I slouched in her chair as she told me, quite kindly, that I was going to be placed on academic probation again. I stared at her. She seemed so gentle and I loved the way she moved her hands as she spoke. Her office was a warm place, full of books, plants, ornaments and pictures. I longed to move into this tiny space and stay forever—the first time I'd felt at home at the university. Where had this woman and this mystical room been three years ago? Why was she just finding me now?

I can't explain why she had such an effect on me, except to say that she genuinely wanted to help me. She saw me clearly: not a Black girl, a smart girl, a dumb girl, or a bad girl, just a lost girl needing guidance. I had rarely encountered anyone who expected nothing from me except perhaps for me to reach out my hand and accept her help.

The more Sally spoke the more relaxed I became, until she asked, "Do you understand?" and I realized that I had not taken in one word she had said. I felt sick. I wanted to confess, *No, I don't understand, because I was not listening. You made me feel welcome and accepted for the first time in this terrifying place. You put me under a spell.*

How the fuck do you expect me to understand while I am under your nicest-person-in-the-world spell?

I swallowed the saliva filling my mouth and sighed. (Ever since I'd gotten pregnant, my mouth would fill with saliva every time my stomach was upset. It was my scarlet letter, the burden I bore for my sins.) I decided it did not matter if I understood Sally or not. I was doomed. I would never be a neurosurgeon and my parents would kill me once they found out about all my lies. I pressed my lips together to fight away the tears and nodded. Yes, I understand.

I understood nothing. I got up and left. It turned out (I learned from Sally later—I stayed in touch and we still meet on occasion) that she had recommended I cut the number of courses I was taking so I could get my average up and graduate with a three-year degree. Maybe I didn't hear her because that was never the plan: I had to graduate with honours.

Instead of reducing my load, I signed up for six fourth-year courses. I ended up skipping even more days and taking more amphetamines in order to cram for tests and papers; as a result, my GPA dropped below the graduation cut-off point of 1.56. At the end of that year, most people who had entered university with me graduated and I was left behind. I'd come from the top of my class in high school to not graduating with my class in university.

What I wanted to do was drop out, but it was too late. My parents had invested too much money and I had told too many lies. And with this fourth-year disaster, I had more lies to tell.

First, I had to forge my marks again. Second, I had to figure out how to explain why I would not be crossing the stage at Convocation Hall to receive my degree.

When I'm in the right mood, I can laugh about the level of ingenuity I brought to bear on this. Forging the marks was no issue: I was a pro at that. I'd saved the transcript template on the computer and a little bit of keyboard work and a short trip to the print shop took care of everything. But explaining why neither I nor my parents could go to the graduation ceremony for the first person in the family to go to university was harder.

The solution: after I presented them with my fake transcripts, I followed up with a fake letter announcing that I'd been accepted into medical school. Then I invented an incident of vandalism that had shut down Convocation Hall so that the whole graduation ceremony had to be cancelled. I even wrote a letter from the administration that sounded as official as a heart attack, requesting that students with any information about the suspected vandalism call a number that looked exactly like a U of T campus number. There were big holes in this story, but having shown my parents the shiny object of my acceptance into medical school, they were so happy they didn't think things through.

Bloody fucking hell. If there was a God, He needed to show up fast and rescue me from this tangled web I was weaving. Or punish me for the liar that I was. I was both shocked and relieved when He eventually did show up in the form of my best friend.

I kept on running my personal Ponzi scheme, believing that if I danced fast enough, I could make reality eventually match the lies I was telling. I wanted to get a real honours bachelor of science degree, so back I went to the university.

Towards the end of second semester of my fifth year—which, as far as my parents were concerned, was the end of my first year of medical school—my best friend, Jessica, and I decided to go to a new club that was opening in downtown Toronto. I was secretly dating one of the owners, behind my steady Brampton boyfriend's back, and he let Jessica and me, along with another friend of ours, in for free.

About an hour into the night, Jessica and the other girl disappeared. I wandered the crowded dance floors for what seemed like hours, but could not spot them. At the end of the night I headed outside, wondering how I was going to get home, and found them both laughing away with a group of people in the parking lot. I lost it, yelling, "Who the fuck do you think you are? Leaving me all fucking night after I got you into the club for free."

Jessica pleaded with me to calm down and just get in the car with her to go home.

"Go fuck yourself!"

I saw right away that I had hurt her badly. I don't know why I was so mad. We had been friends since high school and she had always looked out for me. She had covered for me many times with my parents. I wanted to take the words back, but it was too late.

The next morning, a Saturday, I went to work at the pharmacy. I did not let myself think of the situation with Jessica all day, but when I got home that night and found my mother sitting by the front door, I immediately knew that my behaviour had come home to roost. Any time I found my mother waiting for me like that, I knew trouble was coming my way.

It turned out that in the aftermath of me cussing her out, Jessica had gone straight to my parents and told them everything: the lies, the drugs, the boyfriends, and even the abortion.

The next few weeks were hell on earth in my house. The constant slaps and questioning of my actions over the past five years had my head and every other part of me sore. I explained and re-explained the convoluted mess I'd got myself in, told and re-told the story of how I did not graduate and answered question upon question about my drug use and boyfriends. The truth had finally caught up to me. But instead of being angry with my friend, I was relieved. I should have thanked her (and maybe if she reads this book, I finally can). She did me a favour by telling them everything I did not have the courage to say. My family was devastated, but the truth finally set me free.

In as much as the five-year spiral had been dark and devastating, and my parents' suspicion and disappointment was hard to live through, I was acutely aware that somewhere inside of me a little spark now shone. My best friend's betrayal of my secrets had offered me hope again. For years now, the dominant feeling in my life had been guilt. I was finally able to move forward, still ashamed, but at least in truth.

When I think about the millions of human interactions and experiences that have brought me to where I am today, I end up wondering whether every single one of them, right or wrong, had a specific purpose. Whether we realize it or not, we are shaped by every interaction we have. The good and the bad. The joyful and the hurtful. The mistakes and the triumphs. All of them make us the person we are.

No one is perfect. But I know now what I didn't know then: our failures, mistakes, imperfections and shortcomings define us. In fact, sometimes they help us see the best parts of ourselves. We make such painstaking efforts to hide our faults and failings from ourselves and others. But being vulnerable and open, and owning our flaws, gives us strength; when we share our failures with others, we all learn and grow.

I used to hate mistakes. I used to hate them so badly, I thought of them as a person I wanted to avoid at all costs: Ms. Take. Every time she showed up, disaster followed. This woman comes in unannounced, makes sure you mess up, does not apologize for how badly she makes you feel and just walks away, leaving you to deal with the mess.

Ms. Take has been in my life at some of the lowest, darkest, most incredibly embarrassing moments. She may be sitting beside me right now. Her visits are awful, and the aftermath is worse. She leaves gifts of hurt, guilt, anger, resentment, pity, anxiety, regret, disappointment, insecurity and other feelings that last for a very long time, if not forever.

But Ms. Take is survivable, I've learned. I have come to realize that she is actually one of the smartest women I know. She understands that there are only two things to do with mistakes: make them and learn from them. When she comes around, someone will usually tell you, "Get back up on that horse right away, or else you will never ride again." In my opinion, we shouldn't get right back on the horse. We should take the time to figure out the lesson Ms. Take is trying to teach us.

It is okay to rest, down on the ground, for a little while. I am not saying you need to stay flat on your face. You can turn over, put your hands behind your head and breathe, as you figure out what you did to get yourself into that mess. Don't blame your friends, teachers, parents or coworkers. You need to own your mistakes and understand how you came to make them. If you do not do this, you will continue to blame others—like I used to blame everything on my mother—and the fear, insecurity, anger and resentment will stay with you forever. I know this now, but I had a lot of ground to cover until I learned the lessons my mistakes at university had to teach me.

After the truth was exposed, I was relieved I didn't have to build up any more layers of guilt or spin any more lies, but I was ashamed of myself. The other really hard thing was that, after living dishonestly for years, I was finally finished with the business of only pretending to live my life. Now I had to do it for real.

But I was still stuck at home with my parents. The tension was so thick I thought it would choke me. I also didn't have a best friend anymore, which was awkward, too, because Jessica's parents and mine were still friends.

That first summer, I decided I had to get out of Brampton for a while. The fact that my parents were too proud to have told anyone in the family about my disgrace worked in my favour. My cousin Debbie wanted me to come with her to Grenada for a week to visit Mrs. Caesar. That seemed like a good idea to me: I could celebrate my twenty-second birthday with people who were unaware of all of the drama, so I would be free to breathe. My parents couldn't find a reason to say no that wouldn't blow our cover, so in the end I set off with Debbie and Lisa, another cousin, as well as my brother's girlfriend (now my sister-in-law) for a week in the sun.

My grandmother was glad to have us, and used my birthday as a reason to invite every person in the village of Pomme Rose, St. David's, Grenada, to a party. She baked a five-tier cake and about a hundred of the little loaves she called "pencil bread," killed a goat and cooked a feast.

After the birthday party, we young ladies took the island by storm. We were invited to beach parties and downtown hot spots by the local boys who loved the idea of Canadian girls giving them attention. After hanging around downtown one day, we decided that we would sleep over at a cousin's house closer to the city instead of travelling back to Pomme Rose. Even under my parents' rules, we would be allowed to sleep over at our cousin's house. But in Mrs. Caesar's world, this was absolutely forbidden. Not only would we be sleeping away from home, rumour had made it back to Pomme Rose that her granddaughters were "carrying on" in the streets of St. George's. She was not about to have it and called my cousin demanding that her granddaughters be sent back home.

He told her over the phone that she had nothing to worry about and that we would be just fine sleeping at his place. Whatever Mrs. Caesar said in reply removed the confident expression on his face. "Okay, Mrs. Caesar," he said, "I will let them know."

I started putting my shoes on as he was hanging up the phone. Remember earlier when I said that Mrs. Caesar was unapologetic and unafraid? She absolutely was, and if we did not get ourselves back to her house, I did not know what stunt she would pull.

"Your grandmother wants you home. She also said that you can't take a clean sheet to cover a dirty mattress," my cousin reported. I don't know quite what she meant, but every time I remember this story, I laugh. She was the ultimate family matriarch. All of us regarded her with unconditional love . . . and, possibly, fear. Her number one rule was that family members were required to sleep at home. She wouldn't even allow Debbie, the eldest of us on the trip, to sleep at her paternal Grenadian grandmother's house. She was so strict, it was hilarious; after all, we were adults.

So back we went, and we all joined her on her Saturday morning trip to the market in Grenville. As we walked hand in hand, she negotiated prices for the vegetables she wanted and purchased the treats she thought we needed, totally in her element. The sun was shining brightly on her that day. Her prodigal granddaughters had returned.

When our week was up, and we had packed to go to the airport, my grandmother told each of us that the next time she saw us, she would be dead. It was her version of hugs and kisses, a way of telling us that we had given her the week of a lifetime and she was sad to see us go.

After saying our goodbyes to Mrs. Caesar, we set off with a big caravan of family and friends who wanted to wish us bon voyage. But as we approached the airport, we realized that there were no passengers but us in sight. We found an airline attendant at the check-in desk, though, who took one look at us and said, "If you were not having so much fun at the local restaurant the night before, you would not have missed your plane." We checked our tickets. Our flight had taken off the night before.

The entire caravan drove back home to our grandmother's estate. When she saw us pulling up, the old lady had never looked so happy. Mrs. Caesar laughed and stomped her feet and clapped, as if she had taken lessons from her late husband, Doril. Her grand-daughters had returned home and she was ecstatic.

"Well," I said, trying not to laugh, "you certainly are happy for a dead lady."

That look on her face when she saw us return was well worth the penalty fee the airline charged to book a new flight.

The next time I saw Mrs. Caesar, she was indeed in a casket at her funeral. I would give anything to have another moment or two with her.

four

WIFE? MOTHER? REALLY?

I CAME BACK TO Canada prepared to start my sixth year at university by taking the advice my counsellor, Sally, had given me at the end of third year. I reduced my course load. It was a humbling experience because I was also forced to take a couple of second- and third-year courses to boost my GPA. That semester I received my first B while at the university, which boosted my cumulative GPA to 1.58. Finally, I would be able to graduate. Getting that news was one of the happiest and scariest moments of my life. Partly because I did not know what to do with a degree that would not get me into medical school and partly because I had lost myself in all of the scheming. I was better known for who I was dating than who I was. I had a chance at a fresh start and I did not want to blow it.

The morning of my graduation ceremony, I heard my mother getting dressed and wondered where she was going. I was certain that the shame and anger of the past few months meant she would not want to be seen with me.

Then she knocked on my door and told me that she was taking me to graduation. She said that she was proud that I had graduated and that I should not feel ashamed. I was getting the piece of paper, and that was everything. I wanted to cry, but I didn't. In that moment, I think we both got a glimpse of how much we loved each other.

That June day in 1998, as I walked across the lawn at King's College Circle, I thought a lot about Sally Walker and the advice that had taken me two years to understand. All I had to do was reduce the load to finish my degree and I had finally done it. I also thought about how important it is to ask questions, even ones that shame you. If I had just asked her to repeat herself, and taken the time to understand what she was saying, I could have spared myself years of torment.

As I got closer to Convocation Hall, I remembered how lost I'd been as I'd entered the building the first time, and laughed about the fact that I had finally found myself going in the right direction. And as I crossed the stage, shook the hand of the chancellor and got my degree, I think I might have smirked. I checked and that piece of paper did not have my GPA on it anywhere. I had the bachelor and nothing Ms. Take could do now would take him away from me.

I did not know what I was going to do next, but I figured if I could make it through this, the sky was the limit. Maybe if a challenge scares you so much you want to vomit, it is more than likely worth doing. I had spent the last six years just trying to survive. It was time for me to grow up. The vomity feeling in my stomach—butterflies, maybe, or maybe little cheerleaders shaking their pom-poms, rooting for me—were telling me "It is my time."

As luck would have it, my time alone to forge a path into the future was shorter than the preceding paragraph. Three weeks before graduation, on the May 24 long weekend in 1998, I ran into Vidal Chavannes at a club. You might wonder how I was even out at a club since my parents had grounded me for as long as I was under their roof. But that Saturday night I'd mustered up the courage to ask them to lend me the car so I could go to the night-club, and, strangely, they said yes.

I put on a mini jean dress and matching denim heels, the perfect outfit, I thought, to kick off the summer. As I walked into the club I saw Vidal on the dance floor surrounded by his friends; he had dated a friend of mine and it hadn't ended well, but he had stuck in my mind. I tapped him on the shoulder. When he turned, I asked him if he remembered me. He smiled and said, "I never forgot you." There was something wonderful about the way he took me in. He looked different, too, as if since the last time I had seen him he had filled out to match his oversized hands. He did not need to ask me to dance because I stayed close to him for most of the night.

At some point I wandered off to meet up with other friends and head home. As we were leaving, I saw Vidal chatting with someone. I didn't want to disturb him, so I kept walking. He grabbed my hand as I went past and twirled me around, bringing me close enough to whisper my phone number in my ear. He wanted to make sure that he'd got it correct. I nodded, and then he leaned in close and kissed me. I did not pull away. I wanted him to kiss me, and the longer he did, the better it was. He held me in that moment like I had never been held before and I did not want him to let me go.

For years, I had kept a list of characteristics I wanted in a partner: tall, dark, handsome, Catholic, doesn't have children, bathes with a washcloth or loofah (in my world you need more than your hands to scrub yourself clean), the potential to make a six-figure income. . . . The list went on and on. On those nights when I gazed out the window at the stars searching for the adult version of me, I prayed for my "list person" to come and rescue me. I knew they were out there, I just needed to find them.

A few weeks before I ran into Vidal, I'd added another item to the list. My coworkers at the pharmacy had heard all about my list.

With every person I dumped, they tried to guess which box the last victim hadn't checked. Were they too short? Did they bite their nails? No loofah?

On that particular day, Mike, the pharmacist, was laughing at an article he was reading in the paper and suggested that I take a look. The story was about a billionaire who was searching the world for a bride. The man had two post-secondary degrees, the article noted. Mike asked if he should contact the man in the article on my behalf. He was only half joking. Mike cared about me and wanted me to find someone really great.

"Of course not," I replied. "But I am adding another item to my list! My soul mate needs to have two post-secondary degrees." I lifted the index and middle fingers of my right hand to the ceiling. "Two degrees!" I decreed. "My life partner will have two degrees!" Mike rolled his eyes. He was almost certain that I would never find true love if I kept adding such items to my list.

As Vidal kissed me, I found myself hoping that he was my "list person." I didn't know that much about him, but I knew he was respectable enough to win over my ultra-strict, controlling parents. He was certainly tall, dark and handsome. Did he have two degrees? Did he meet all the other criteria? I pulled away slightly to look into his eyes. I hoped so, and I let him kiss me again.

The next day I was at Ontario Place with my niece when Vidal called. He was reassured that I had not given him a fake number and I was reassured that he called. There was something about him that made me feel secure, a feeling I am not sure I had ever known.

During that first phone call, Vidal calmly said, "You know you'll be my wife."

I was busy balancing the phone on my ear, holding my niece with one hand and scaling an angled rock-climbing structure at the time, and responded, "Sure you will, buddy. Remember I know who you are. Do you recall that time when your old girlfriend returned all of your gifts? Well, she was at my house an hour before that, begging me to go with her. I happened to look at some of the stuff you bought for her. That bracelet was horrible. But I did ask for that big white stuffed gorilla you won for her at the CNE, and she gave it to me. I have it in my room. All I am saying is that you cannot afford for me to be your wife. I won't accept your shit."

He laughed. "We'll see."

I could not believe this man was speaking to me about marriage. No one had ever done that before. If I could blush, I would have. My niece was demanding to go to another part of the park and so I said I had to get off the phone. "Can I take you out?" he asked before I could hang up. He really did not need to ask.

As the evening of our first date drew closer, my pharmacy gang peppered me with questions. Vidal was driving from where he and his family lived in Pickering to Brampton to pick me up after work. It was a one-hour drive across the top of Toronto on a good traffic day, and a lot longer during rush hour. I had never brought a date around, and they were wildly curious. "Is this one the list guy?" they all wanted to know.

When Vidal walked in near the end of my shift, everyone behind the counter froze. "Is that him?" my colleague Fran asked. "Holy shit," said Judi. Even Mike the pharmacist seemed mesmerized.

This is corny as hell, but I felt as if everything was happening in slow motion. Our eyes locked as soon as Vidal walked in. He was smiling as he strode towards me, wearing his usual button-down shirt tucked neatly into his pants. Not even a trace of bad boy in this man.

I smiled back and somehow managed to finish whatever I was doing without losing eye contact. Then I opened the release on the gate to let him behind the counter. "Vidal, these are my coworkers—Fran, her daughter Andrea, Judi and Mike. Everyone, this is Vidal." They acted like I was introducing royalty.

I had a few minutes left of my shift, and Vidal spent the time chatting easily with my coworkers. It pleased me that they were getting along. When I was done, we hopped into his light blue Dodge Caravan and headed to the movies. We had some time before the show, so he suggested we go to Chapters for a while. *Chapters?* I thought. He was actually a nerd. I loved it.

As we strolled through the aisles of books he pointed out the ones he'd read, giving me the Coles Notes summaries. I rolled my eyes at his cockiness. Could he be more arrogant? Did he think I did not read? I graciously let him continue.

He rattled on, book after book. I was intrigued by how well read he was, but goodness gracious, he loved the boring sections: American History, Canadian History, English Literature and every book written by a prominent Black thought leader. I'd read some of those too, but don't think I had appreciated them in the way that he seemed to appreciate them. I looked at my watch. Thank goodness the movie was starting.

It is interesting that Vidal and I can both remember what happened before and after the movie, but to this day, we cannot remember what movie we saw. When it ended, we headed back to Brampton with plenty of time to spare before my curfew. I suggested that we "park" at Chinguacousy Park for a while. I wanted him to kiss me again, and this kiss was better than the previous ones and it started to get steamy . . . until it didn't. Vidal wanted the moment to be right and he did not want us to get hot and heavy in the back of a Dodge Caravan.

Something about him made me quiet in a good way. Not silenced, but peaceful.

We got out of the van and took a stroll through the park instead. We chatted about everything, and I started to ask questions related to "the list." And when he answered every single one perfectly, I started to believe that the marriage thing could be real.

Shortly after our first date, my parents threw one of our big family parties. Big family parties were not out of the ordinary. Our family members tended to drop in on each other and "stay a while"— basically until there was enough food cooked and music playing to call it a party. However, this time, my female cousins were all inviting their boyfriends—a first. I figured there would be no better opportunity to introduce Vidal to the Caesar clan. I had never introduced anyone that I was remotely serious about to my parents. But there was something different about Vidal.

And sure enough, all went smoothly. He hit it off with my parents. We laughed, danced and ate our way long into the night. I was falling and falling fast.

By the time my twenty-fourth birthday came around on June 24, Vidal and I were an item. He planned the perfect celebration and came to pick me up in the van. I was wearing a black velvet mini halter dress, and had my hair styled in a bob. We took a couple of pictures of us looking good and then headed for Toronto. First we saw *The Phantom of the Opera*. I'd told him that I really wanted to see that show and I was excited to see it with him. When it was over, we walked over to the Top o' the Senator restaurant where he had booked us a table. I did wonder how he was paying for everything. He had a teaching job starting in September, but his summer job was doing the photocopying for a law firm, and that didn't pay a lot.

The host showed us to a cute little table for two in a little nook of the restaurant. I was beaming as I looked at Vidal. Nobody I had dated had ever done anything this special for me. Vidal, however, was looking pale. "Is everything okay?" I asked. He nodded as he looked over the menu.

The host came back to the table. "Can I get you anything to drink?" "Water," Vidal said promptly. "We will just stick to water."

"Everything okay?" I asked Vidal again. He was even paler and admitted that he really could not afford the restaurant. I didn't mind. We were a team, and we came up with a plan. We would drink water and order one plate of rosemary chicken to split between the two of us.

When the host came back, we ordered and even had the audacity to ask him to take our picture. He knew we were children playing in the adult world, but we didn't care.

The closer Vidal and I grew, the more he wanted me to meet his parents too. No matter what I've just written, at the time, I was still under the impression that Vidal and I would date for the summer, and then call it quits in October. As a way to finally get out from under my parents' roof, I had planned an exchange trip to Australia. I'd even partially paid for it. Still how could I say no to this request?

We were chatting on the driveway in front of Vidal's Pickering home when his father, John, pulled up, having driven back from a job in northern Ontario. A tall, handsome fair-skinned man, he got out of his car and greeted me warmly after Vidal introduced us. Then he started to tell Vidal about his trip. I was instantly drawn to the relationship they had. Their ease with each other was foreign to me. It was as if I had never learned the correct way of communicating with my own parents. They were two men, who respected and loved each other, talking on the driveway as if they were old friends. I loved to see it.

I felt drawn to their conversation, not to be a part of it, but to be part of their world. I could have watched the interaction forever, but my trance was broken when Big John (as everyone affection-ately calls him) suddenly switched into patois when Vidal told him about his new job; we could have been on the street in Kingston, Jamaica. I burst out laughing.

"So wha," Big John said. "Yuh laughin' a meh accent?"

I shook my head no, but I couldn't stop laughing.

That was the start of an amazing friendship with my father-in-law, one I cherish to this day. When I eventually told Big John about my disappointment with my years at university, he gave me a piece of advice that I will never forget, and that I have repeated often. He said I shouldn't be too hard on myself. I could live my entire life all over again, start from scratch, and not be as old as he was.

I was so ashamed of my past mistakes I had never taken the time to realize that I could start fresh. If I wanted to, I could start over again at kindergarten, or more realistically, go back to school. I had no control over the past, and couldn't change it. But I could go forward.

Fat chance. By the end of the summer, I was pregnant. Given that they knew Vidal, and he was ecstatic, we had to tell my parents, whose glares of disapproval could have etched a scarlet letter in my forehead. As if my university performance and shenanigans were not disappointing enough, now I was pregnant out of wedlock.

I could not catch a break. I needed to find a direction for myself, and here I was breaking a major vow I'd made to not have children. A baby. Could I protect her? Given what I'd seen in my life, what chance did I have to be a good mother? What if I hit her?

The tension at home was stifling, and my own self-loathing did not help, so I left home to stay with Vidal for a few days. He was living at a friend's house, but they were away for a week, so we would have a little privacy.

I sat on his bed and cried. I was not ready to take care of a baby. I could hardly take care of myself. Vidal stroked my head, and then my belly. He begged for me to stop crying: "You are going to make yourself sick, and that's not good for the baby." His concern made me cry even more. How did I get so lucky? I found the perfect guy. The list guy. The scrub with a loofah guy (yes, I asked). The man who said all the right things, at exactly the right time. As I sat on the edge of the bed, I heard Vidal open the closet and rummage through some stuff. When he came back to me, he knelt holding a little red box. "I was waiting to give this to you at the perfect moment," he said, "but I want you to have it now. I will take care of you and this baby too. Please be my wife."

Then he opened the box to reveal the engagement ring I had designed in jest shortly after Vidal told me he was going to marry me. I did not like rings with the claw grip on the diamond and had drawn one that looked like an upside down omega, with the diamond cradled in its centre. He must have ordered the ring just after we started dating.

I stared at the box, and then at Vidal, who was wearing a white T-shirt and boxer briefs. (We would laugh about that outfit later. *So romantic.*) I'd been so unsure about everything in my life for so long, the moment seemed surreal. He had said from day one that I was going to be his wife and he had prepared for this moment.

I knew he loved me, and I loved him, but I was terrified. I thought we'd been playing when it came to getting married. I had so many unresolved issues it seemed unrealistic to get married. I had barely processed the bullshit of the previous six years. When was I going to have time to deal with my issues with a husband and a baby on the way? When was the adult version of me going to show up?

I was shaking and Vidal's big brown eyes, filled with tears, drew me in with the promise of protection, love and happiness. I couldn't hurt him by saying no, but I felt like I did not deserve him, so I couldn't say yes. So I said nothing and just nodded. We were getting married.

Still, I could not shake the unsettling feeling that everything was moving too fast. On top of that, I had morning sickness that lasted most of the day, every single day. My parents were not completely on board with the shotgun wedding—we wanted to get married as soon as we could—and I could not bear the thought of disappointing them again or letting Vidal down.

One night, during all this turmoil, I had a dream that I was in a house that my grandfather Doril had built in heaven. It was a beautiful, golden, shimmering building with many rooms. In the centre courtyard was a large pool. My cousins were all gathered around it, including my cousin Donna, who was pregnant (in real life too). I waded into the pool and somehow fell asleep. I dreamed that when I woke I was lying beside the pool in front of something that resembled a narrow altar. I looked up, and there was Vidal, leaning over the altar, looking down at me. What appeared to be an angel stood behind him and gently placed a white cloak over Vidal's shoulders. Then Vidal said to me, "Your grandfather has sent me to take care of you."

After that dream, I relaxed a little. And everyone else seemed to lose their reservations, too, and got into planning the upcoming nuptials. My dad's older sisters, Aunt Liz and Aunt Louisa—inseparable, highly opinionated and influential in the family (if they shun you, you are done)—were surprisingly excited about the wedding, and put everyone to work making invitations and wedding decorations. My mother got into the spirit in a big way: she sewed my wedding dress, complete with a little extra room around the belly, and the bridesmaids' dresses too. It was like my grandfather was making miracles of harmony happen from beyond the grave.

Then my body decided it would throw another little wrinkle into the works, just in case I was tempted to fully relax. About a month before the wedding date, in early December, I started to dilate prematurely due to an incompetent cervix (yes, that is the medical term); the medical team thought it best to have me on full bed rest. This meant no standing, let alone dancing at my wedding.

Our day, January 2, 1999, was memorable to say the least: it was the day of a blizzard that was the first of two major storms that caused the mayor of Toronto at the time, Mel Lastman, to call in the army to help deal with the snow. The large snowflakes made our wedding pictures really beautiful, but the storm turned the drive home after the wedding into an eight-hour ordeal for our guests from Pickering. During the reception the snow had buried the cars in the parking lot and made the exit out of the northwest Brampton reception hall impassable.

At the end of the night Vidal changed into my father's work boots and joined a group who were shovelling out the driveway of the hall. I was helped out of my dress and into track pants, then four people carried me out to our car. Since there was no way, in my condition, we could attempt the drive across the city to our newly rented basement apartment in Scarborough, we spent our honeymoon night in my childhood bedroom. Even if my incompetent cervix hadn't ruled it out, we were not having sex in my parents' house. It was a couple of days before the roads cleared up enough for us to go home.

Telling lies to others, like I had to my parents for all those years, was bad. Not telling Vidal how I truly felt about getting married and having a baby before I was ready was worse. But the potentially fatal lies are the ones we tell ourselves. We are not good enough. Not smart enough. Not pretty enough. Not worth love. I had been telling myself these lies for years.

Though Vidal was so willing, I did not need my list guy to rescue me. I needed to get out of my own way and learn to stand in my own truth, flaws and all. I needed to form a perfect union with me. I needed to rescue me. The blizzard of our wedding day foreshadowed more life storms ahead.

five

YES, REALLY. A WIFE AND A MOTHER

VIDAL HAD SPENT NIGHTS and weekends before we got married fixing up the basement apartment in Scarborough. He painted Desiray's nursery lilac and added a Winnie-the-Pooh wallpaper border, painted the master bedroom blue and the rest of the apartment a light pink. Not sure what we were thinking with the colours, but thankfully we eventually refined our colour palette.

I was anxious about moving into our new place, and the wedding-day storm had delayed us from spending the first couple of days there. Though I was almost twenty-five, this was the first time I would be living away from home. As much as I wanted to leave my parents' house, it had offered me a protection from the outside world that I hadn't appreciated until now. I'd never thought about bills or buying furniture or taking care of another person's needs. And although my parents were strict with me, I never had to worry about anything material. Our house had all the bells and whistles and all the new gadgets. We had more volumes of the *Encyclopaedia Britannica* than the local library and my bedroom had matching designer furniture. In our basement apartment I would be starting from scratch.

But once the snow had been cleared off the highways, I couldn't put it off any longer.

Since I was still supposed to be taking it easy in order to hang on to my pregnancy, Vidal really had no idea that there were some more surprises in store for him when it came to how I saw myself as a wife. At that point, I actually couldn't do all that much around the house, but there were a couple of things I never intended to do: ironing and cooking.

My mother had taught me to iron, and I often did so without fuss. But when she still lived with us, Gramsie told me one day that I wasn't ironing a shirt correctly. She took over, pulling the sleeve over the slender end of the ironing board and folding it such that the pleat along its length was perfect. She made sure that even the spots between the buttons were smoothed flat. She spent so much time on that one shirt, I thought we would be ironing it for days. When she was done, she looked at her masterpiece and said to me, "When you grow up, this is how you should iron your husband's shirts."

As-fucking-if! That was not my picture of how I was going to live my life. That day I swore I would never iron for a man. Ever! And I have kept that promise. To this day, I do not own an ironing board. Well, actually I do. Once, when my father-in-law was visiting, he asked one of the children to get him the iron and they fetched him the iron tablets I take for my anemia. Out of embarrassment, I purchased a small ironing board, but I keep it in storage except when he's staying with us.

Then there was the idea that a woman's place was in the kitchen. When I visited Grenada, my aunts would cook the most amazing meals—combinations of fried or stewed chicken, rice, macaroni pie, and greens. For Sunday dinner, it seemed like they cooked everything there was to cook. One day, as my aunt and I were waiting for my uncle to come home, I watched her prepare his plate. She actually took the time to place steamed rice in a small bowl and turn it over on the plate so that it formed a nice round dome. It was amazing. My dad would be lucky if my mother slapped the rice on the plate.

My aunt then added the best pieces of chicken, some greens and a mound of yams and other ground provisions. I salivated. At the time, I did not realize she was taking such care for someone who was not even home, and rushed forward to grab the plate.

She held up a warning hand. "That's not for you, dear. That is for Uncle."

I looked at the chicken pieces left for the rest of us—the dark meat and a few pieces of chicken back. What in the actual fuck was chicken back?

My uncle returned home after I'd gone to sleep, but I woke up when I heard them arguing about something. I got out of bed, crouched down and peeked around the door. I saw my uncle stumble over to the table, pick up the plate and smash it on the floor. I froze. How disrespectful! If this was the way things could go, there was no way that I was ever going to consider it my duty to feed my husband, and the day that husband demanded I cook for him would be the last time I ever did.

Those weren't the only rules of engagement I'd decided on. I did not want to start our marriage in the same way that I started my life—being left behind. Undoubtedly, this is no way to begin a marriage, but no one had given me the rule book where it said, "Do not start your marriage with threats." So I proceeded to give Vidal some instructions. In addition to no ironing and no expectations of hot meals when he came home from work, I told him that if he ever stopped loving me or was no longer interested in being with me, he could and should leave. That may sound like the opposite of not wanting to be left behind, but it wasn't. If he did not want to stay with me, I wanted him gone. I loved him enough to know that sticking around in order to stick around was no way to live, but

I was not going to make it easy for him to want to stay. To be honest, I think I was trying to push Vidal away from the moment he said, "I do."

For instance, I would still drive to my parents' place in Brampton when they asked for help with the simplest of tasks, like I was under a spell. I am sure it was confusing for him. The woman he loved did not fall under spells or acquiesce to the demands of others. She was fierce, unapologetic and bold, and didn't suffer fools. Now he was seeing the side of me that had always been under her parents' control. The more I went to Brampton, the more strain it put on our marriage. When Vidal asked me to think about not going so much—he wanted to see me on nights and weekends, after all—I was hard on him for not understanding. How could I say no to my parents?

In those early months of our marriage, waiting for our daughter to be born, I knew what I didn't want to be as a wife—or at least thought I did. I also knew what I did want to be as a mother. The problem was I didn't know what to expect when the child was actually on her way.

Nobody had ever talked to me about pregnancy or the pains of childbirth; I was in the dark. I needed the extended version of the story of the birds and the bees, the one that included the woes of pregnancy, because I was having a tough one.

I was nauseous for the entire nine months (something that happened every other time too), so nauseous that saliva constantly accumulated in my mouth. When I finally went into labour at the end of April, I could not make sense of the degree of pain. In TV dramas, women sweat and scream for a bit, the baby comes out and, suddenly, they are smiling. I was not smiling. The labour was so long and painful I did not want to hold my baby after she was born. The disconnect I felt as I watched the attendants clean Desiray and weigh her was so strange. When a nurse at last handed her to me, I held her as if she was a small pumpkin, and I wanted nothing more than to give her back.

In the following months, I waded through a fog of postpartum depression (which may be a natural reaction to having your vagina stretched in such unthinkable ways). I had lots of fears about becoming a mother, but high hopes too. This was not what I'd imagined. I'd gone through six years of relentless failures and lies, and now I felt like I was failing again.

I went back to work within weeks of Desiray's birth. At least work was a break from feeling badly about feeling badly about my daughter. Because we had moved to the east end of Toronto, I'd had to quit my job at the pharmacy. Yet when my parents told me I shouldn't be sitting around and should go to work in their warehouse as a forklift operator and part-time receptionist, I said yes. So as well as visiting them on weekends, I started driving to Etobicoke, where the warehouse was, every workday. It was not as far as Brampton, but during morning and evening rush hour, it may as well have been.

To say Vidal was confused by my choices was an understatement. The upside was that I could bring Desiray to work with me, so we didn't have to pay for childcare. The downside was that I was working for my parents and in their grip. Again. I'd had low points in my life, but this was one of the lowest points. Vidal, who was teaching high school in Pickering, a job he loved, saw how miserable I was and didn't understand why I didn't quit, especially since the pay wasn't all that great. "Why are you doing it?" he'd ask. I had no answer.

Every morning as I drove to work, I'd dream about getting out of that warehouse, which I knew was no place for my baby and me. I'd think about the fact that U of T had given me the piece of paper. I did graduate. Though maybe they only gave the degree to me to get me out of there because my abysmal performance was causing their international rankings to drop. I desperately needed to find that fierce and confident child who sang naked at the top of the stairs. I now had a family and a daughter who looked up to me. I couldn't just wish for a better world for her, I had to be a part of the team creating it.

I'd remind myself that my GPA was not printed on the degree. Nobody would know what my score was except me. But that was the problem—I knew that score, and the whole shameful performance that led to it.

After a couple of years of feeling completely stuck, barely hanging on from day to day, I finally decided that the first move I needed to make in reclaiming myself was to go back to U of T. I was acutely aware that I was deliberately choosing to go back to the same university that chewed me up and spat me out. But this time, I was going back on my terms, and in an entirely different situation. I needed to prove to myself that I was capable of succeeding in university and that my past was not going to get the best of me.

One night after the baby was asleep I went on the university website and looked through all the courses offered to mature students. As I sat in front of the screen, tears streamed down my face— the imposter rearing her ugly head. I could not believe I was married with a child and looking through undergraduate research programs like I had in high school.

I searched and searched, continuing to beat myself up, until I finally clicked on the Department of Nutritional Sciences. Although I cannot accurately describe why I reacted this way, I stopped crying immediately, feeling a wave of comfort coming from the screen. I wrote down the name and number of the course director, Dr. Thomas Wolever, and called him the next day. He picked up the phone! I told him I wanted to come back to school to take a fourth-year research course. He responded that two professors in the department were accepting research students. I could go with Dr. X, he said, but "that guy is a bear—you do not want to go with him." He was right—no way could I deal with a bear in my state. I opted for his second suggestion, Dr. Carol Greenwood. I called her later that day and she told me to come in for an interview the following Tuesday. Huh? Just like that?

And so, the following Tuesday, I walked into Dr. Greenwood's narrow office at the Rotman Research Institute, on the grounds of Baycrest Centre for Geriatric Care in Toronto. She had no receptionist, just a desk and a couple of chairs in a space crowded with books. I cannot remember if she looked up at me when I arrived at her door, but before I could say much of anything she told me that it was a bad time and we needed to reschedule. I wanted to protest, but I was too scared and crushed. I just put my tail between my legs and left. By the time I reached the lobby, though, I'd gathered my resolve and called to make another appointment.

At our next meeting, Dr. Greenwood simply asked me when I could start.

"Now!"

Although I was a research student, the position paid minimum wage. Bonus! Not only would I get to continue my education, I would be getting paid. We enrolled Desiray in a French daycare, not far from our basement apartment. She was a bright child right out of the womb. Leaving her at a French daycare meant that if they taught her nothing else all day, at least she might pick up a second language (which she did).

My shifts were eight hours a day, five days a week, supporting the research of a doctoral student named Karen Young who was completing her thesis on nutrition and cognitive impairment in the elderly. I was required to serve weighed portions of food to the residents of Baycrest's Alzheimer's disease unit at breakfast, lunch, dinner and snack. Once they were finished their meal, I had to weigh the portion they didn't eat then calculate the difference between that, and the whole offering, to evaluate their individual caloric intake. These leftovers included anything remaining—the chewed-up bits the residents threw against the wall or wrapped in a napkin or tucked into a drawer. Wherever it was, I had to find it, weigh it and perform the appropriate calculations.

Learning about the different fridges and separate services for dairy and meat dishes necessary to keep kosher for the Jewish patients was fascinating—my life to that point had not brought me in contact with Jewish traditions—but not as fascinating as learning about each of the residents. During my breaks, I would sit with them. They might not remember what happened half an hour earlier, but most of them had their long-term memories intact, and they would tell me stories of the Second World War—harrowing tales of the concentration camps, but also of survival and love, and the triumph of the human spirit. I would often hear them screaming in their sleep, their dreams interrupted with nightmares, maybe of the camps. I grew to love and appreciate their gentle spirits and mourn the forgetfulness of their minds.

Every day, after I worked my full shift, I would stay on to complete the data entry and learn the appropriate statistical analysis. I picked Karen's brain and talked to other PhD students in the building about how best to interpret and present the data. Student after student gave generously of their time as I learned my way around the statistical software. One student spent an entire evening teaching me Excel, showing me how to graph the outcomes, how to account for outliers, how to change variables and other functions.

Those unpaid hours I put in not only gave me the experience I needed to get the next job, they were appreciated by those around me, especially Dr. Greenwood. She soon made me responsible for a small component of the project and told me that she wanted me to present the results at an international nutrition and ageing conference in Albuquerque, New Mexico. I blinked at her when she announced this and tilted my head—was she really speaking to me?

Dr. Greenwood did not take back what she said, she did not ask again, and she certainly was not waiting for my response. I was going to take the assignment and go to New Mexico to present it.

I got to work. I prepared a case study on one of the residents to determine the best time of day to offer a nutrient-dense snack, such as an energy bar, to ensure they would eat it. It was often difficult to get residents with dementia to eat extra calories. They would either insist they'd just eaten and didn't need a snack or preferred candies or cookies to the more nourishing option. Dr. Greenwood supervised from a distance as I completed the research and prepared my findings. She never hovered or made me feel like I did not know what I was doing. She allowed me to fully appreciate the research process, including making mistakes. When my analysis went awry, I asked questions, got answers and course-corrected. When I was ready to prepare the poster for the conference to display my finding that a mid-morning intervention provided the best result, she was beside me to help. I had never had anyone willing to put so much energy into simply helping me.

The experience of New Mexico was fantastic. I listened to other presenters share their research, visited some tourist areas, ate some great food and had wonderful laughs. When my poster was placed in the main conference hallway, I stood beside it hoping no one would come over and ask questions at the same time as hoping everyone would come over and ask questions. I was a nervous wreck. Karen and another student stayed with me, standing at a distance and reminding me to breathe. Soon, there was one person in front of me staring at the board. I remember letting them stare, as if they were browsing a rack at a clothing store. Then another came over, then another. I glanced at Karen, who gently waved her hand, indicating that I should talk to them. As simple as the case study was, people were genuinely interested in the results and congratulated me on my findings. For the first time, since high school, I felt at home.

Dr. Greenwood became one of my greatest sponsors. More than just a mentor, she invested time and resources in my development and was not afraid to push me beyond my limits. As eager as I was to learn, I am sure she recognized how the shame and guilt of my past mistakes weighed on me. In telling me to present my research myself, she nudged me to the edge of the deep end and ever so delicately pushed me in. She knew full well that I could swim on my own, but that I had temporarily forgotten how. And she stayed at the edge of the pool, patiently waiting for me to remember that I was actually good at it.

I finished that year with the only A grade on my University of Toronto undergraduate transcript. And on top of the boost that gave to my damaged self-esteem, that year I encountered someone else who lifted my spirits and made me think differently about my future. One day I had to go on an errand—I forget what—to the top floor of the Rotman Institute and walked past an office that was so bright and beautifully decorated I stopped to peer in. It was a huge corner office decorated with pottery and plants of every kind. There was art and photographs and . . . hold up . . . there were Black people in the photographs. Whose office was this?

As I poked my head farther in, I saw her. A beautiful, dark-skinned woman whose natural curly hair was accentuated with the most brilliant grey. I looked at the nameplate on the door: *Jean Lazarus, Director of Research Operations.* Director of Research Operations? I did not realize a job like that was possible. That first time, I did not dare to interrupt her, but I made a point from then on of walking through the top floor every chance I got, hoping she'd notice me. When we finally were introduced, I was ecstatic. My conversations with Jean were the bonus on top of an already life-changing experience. She became the big research sister I never knew I needed. Knowing that a Black woman was in charge meant everything to me. She sat at the table with the other directors, and I felt like she represented me at that table. I wanted to make her proud of everything I did, and I worked my tail off so that I would not embarrass her and could show others that all Black women were as amazing as Jean was.

Representation matters. But Jean taught me that access to representation is even more important. Not only did she allow me to watch her in the position, she allowed me to ask questions and make decisions about a career in research. During my time in politics years later, I would insist on such access for everyone, but especially Black women and girls. Not only did I want them to see me in that public sphere, but I would invite them to Parliament, to my riding office and to my home. I made myself, and the position I held, accessible to them, just as Jean had done for me. I knew that the impact of seeing me interact and be a regular human being in politics would last them a lifetime—giving them permission to be their authentic selves, too, wherever they ended up.

Jean's example made me want to dream bigger. So when I saw a job posting for a research assistant, I decided to apply. Such opportunities were rare and, when one became available, every student pounced on it. The posting called for someone with a background in psychology and statistics. I had neither. I'd never studied psychology and the after-work guidance I'd received from the other students did not make me a statistician. But I needed the job. I was falling in love with research and wanted to pursue it as a career, and you cannot become a research coordinator without having been a research assistant, and you cannot become a research manager or director without having been a research coordinator.

When I showed up for my interview with Dr. Donald Stuss, the head of the Rotman Research Institute, and his own research assistant, he asked me off the top to tell him a little bit about myself. I immediately blurted out that I did not have any training in psychology or statistics experience. He and his colleague looked perplexed. They must have been thinking, *Can she even read? Did she not see what the posting said?* But I was in survivor mode—everyone wanted the job but I needed it—and before they could show my unqualified self out the door, I said, "Look. I may not have any psych, and I certainly do not have enough stats, but I have passion and drive and am a quick learner, and you can't teach that. You can teach me stats, and you can teach me psych, and I will learn it. Fast. But you cannot teach passion and drive, and I have that in abundance."

I got the job. The only way I can explain why Dr. Stuss took such a chance on me is that he was not a manager or a boss, he was a leader, and as such he wasn't afraid to trust his own judgement no matter my lack of credentials.

It was a real turning point. The next week I went to work for Dr. Stuss as a critical part of his cognitive neurorehabilitation research team, funded by a million-dollar grant. The work involved testing participants with mild cognitive impairments or traumatic brain injuries to determine if training could improve their executive function and short-term memory. We take for granted how things such as writing lists, self-talk and putting our keys in the same spot when returning home keep us on track. But for a PhD who couldn't remember how to make a sandwich because he hit his head when he fell off a ladder putting up holiday lights or a senior who was worried about their partner's inability to remember simple tasks, such little lessons and tactics helped make their lives better. (Understanding how a seemingly innocuous bump on the head could damage the brain has made bike helmets mandatory in our household.)

Dr. Stuss paid keen interest to what his team members wanted out of their work, how we wanted to develop as researchers and in our careers. Like Dr. Greenwood, he took the time to ask questions and get to know everyone on the team. Every time he called me in for a meeting, I would get to his spacious office early. I loved looking at the trinkets and books he'd collected over the years related to the brain and found myself smiling at the serendipity of ending up studying the brain, even though I wasn't, and would never be, a neurosurgeon. It was as if the universe was giving me a hint that I was on the right track by keeping the brain in my life and I was so grateful for it.

The research was challenging, and when the study was complete and the manuscripts prepared, there was my name, listed along with the lead researchers and other team members, on publications in several medical journals. My hard work had been recognized and credited. Figuring that all signs were pointing to me staying in the brain lane, I went to see Dr. Stuss, hoping he would write a reference letter recommending me for a master of science degree program, so I could continue working with him. I sat on the chair across the desk from him and pleaded my case for the endorsement, confident he would write a stellar letter. Dr. Stuss agreed to write me a letter, but not to the science program. The thing about true mentors is that they see something in you that you often don't see in yourself. Based on my performance and what he'd observed during the time I worked with him, he said, he believed that my skills were suited best to business.

I felt like I had been transported back to Sally Walker's office. Words were coming out of his mouth and I was not hearing anything. I was crushed—but only for a minute. The person sitting in front of Don Stuss was not the same girl who'd flamed out in undergrad.

"Why are you saying this?" I asked.

It turned out that Dr. Stuss could not envision me sitting in a lab running cognitive tests on willing participants for the next few years. He saw someone who was analytical and strategic, someone who had helped to make his whole project a success. Like Dr. Greenwood, he cared enough about my future to steer me towards challenge and away from complacency.

I swallowed hard. Could I study business? The thought was completely foreign to anything I had ever imagined for myself. What if he was right? What if he was wrong? Usually, Kenny Rogers' voice pops into my head when I have a tough decision to make: "You gotta know when to hold 'em, know when to fold 'em, know when to walk away and know when to run." But Kenny wasn't helping. I did not want to do any of those things. I wanted to follow Dr. Stuss's advice. He'd taken a chance on me when he knew nothing about me and I knew nothing about the project he was running. He knew me now, and I knew that he would not steer me wrong. So I took the offered reference letter and applied for a master's in business administration at the University of Phoenix, a program that was all online, meaning that I could keep working while I was doing it.

When Don Stuss died in September 2019, it hit me almost as hard as when my grandfather Caesar passed. He taught me so much about my own capabilities, I will be forever grateful. He showed me that mentors don't have to look like you, or come from where you come from, to be able to see you clearly. He showed me once again, just as Sally Walker and Carol Greenwood had, that people can be selfless.

six

BECAUSE NOTHING EVER RUNS IN A STRAIGHT LINE

I HAD A ROAD map now. I'd ticked off the research assistant box, had my application for my MBA in, and now I landed a job as a research coordinator with the University of Toronto, working on an Alzheimer's registry, tracking generations of families with the disease to see what patterns could be discerned. I was also seconded to work with two physicians at Toronto Western Hospital's Memory Clinic, a hospital role that gave me my first opportunity to see the pharmaceutical side of memory research. When we couldn't recruit enough participants for the study at the hospital, the lead researchers asked me to visit Ontario Shores Centre for Mental Health Sciences in Whitby to recruit more. During one of the early visits to the Whitby site, my blood pressure dropped suddenly and I fainted. It turned out I was pregnant with baby number two and, due to complications similar to the ones I experienced with Desiray, I was immediately put on bed rest. My stint as a research coordinator was over.

No good could come from me being on a second bout of bed rest. I was restless and agitated, and since I couldn't take care of Desiray in this state, she stayed on at daycare and I was alone all day, going stir crazy in our basement apartment. To pass the time, I spent hours on the internet.

One day Vidal called home from work, completely confused about a phone call he'd just received. "Babe, I just got a call from a high school in England," he said. "The person told me they were glad to receive my application and thought I would be perfect for the job. They want me to interview for a teaching position there. What is going on?"

The words couldn't come out of my mouth fast enough. "Did you say yes? Please tell me you said yes." While I was noodling around on the web, passing the time, the recruiting pitch for the position had caught my eye. It had been easy to fill out the application and send in a résumé on Vidal's behalf. I would be off for a year on maternity leave after our baby was born. This was our chance to see the world.

"Baaaabbbbbe-uh!"

Whenever Vidal made the word "babe" sound like it had more than one syllable, I knew I was in trouble. I didn't care. Trouble was my middle name and at least here I felt like I was using my talent for deception for good, not evil. Though, when I reflect on this now, I see how much I took it for granted that Vidal was mine to control, that he would always follow my lead. Our marriage would suffer for it down the road. But Vidal, as always, was kind.

"Babe," he said again, more softly. "You are seven months pregnant. This job starts in September. What are we going to do, have the baby, pack up Desiray and all our stuff and move halfway around the world for me to teach English to the English?"

"Absolutely," I said.

And that is exactly what we did.

Two months after our second daughter, Candice, was born, Vidal arranged a leave from his job at the Pickering high school where he taught, and there we were, landing at Manchester Airport with way more suitcases than four human beings should carry. All the new teachers had arrived at the same time and the school had sent a bus to pick us up.

The one thing neither of us wanted to do was leave a basement in Scarborough to live in another basement flat. Vidal and I had spent time on the internet to find what we thought would be a comfortable home. One by one, the other families were being dropped off in front of places that looked small and cramped with nonexistent yards. When the bus finally stopped at our new address on Brooke Drive in the little town of Astley, we both breathed a sigh of relief. It was a cute, fully furnished, two-bedroom, semi-detached house with a small front yard and more than enough space in the back yard. The landlord renting us the place welcomed us with some freshly baked bread and a pot of soup; we were hungry and tired and grateful for the thoughtful gesture. Already the place felt like home. Before I knew it, the children and I were all asleep.

I woke up to the sounds of laughter and loud talking coming from outside. Too timid to go out and investigate, I peeked out the bedroom window. There was Vidal and a crowd of new neighbours in the middle of the street with a good dozen empty beer bottles at their feet. Desiray was riding around on some other kid's bike and little girls and boys were squealing as they chased her. I sighed and tried to step back out of sight, but Vidal saw me and waved for me to come meet our new friends.

I hate that sort of thing; even now, I find meeting a new crowd of people all at once totally overwhelming. Besides, what did my hair look like? I'd just spent seven hours on a plane and had fallen asleep without wrapping it in my headscarf. But if I didn't go out there, Vidal would come to get me or, worse, invite all the neighbours in.

I quickly went to the washroom, smoothed out my wild mane as best I could and rinsed my mouth. There were bags of toiletries and house supplies everywhere. Where did we get all the stuff? I changed the baby, then carried her outside in the crook of my arm, waving hello to everybody and nervously patting my head to try to tame my hair further. I shot a wide-eyed glare at the empties and then at Vidal, trying to will him to tidy them up. "I see you have made yourself right at home," I said, but Vidal ignored my hints and calmly introduced me to the Brooke Drive crew, including our immediate neighbour who had taken him to the shopping centre to get all the bags of stuff in the house, as well as the beer. It seemed that Astley was abuzz about the new Canadians who had come to stay.

For the rest of 2004 and the first part of 2005, Vidal taught at Moorside High School in Swinton, a town in greater Manchester. The kids and I would wake up early to watch him walk to the bus stop in the morning. Then I'd take Desiray, now five, to school, and spend the rest of my day going on outings with Candice, having tea with neighbours, and, when the baby was napping, completing my MBA online.

It was just the break Vidal and I needed—an opportunity to shape our little family away from the competing influences of family and friends. In the evenings, I'd put the baby down for the night, and Desiray and I would amuse ourselves by giving Vidal facials or waxing the hair on his arms. He put up with it all, even the pain of hair removal; his students went crazy over what their new teacher was getting up to. The news that "Chavannes waxed his arms" went viral before going viral was a thing.

We watched television at night after the kids were both in bed until the cable man came around to collect the television tax. A tax for watching TV? I wanted to get rid of the set, but Vidal convinced me to keep it, so we could invite the other Canadian teachers over to watch the Super Bowl.

We could not afford a car, so we explored our new world on foot or by bus. We bought our produce from the farm at the end of our street, purchased meat from the butcher down the road and got the Tesco supermarket to deliver everything else.

And it was intoxicating that Europe was so close. I'd never been anywhere but the United States and the Caribbean. So, in addition to travelling around England during school breaks, we spent the holidays travelling through Venice, Milan and Rome. We had Christmas dinner at a Venetian Burger King. And when we fell prey to a telephone credit card scam that charged us $30 a minute to call home on Christmas, maxing out our credit, Vidal's parents paid for tickets on Alitalia to fly us back to the UK.

We loved the freedom we'd found, but even Vidal, who had a lot of patience when it came to tough kids, had a hard time handling the job. When foreign schools come looking to recruit Canadian teachers, we now know the glossier the brochure, the rougher the school. One of the new hires had gone on stress leave almost immediately; one by one, as the months passed, the others started to return to Canada. Although most of his students liked Vidal, when they set his classroom on fire after throwing fireworks through the window, we knew it was time to go back home too.

Vidal could pick up his old teaching job where he'd left off, but we'd given up our apartment and re-entry was rough. The four of us stayed with family and friends until we found a ground-floor apartment to rent in Ajax, Ontario, which was close to Vidal's school in Pickering.

I'd finished my MBA, and I needed a job too. I started looking for work as a research manager, the next step up the ladder I'd imagined for myself. Yet every time I sent out a résumé, I would feel my spirit pulling me in another direction. It was easy to put out résumé after résumé. It was the comfortable thing to do. But my capstone project for my degree had been putting together a business plan for a start-up and I couldn't stop thinking about what it would be like to actually follow through on all that planning and try to pull it off. It was unfamiliar and scary territory for sure, but it sparked the same feeling I'd had crossing the stage at Convocation Hall. The cheerleaders/butterflies were back, and I could not get rid of them.

I had enough contacts in the research world to start the business I'd mapped out—taking on the management of clinical trials for pharmaceutical companies or big academic research projects. But I told myself I was dreaming and kept sending out my résumé—in the end, 732 times. When all that effort resulted in four interviews, two second interviews and zero jobs—I was told that I had no managerial experience and now that I had my MBA I was over-qualified—I realized that no matter how hard you try to go in another direction, nothing meant for you can ever pass you by. I pulled out my plan and got down to the business of being an entrepreneur.

I incorporated ReSolve Research Solutions in 2005, and just as I'd planned, it was a healthcare-focused research management firm. The first year was a grind. Vidal, who believed in me and in the idea (he was the one who came up with the name for the company), started teaching night school, too, and on the weekends got a job in the paint department of a local hardware store. We worked hard and prayed even harder, but still had a difficult time making ends meet with two kids to support as well as the new business.

We'd sold most of our furniture before we moved to England; the only two items we had brought with us to our new apartment was a mattress, which Vidal, Candice and I shared, and a bed for Desiray. Friends gave us some small items, but every Monday evening (garbage night in Ajax) we would go for a walk around the neighbourhood looking for treasures people had thrown away. If we spotted something great, I would guard it while Vidal went to get the car. We would struggle to load the item and then Vidal would drive it home while I walked back with the girls.

One such evening, a little boy watched from the window as we stood in front of his home considering whether we could use something his family had discarded. I don't remember what it was, but from the way he was staring at us, it must have been something he didn't want to part with. When Desiray asked me why we were taking that little boy's stuff, my eyes welled up. I hate that I am such a crier. I cry over everything. But this was not the time to cry. I put on my game face. We needed the item, and one day Desiray would understand.

Still, I was frustrated and tired of living in an apartment furnished with other people's shit. As with every other time when I was in trouble or needed help, I asked for help. If you don't ask, you don't get. Even the Bible says "seek, and ye shall find, knock and the door shall be open." I was not sure that my faith was strong enough to believe that a miracle would happen, but my faith was strong enough to know that I deserved to ask.

"Lord," I said, as I leaned dejectedly on the kitchen counter one afternoon, looking around our place. "I need a miracle. I need a miracle now. Not the burning bush kind where I have to work to figure out what you're trying to tell me. I just need a good, old-fashioned, clearly articulated miracle. I need a house. I need a real home for my family." I cannot remember if I said please at the end, but I did drop to my knees and let all the tears out.

When I got up from the floor, I called our accountant, who was a family friend. I wondered why I hadn't thought to consult him before. I explained the situation. He said, "No problem. Call Rita. She's a mortgage broker and I'm sure she can help." So I did. After speaking to Rita, Vidal and I gathered the documents we needed to fill out a mortgage application, and within a couple of days, we pre-qualified for a $200,000 mortgage. This time I cried tears of joy. We were movin' on up like the Jeffersons. But nothing worth getting is easy—we still needed to figure out how to put together a down payment.

I started hustling harder with ReSolve. I worked dawn to dusk, never taking a break, and sent thousands of faxes to every pharmaceutical company in North America describing the services I offered. Not a lot of companies at the time were operating in the field I'd chosen for ReSolve, and I was confident that someone, somewhere would soon see the advantage in hiring me.

At last, I received a call from a major pharmaceutical company that was looking for a company based in Canada to manage a paediatric epilepsy clinical study. The woman at the other end of the line asked if we were interested in being the management site in Toronto for the research. "Of course," I replied. She then asked if we had experience with epilepsy clinical research and access to a local network of paediatric neuropsychologists. "Of course!" I replied again.

I lied. What and what? I did not have that experience and I did not have that specific network, but I needed the money. And of course I had passion and drive.

I worked even harder after that call, sometimes eighteen to twenty hours a day. Desiray was at school, but I still had Candice at home. She seemed to understand the pressure I was under and did not cry at all—until the phone rang. She also timed her demands for cookies or juice precisely. Stuffing her with cookies so I could to start a research study was all right by me. Changing diapers, laundry, bottle prep, marketing, advertising, client engagement and reception—no job was too big or too small. Although I had worked as a research coordinator, this was an entirely different beast.

I needed to learn everything I could about running a clinical research project with multiple sites. I needed to prepare a contract and a budget so the physicians I hired got paid, and I got paid as well. I needed to submit regulatory documents to the FDA and Health Canada, as well as make submissions to ethics boards to get the study approved. Crucially, I needed to recruit the doctors. I quickly realized that finding a paediatric neuropsychologist in Toronto who had experience with clinical research was like finding a needle in a haystack. I could not have asked for a harder first client.

The challenge was daunting, but there I was emailing and faxing and calling and driving around to visit physicians and asking questions and preparing budgets and submitting regulatory documents and getting ethics approvals and, and, and . . . successfully running the research study. I was doing it. I was levelling up. In May 2006, a week before the closing date on our first home, I opened the mail to find the first major cheque addressed to ReSolve Research Solutions, Inc. It covered the entire down payment.

When it came time to move, we had started to load our furniture into the truck when Vidal came running into the apartment and announced that he'd found something in the building's garbage room for our new home. I could not believe it. We were moving on up, and he was bringing in another dumpster-dive item. Those days were supposed to be behind us. I stopped packing to watch him manoeuvre a beautiful, wood-framed mirror through the door. It was exquisite. That mirror has moved with us from house to house. It is a permanent reminder that we should never forget where we come from, and that humility is the best way to stay grounded.

The first ReSolve cheque drove me to want bigger and better for the company. But bigger and better is expensive, and we did not have that kind of money to reinvest in the company. I needed to be smarter about gaining the competitive advantage I needed to keep it growing.

I knew I was one of very few site management organizations helping pharmaceutical researchers run clinical studies in Canada. Early on, I decided that I did not want anyone to be distracted by my gender or race, so I chose to exclude any images of me on the promotional material. Instead, I used a logo I designed myself, customer testimonials and their pictures.

Since I couldn't afford an advertising budget, I signed up to receive all the free industry periodicals and read them from cover to cover. Then I would write letters to the editor explaining why I agreed or disagreed with an article, making sure to include my company name and coordinates after my signature. Bit by bit, through such efforts, I started to be viewed as an expert in clinical research management. However, I didn't want to be just an expert. I wanted to be the go-to voice on issues related to research management. So I decided to conduct a small study on the inclusion of marginalized people, especially people of colour, in research studies. Very few people were in this territory at the time, and very few, if any, Black women were speaking about it.

The work was a hit. I was invited to speak at the top conferences across Canada and in the US. I was turning nothing into something spectacular. I kept my focus on getting clients, as I believed that grants and loans would enable the business, but clients allowed it to grow.

To save on overhead, I ran the company out of the front room in our home. We all know that room—the one that our parents never let us enter, where the vacuum lines stayed perfect from Saturday to Saturday and the plastic stayed on the furniture for eternity. I was working with some of the best physicians in Toronto. When we needed to, we could host meetings with pharmaceutical representatives in their fancy boardrooms. Nobody needed to know I didn't have one. And I did not allow my ego to pressure me into renting an office and putting "ReSolve Research Solutions, Inc." on some fancy sign.

Coming up with creative ways to make the company appear larger than life at the same time as saving every cent I could and never hiring the help I needed for the work, came with a cost. I spent most of my time on the job. I decided that seeking out contracts from big pharma wasn't enough, and I started doing secondments with various charitable neurological organizations. When we went on vacation, my phone, computer and all other necessary notes and supplies came with me. I felt I couldn't miss a call, text, fax or beep. If (and when) I did, I would melt down in a panic. One missed call was one missed call too many.

It put a strain on everything, especially my marriage. No amount of zeros on the cheque could buffer that. I was making a success of my business, but I had so much left to learn about how to live my life.

seven

THERE'S NO SUCH THING AS BALANCE

THERE ARE PAINFUL EXPERIENCES that happen to each of us that no one else will ever know if we don't tell. Sometimes it's shame that causes us, wrongly, to keep what happened a secret, but sometimes we push things down in an attempt to avoid reliving the pain. No matter how hard we try to ignore it, though, such pain will eat away slowly at our reserves of love and kindness. That's what pain does: it shuts you down and closes you off. The challenge is to acknowledge it and let the pain go. From my own experience, some of the most painful stories many women never tell are the stories of miscarriages. I had two between the births of Candice and our third and last child, Johnny.

On the morning I had my first miscarriage, Vidal and I had had a terrible fight. I was still yelling at him as I left the house and I stayed mad as I drove to Toronto for a meeting. In the car, I felt a heaviness in my stomach and chest. I knew I needed to calm down, but in the moment staying mad was a more important priority.

ReSolve Research Solutions was taking off and I was in the middle of that first major contract, running the paediatric epilepsy clinical trial. I arrived at the site still enraged, though to be honest, I had forgotten what we had been fighting about. I was there to meet with a young research participant and his mother to review some of the study protocol and do some preliminary tests. As I was in the examination room with them, I felt something strange pass through me, as if I was on my period. I froze. If I ran out of the room, I could jeopardize the care of the child, the research results and the reputation of my company. I remember thinking, "If what I felt is what I think I felt, then there is nothing I can do about it."

I finished the examination. I took the time to enter the data and complete the patient chart, and only then did I allow terror to take over. I walked to the washroom, sat on the toilet and did the kind of crying that many women are familiar with—the kind where the tears are falling, your mouth opens wide as if to scream, but no sound comes out. I did that again and again, screaming so nobody could hear me, as the blood fell into the bowl.

When I calmed down a little, I called my cousin Debbie, who worked at the high-risk pregnancy unit of the hospital where Desiray and Candice were born. She tried to tell me that nothing was wrong, but that I should come in for a pelvic examination.

"I am having a miscarriage, aren't I? Don't lie to me, please."

"I can't tell if that is the case over the phone. You need to come in. Don't worry. Spotting during pregnancy is normal."

"This is not spotting, these are clots."

"Just come to the hospital and let's check it out."

I cleaned myself up as best I could, and drove towards the hospital. On the way, I called Vidal. I did not want to call him, because I absolutely felt like the miscarriage was my fault. I was such a hothead (still am) and was always looking for a fight with him (still am), and now it had cost me our pregnancy. He didn't have to say a word, though—I knew immediately that he understood how I felt. We both stayed silently on the phone until I arrived at the hospital. Too many unnecessary and hurtful words had been expressed that morning. Any more words, even pleasant ones, wouldn't help much.

I waited in the entrance for Vidal to arrive. I didn't want to go up to the unit until he was there. I knew that he would need me during this experience as much as I needed him. We had both been looking forward to growing our family. There was a five-year gap between Desiray and Candice, and we'd wanted our next child to be closer in age.

It did not take long to confirm what I already knew. The obstetrician gave me a couple of options. I could either be checked in to have a D&C to complete the miscarriage, or go home and take a drug called misoprostol that would allow me to pass the remaining tissue. The mere thought of a D&C awakened the old ghosts, so I opted for the drug.

When we got home, I used the medication as instructed and waited. What happened next felt worse than childbirth. The pain of the contractions caused me to contemplate suicide for the first time in my life. I was a wreck. We were a wreck. There was no consoling me and the physical and emotional toll was unbearable. I was not sure which hurt more, the contractions or the heartache.

I miscarried for the second time only a year later. During the second one, I faced my fears and opted for the D&C. Physically, I handled it much better. Emotionally? Not so much.

I felt terrible for months after each miscarriage. The medical staff told me that they were not my fault, and that there was nothing I could have done to prevent them from happening. But their reassurances did not matter to me. I was certain that my temper had something to do with them, or that I was being punished for past mistakes.

While I was still in the grip of despair after the second one, I ran into a friend who asked why she had not seen me for a while. I had not talked about what I was going through with anyone, but found myself telling her not only what had happened but how sad and guilty I was feeling.

"I felt that way after my miscarriage, too. You know it is not your fault, right?" she said.

I felt a weight lift off my shoulders. "Really? You had a miscarriage? When? Where?" I reached to touch her leg as if I was about to examine her southern region. I am not sure what I was thinking! I was just so relieved to share the experience with someone who had been through it before herself and could empathize. Of all the people who spoke to me about the miscarriages and told me how I should be feeling, she was the only one who admitted to going through the experience herself.

That one story gave me what I needed to no longer feel alone and ashamed. Stories are sticky, which is why we need to tell them. True, sharing our experiences helps others feel like they are not alone in a given circumstance. But I also believe that the vulnerability we show in telling our stories gives other people hope. It was in that moment that I realized the power of using our most vulnerable moments to build strength and resilience in other people, as well as ourselves. To empower others and create the sense of humanity that is so often lacking in our society because we are too busy trying to show off to our neighbours instead of trying to show up for them.

When Johnny was born in 2008, our family was complete. Unlike most mothers I've talked to, I do not think that the best days of my life were the days my children came into the world. The pain, the sadness, the losses, the morning sickness, the horrible labours: they always say that mothers forget all about them. I haven't forgotten any of it.

But my children are my touchstones, my energy source—they drive my determination and willingness to do whatever it takes to be successful. My greatest honour and joy is being a mother to these extraordinary children; the Lord knows that I need them as much as they need me. They kept me pushing forward and striving for better then, and they still do. I did not want them see me the way I often saw myself, as a failure and a fraud. I wanted to be the strong Black woman that they could model themselves on and be proud to call Mom.

Just as I'd vowed as a teenager, corporal punishment is not part of our home—I had received enough beatings to last my own and a hundred more lifetimes. And after they were born, I added one more vow: I would keep nothing from them. I was going to tell them everything. They were not going to be surprised by anything life dished out or ever wonder why their mother had kept an important insight from them.

And when I say everything, I mean everything. Whereas Vidal always stuck to the script about the birds and the bees, I gave the children all the gritty details. For instance, while taking a drive one spring a couple years ago, I overheard Desiray whispering to Candice.

"What are you saying about tampons?" I asked.

I had a captive audience in the car, so it pleased me to enunciate every letter in the word "tampons" to the point where it sounded like I was speaking in slow motion. Vidal gripped the steering wheel harder and I could see Johnny perk up in the rear seat. He loved these awkward conversations. Desiray shot Candice a look—they knew what was coming.

I reiterated for them that my mother gave me the basics, but she certainly never taught me how to use tampons. I used one for the first time late in my teenage years, I said, and my cousin Vanessa had to teach me how.

Well, to be clear, she did not actually "teach" me anything. I had gotten my period while visiting family in New York, and had asked her if she had any pads. She went away and came back holding a stick wrapped in paper. "Here," she said, handing the thing to me.

She knew very well that I had no idea what it was, but I didn't give her the satisfaction of asking any questions. Vanessa was loud and larger than life. She would have laughed uproariously while telling the entire household and everyone on all of East 82nd Street, where she lived, that her dumb Canadian cousin did not know what a tampon was.

I had already started to stain my underwear and I needed to fix the situation before it got worse. In the bathroom I opened the package and looked at the strange device. What was I supposed to do with this? I cringed at the thought of touching myself down there, but I found the right location and pushed the device in. I think I bruised most of my insides trying to complete the task and I walked around for the rest of the day as if I had ridden a horse.

At this point, one of my girls interrupted. "We can learn this on Google or YouTube. We don't need the whole lesson."

Learn from Google or YouTube? Hardly! I was their internet and encyclopaedia, and was not deterred by the comment from the back seat. I pressed on, explaining how to insert the tampon by holding on to the ribbed portion of the head, inserting it fully and then (and only then) placing your other hand on the stick and pushing upward.

Candice squealed, "OMG, Lady! That sounds like it hurts!" (Candice always calls me Lady.)

I pressed on to explain that one should purchase tampons with the pearled rounded top. But even those can pinch a little, so it might be necessary to rub the top portion of the tampon on your clitoris to help provide some extra lubrication in your vagina.

At that Vidal swerved the vehicle. Everyone but Johnny, who seemed pleased with the educational content, was screaming! "Babe!" (from Vidal), "Mom!" (from Desiray), "TMI, Lady!" (from Candice).

Since when did such practical advice equal too much information? I knew that one day, the little vice grips on the top of a tampon would catch their delicate flesh and I wanted them to be able to avoid that pain.

"Johnny certainly does not need to hear any more of this," Vidal warned.

"Why?" I demanded, "What if he has daughters? We have had discussions about his balls dropping and he told all of us about the length of the hair on his scrotum." A few weeks before this particular conversation, Johnny had announced that he had found three-centimetre hairs growing on his self-named "sack of toys." We investigated, and found no such hairs. At the dinner table that night, Johnny explained that his three-centimetre announcement was a "hyperbowl."

I looked at Desiray and Desiray looked at me. A hyperbowl? During those split seconds I tried to remember if the term described any part of the male genitalia. Johnny is a gifted child, so most of what he says makes me question my own intelligence. He often speaks about issues I have never heard of.

"Do you mean hyperbole—hy-pur-bow-lee?" Desiray finally blurted. The girls have no patience for Johnny's gifted brain and both of them welcome any opportunity to bring him down a few pegs. Everyone burst out laughing. A three-centimetre hyperbole was something we could all understand.

In addition to talking openly with my children about any subject, I was also the mother who followed the recommendations of all the reports that said that we, in the Black community in particular, need to show up and be present for our children at school. Vidal or I or both of us went to every parent-teacher meeting, school event and concert, volunteered for trips and the occasional drop-in to the classroom.

Even though the teachers, administration and support staff knew who we were because of all the showing up we did, our children still faced barriers in the system. I cannot imagine what it is like for

THERE'S NO SUCH THING AS BALANCE • 101

children who do not have a parent present to defend them or advocate on their behalf. Sometimes, when I went into the school office and saw other Black children there, I would ask them why they were in the office. If they were in trouble, I would pretend that I knew their parents and say (loud enough for the administration to hear me) that I was going to call their mothers later and let them know I saw them in the office. The children usually looked at me as if I was crazy. I didn't care. The point was to make sure that everyone in authority at the school knew a parent was paying attention to what was going on. If it takes a village to raise a child, sometimes the village simply needs to show up unannounced.

Rarely were my children in the office without us knowing about it. In our house, the rule was, "Tell us the whole truth immediately and there will be no consequences. If we hear the story from someone else, there will be consequences." Our children would come home and tell us everything, even if it was inappropriate and/or had nothing to do with them. Once Desiray was on a school trip and called me to say that she had been pulled aside by a teacher who wanted to talk to her about entering a restricted area. She told me that she had not entered the area herself, but had seen one of the other girls doing it and told the teacher. "So why did the teacher pull you aside?" I asked. Desiray explained that the other girl had implicated her in the situation. When Desiray got home, I asked her twice if there was anything she wanted to add or change about her story, but she reassured me that she was telling the truth.

"Get your shoes on," I told her.

"Where are we going, Mom?" I shot her the look that all Black parents give when their children are told to do something and they talk back.

She put her shoes on and followed me out the door. I made a right turn, then a left and stopped in front of a familiar house.

"Mom! What are you doing?" Desiray was in full panic.

"I am going to ask this young lady why she did not tell the teacher that you were not in the area. That's all." I tilted my head at her, smiled and rang the doorbell. When the young woman's father answered the door, I greeted him with the necessary pleasantries, then proceeded to tell him the story. When I was done, I asked if I could talk to his daughter so she could explain why she lied to the teacher about Desiray.

He looked at me in shock, then said his daughter was tired after the trip and had fallen asleep. However, when she woke up, he would come over to discuss what happened. I wanted to say, "Wake her ass up," but agreed to the terms.

On that doorstep, Desiray had gone from Black to pale white. On the walk back home she was a grey colour. "Seriously, Mom. Why did you do that?"

Silence.

By the time we got home, she was a post-mortem green. "Mom! Why are you doing this?" Even after the girl and her father had come over and the girl apologized for trying to get Desiray in trouble, my smart daughter still didn't know why I had behaved the way I had, and asked, again, "Mom! Why did you do that?"

I took a breath to calm myself; to her it probably looked like I had blown a minor incident way out of proportion, but I didn't see it that way and I still don't. "Desiray," I said, "one day you will have a daughter, or a son, and you will want them to know what I want you to know now. I have your back. Even when you think you do not need me, I will be there for you. I will protect you. It was important for the truth to come out and it was important that your name was completely cleared. I did not want this incident to be on your record or to prevent you from achieving your goals." I hugged her then, extra tight. As usual, I wanted to cry. I'd seen myself in the girl who had just left my house, who had been trying to protect her own image so she didn't disappoint her parents. I also saw myself in Desiray and worried about her. She was on track to be the class valedictorian, and was working hard for the honour, yet she was oblivious to the fact that if the situation hadn't been cleared up, it might have derailed her. At that moment, I was transported back to my high-school graduation, where I did not receive any academic awards despite having been on the honour roll for four years and getting accepted to all the universities I'd applied to. Instead, other students, who were way less qualified, received award after award. I was angry at the time, but it didn't occur to me that I was being overlooked because of my identity, even after all my reading and protesting against police violence and inequality. I knew better now. I had taught Desiray that, like most Black girls in school, she needed to be twice as good and twice as smart. Now I had to teach her to be strategic and look twenty steps ahead of herself too.

When Candice found herself in similar situations, I responded just as protectively, though with my second daughter, it was usually the teachers giving her a hard time, not the other kids. Take a minute to imagine Candice, a tiny girl with glasses—the sweetest little thing you have ever seen. In kindergarten, she was reading at a fourth-grade level. At one point, she was fascinated with the solar system. As my little five-year-old was exiting the library with a book on Saturn, the school librarian stopped her and asked her why she was taking out such a book. Candice told the woman, quite proudly, that she could read and explained that she was studying the solar system by reading books about each planet, one by one, in order of their relationship to the sun. The librarian proceeded to remove the book from Candice's hands, saying, "I am sure you can read, but not that well." Candice was crushed. When she came home and told me what had happened, I confronted the librarian, who denied it. That didn't wash with me and I told the woman so. I always believed my child.

By the time Johnny got to kindergarten, I was more than fed up with the school. And soon he was too. In second grade he came home day after day frustrated with his teacher. One time he complained, "She is not letting me do my presentation on the difference between DNA and RNA. She said the class is not there yet." Why wouldn't she just let him do the presentation? Whether the other kids got it or not, he was not teaching them anything dangerous, just a simple introduction to genetics.

We decided to get him tested to see if he was "gifted." The tests confirmed what we already knew, that Johnny was an extremely smart boy. To his delight, he was able to transfer schools to enrol in a gifted program, where he excelled in math and science.

However, he also soon learned that he was not the Black boy everyone assumed him to be. When someone asked, as they almost always did, what sports he liked, he would respond that he didn't like sports. He was interested in math and science and was a competitive dancer in ballet, jazz and contemporary. He understood why they were almost always surprised by his answer and he spoke to us often about how it felt not to conform to the standard image of what a Black boy was like. He wore his sneakers with pink laces, because he believed that there should be no such thing as boy and girl colours. At ten, he was invited to join the #aboycantoo photo series campaign that dispelled gender stereotypes about boys, and was an invited speaker on the subject at the Vanier Institute's Families in Canada Conference.

Yet even with all of Johnny's strength of mind and smarts, and his resisting all the stereotypes, Vidal and I still made sure to teach him what a Black boy needs to know when dealing with authority and, more particularly, when dealing with police. We continuously reinforce the fact that during those first few seconds or minutes of an interaction with police, nobody will care that Johnny is a gifted boy or that his mother was a member of Parliament or that his father is a civilian who works with the local police services. They will just see a Black boy, who they will often perceive as bigger than he is, and more threatening, guilty or criminal. We taught our children about the criminalization of Black bodies in a way that a child should never have to understand, but needs to understand in order to survive an interaction with the police or with racists—physically, mentally and emotionally. I hate these conversations, because they rob them of the innocence that is necessary for children to be children and teleport him into the space of adulthood. A necessary evil in a world of growing populism, racism and the continuing destruction of Black bodies.

Such difficult conversations are hard to have because they expose a piece of me that I would much rather hide, forget or ignore. I never want my children to know the sting of racism, but racism exists. I cannot ignore it and leave them open to being blindsided by its ever-reaching tentacles.

When Desiray was in grade school her teacher asked the class to write the questions for a mock interview with a celebrity and then research the answers. My daughter chose to do this project on me. When the teacher dismissed the idea, telling her that her mother was not a celebrity, Desiray went over to the classroom computer, opened up Google and typed in my name. Hundreds of entries came up related to my business awards, speeches and research. She pointed to the 2007 Black Business and Professional Association's Harry Jerome Award in the "Young Entrepreneur of the Year" category, and then to my role as speaker and session chair at the Drug Information Association's annual conference, one of the biggest pharmaceutical industry events in the world. "Is this celebrity enough for you?" she asked. Her teacher shrugged, gave the thumbs up and Desiray was on her way.

But she annoyed me with her first question: How did I create work/life balance?

"First of all," I said, "I do not think you would ask your father that question, so why are you asking me? Is it because I am a woman? In any event, I'll give you an honest response. When you create a balance, how much does each side get?"

I held my palms up like scales, for dramatic effect.

Desiray responded that both sides get 50 percent each.

"Exactly!" I said. "Fifty percent on each side. Would you like me to give you only 50 percent of my attention when I am with you?"

She shook her head. No, definitely not.

"Right! When I am with you, you want 100 percent of me. So, I put my phone away and we have dinner as a family, we do home-work, watch movies and go out together. Most of the time, I make a conscious effort to not have my phone out or do any work. When I am with our family, I want to give us 100 percent. Similarly, when I am at work, I need to give my clients all my attention. That is why I cannot have you calling me when I'm working. My clients are paying me good money to do a job, and they need to know that they have my undivided attention. At work I do not think of you, your sister or your brother. I know that you are at school or being taken care of."

My mind drifted as I recalled scolding Johnny for calling me after school to ask where the bread was. I needed to be emphatic and make sure that what I said stuck with him. "Only call me if some-thing is severed from your body. Okay?"

"What is 'severed,' Mommy?"

"'Severed' means that your arm or leg or another part of you is now on the floor and there is blood everywhere. Only call me if that happens. If not, talk to Ms. Michelle." Michelle was our nanny—a lifesaver—whom we hired when the business started to take off. Johnny looked afraid, but appreciated the gory example.

"So, Desiray," I said. "There is no such thing as work/life balance. There is work and there is life and there are the priorities you place on each. When I am with you, you are my priority. When I am at work, my clients are my priority. Balance would be unfair."

I was expressing the guiding principle I was trying to live by, but was it the truth? I did think that work/life balance for women is a ridiculous, unattainable idea, but if I was honest, I had to admit that the amount of attention I was putting towards my clients was increasingly disproportionate in their favour and not my family's. Before I started ReSolve and in the early years of building the company, Vidal and the kids and I spent a lot of time travelling during the summers and holidays. We scraped together whatever cash we had, and sometimes even blew the rent money, to make sure we had a nice vacation. Some of my favourite moments of giving 100 percent to family came on vacations. Life experiences were so important to us that my children got their passports right after they received their birth certificates.

Travelling was our passion. We started a tradition of not purchasing Christmas gifts, but instead using what we might have spent to donate to another family. Our gift to each other was to travel together to amazing destinations. Europe, the Caribbean, Costa Rica. The warmer, the better. When work took me somewhere new, I'd bring the whole family too.

Vidal and I rarely travelled without the kids, but one of my favourite trips was just the two of us, to a less than exotic location—New Jersey. In December 2010 we flew there to see my favourite artist of all time, Prince, in the opening show of his Welcome 2 America tour. When Vidal decided that he would buy $36 tickets in the nosebleeds, I made him return them and put out the cash to buy VIP tickets.

The move worked. Midway through the concert, Prince called all the "sexy people" on stage, so I jumped over the barrier separating the VIP section from the more expensive "Purple Circle" seats and headed straight for him. Standing in front of my idol as he strummed his guitar, I told him how much I loved his music and how I had waited my whole life to meet him. As I reached out to touch him, the woman playing tambourine in his band looked at me like, "Honey, don't be stupid." I quickly retreated, even as Prince gave me a slight, seductive smile. At that moment I realized that I had abandoned Vidal without telling him where I was going and I ran along the edge of the stage, waving my arms so he could spot me. A woman named Michelle from Dallas (we are Facebook friends to this day), who was sitting next to him, tapped Vidal on the shoulder and said, "Isn't that your wife?" To Vidal's shock, there I was— his crazy wife on stage dancing in the purple rain!

Vidal ended up buying us premium "Purple Circle" tickets for the tour's stop at the Air Canada Centre in Toronto. As we drove towards the city for the show, I told Vidal that this time I was going to shake Prince's hand. For sure. He looked at me sideways. I said if anything untoward happened I would run really fast and meet up with him at the intersection of Front and Bay, a block from the venue. Hey! Let's Go Crazy, right?

We took our Purple Circle seats right beside the stage, and as he'd done at the New Jersey show, partway through the night Prince called all the sexy people to the stage. I bolted. Ran straight towards the little man, calling, "Hey, Prince. Do you remember me? I saw you in New Jersey!"

This time the tambourine lady looked at me with pity, no doubt thinking, "Chile, please! This little man doesn't remember yo ass." But I didn't care. I reached out a hand for him to take. Now he was the one looking at me, no doubt thinking, "Lady, please, I don't know where your hands have been." I looked deeper into his eyes, extended my hand farther and said, "Please, Prince, please."

Well, my idol took pity on me and shook my hand. I got an instant massive headache. I screamed, jumped back from him and started shimmying across the stage. The moment was epic. I could not ask for anything more.

Vidal and I would laugh about that moment for years, but we both knew that moments of joy between us were happening less and less.

I loved him a lot, but I admired him even more. I often say that while I have three children, Vidal has hundreds. Every one of his students loved him, and especially the Black kids. He would be there for them at recitals, athletic competitions or their first gig as a DJ. He would show up for them when they were in trouble. He would go with them to court. He was involved with their parents and would often act as a liaison between the school administration and a Black parent not sure how to navigate the system. He spent countless hours tutoring, mentoring and trying to raise a generation of children to take pride in who they are and the rich history they come from.

In the summers, Vidal would organize leadership camps for youth, lining up sponsors so parents would not have to pay too much. In 2006, he organized the Black Family Summit in Toronto, to get the community politically engaged and looking for solutions to some of the problems that plagued us. In 2010 he outlined some of his thoughts about those problems in a book he called *Detox*. Many of these initiatives came out of Vidal's heartfelt response to what people called Toronto's "Bloody Sunday"—October 27, 2002—when four young Black men were killed in separate incidents before the sun came up. This work was a natural extension of the way he advocated for Black students. Ultimately, Vidal decided to pursue a doctorate in higher education leadership, focusing his thesis on the factors that influenced Black students who chose to go to university. He wanted to see more students succeed. He was all in when it came to helping the Black community.

Then there was me. Although I helped Vidal with the organization and promotion of the events he was interested in, I was not that involved. I helped through donation. I also insisted that we donate to programs that assisted students, like the Imani Academic Mentorship Program at the University of Toronto. We made additional donations to the Aroni Awards and to support Congress of Black Women scholarships and to the Royal Ontario Museum.

ReSolve Research Solutions was doing well. While nobody knew who I was when the contracts were signed, I wanted to ensure that people knew who I was when thousands of dollars in donations were being made. Call it ego, I could not care less. I was building a brand, and philanthropy helps in that effort. But more importantly, I wanted people to see a Black couple making investments in our community and in organizations outside of the traditional spheres. I wanted people to see a married Black couple show up at events and galas and know that we were more than stereotypes. We were lovers, and contributors, and an important demographic in our society.

Except we weren't really such great lovers anymore. The truth was that there were a couple of things in my life I really needed to prioritize but didn't—my marriage and myself. I was running too hard. I was cracked and bruised. Some parts were clearly broken and were being held together with duct tape. Other parts had dropped off and were rolling down the road, even as the surface of me was staying nice and composed. I could deal with my children and my business, but the rest of me was taking a hell of a beating. And Vidal was drifting away. Even brilliant gestures, like gifting me with

Prince tickets, weren't enough, and if I'm honest, he was the only one making them.

I'd been engaged in contract work for Parkinson Society Canada off and on for a number of years, and in the summer of 2011 they asked if I would consult on a national epidemiology study related to neurological conditions, which the society was leading in partnership with several other organizations under the umbrella of a national group called Neurological Health Charities Canada (NHCC). I would work alongside the NHCC's director, Shannon Pugh-MacDonald, to study the impact of various diseases, their scope throughout Canada, risk factors and the health services available to people living with neurological conditions like Alzheimer's, Parkinson's, MS, ALS and epilepsy.

Over the months of working together, we had gotten close. Shannon is a tall, blonde, stunning woman. When she walked into a room, you noticed her. I am an average height, gorgeous, chocolate woman. When I walk into a room, people notice me. Together, we were invincible, and we worked together seamlessly and effortlessly. It felt like there was nothing we could not accomplish.

Soon it felt natural for us to tell each other secrets most people would keep to themselves. It was as if I could suspend the Black girl code, where we talk only with each other about things like our hair (or purchasing our hair), our attitude or mood, love life and family life. When it came to Shannon, she understood me, and I understood her.

When Shannon left to join another organization that October, she asked me to take over for her and I was named the co-chair of Canada's first national epidemiology study of neurological conditions. It was the first national research study I had managed, and the work was exhilarating. I was meeting new people, flying across the country, and building on my successes.

At the same time, however, I finally really noticed something strange going on with Vidal. When I asked him what was the matter, he would usually say nothing or brush me off. At one point I remember asking him if he was still passionate about me. (Remember my newlywed rules?) He was, he said, but not like he used to be. As it turned out, if I was honest, I felt the same way. For months we kept on growing further and further apart. Communicating less, rarely being intimate. Vidal finally moved into the basement, which he made into the perfect man cave. With that move, it was as if he left me, and it didn't me take long after this to meet someone and have an affair.

I felt horrible. But I told myself the attention I was getting made up for Vidal's lack of passion. By June 2012, I'd had enough. I could not continue with the affair and I could not stand that Vidal and I were falling apart. I packed a bag and left for a downtown Toronto hotel with the intention of making the separation permanent.

Did I really want to leave Vidal? Of course not. Being actually alone would be more painful than being with someone who made you feel alone. I decided to call Shannon. We met in the lobby of the hotel, which was just minutes from her home. When I finished telling her what was going on, she said, "Give your head a shake. Vidal needs to own his mistakes in the marriage, but you need to own yours too. You are constantly trying to make Vidal take centre stage with you in your world. From what I have seen, he doesn't want that. He doesn't mind supporting you and loving you from behind the scenes. You do your thing and take your hand off his wheel. Let him drive his own life and you drive yours. He just wants you. And you want him."

Her voice softened. "And I know you want to go home." She hugged me then, and said goodbye. I knew what Shannon was saying was right. I had been ignoring Vidal, and when I wasn't ignoring him, I was pushing him away, not deliberately, but doing it all the same. We had loved each other so much, though, wasn't it worth fighting to try to get that love back? Falling in love is easy. The hard part is the landing. You fall fast and hard through a distance that is uncertain. And then you land. Vidal and I were at that landing. But, instead of holding onto each other as we braced for impact, we'd let each other go.

Long gone were the children, sitting in a restaurant, playing in an adult world; we were adults with children who needed us both. So, after several days, I went home, and talked to Vidal, and he and I put a plan in place, the first requirement of which was a commitment to stay together. And while some may ask why we would do that, I ask, why not? Vidal and I were good together, but we had lost our way and we needed to give each other a chance to forgive ourselves and each other. It had nothing to do with the children, or our families. It was just about us. A marriage does not break down by itself and it needed both of us to be accountable, to figure out how we got here, how each of us contributed to the mess we were in.

The second step, we decided, was to go away on vacation; sometimes running away from reality is better than staying and fighting with each other in it. We flew to the Caribbean and rented a hotel with two adjoining rooms, one for the children and one for us. A separate bedroom would give us enough privacy to reconnect and be intimate, while having the children on the trip with us protected us from fighting like a couple of crazy people.

Admittedly, I'd been missing Vidal. So those few days of intense love on our vacation turned out to be easy. The hard part began when we returned home and started counselling. Telling our secrets to each other in front of the counsellor was sobering. I felt ashamed, but I was determined to tell Vidal everything. I dug into my past and told him stories I had buried, many of which are not contained in these pages. He dug deep, too, revealing his own fears and wounds. When he found he could not talk about something in counselling, he wrote to me instead.

As we did the homework required to build our relationship again, I finally understood how big a role unresolved issues from my past were playing in our present. I had been pushing Vidal away exactly because I was worried he would leave me, and wanted to feel like I was in control of things.

The magic was that after several counselling sessions, working hard on our lessons and completing the homework assignments, Vidal and I stopped trying to fall in love again and we started just being in love. Somehow we had managed to plant a seed of a healthy relationship that we would nurture together, growing in sync rather than growing apart. We needed to take care of each other and we committed to not hurting each other any more. If this sounds like it was simple, it was not.

eight

GET OFF THE DAMN BUS AND OUT OF YOUR OWN WAY

AS I REFLECTED ON THE events that led me to this point in my life—the work, the kids, the ups and downs of marriage—I imagined myself on a bus. Not a school bus, but the kind with the comfy, reclining seats and the washroom in the back. Everything I needed in life was with me, familiar and comfortable. I was fed, clothed, and the temperature was perfect. I had no need to leave my seat, let alone get off the bus. The windows were tinted so the sun didn't glare in on me and the hiss of the tires on the road was soothing.

I imagined myself wriggling my butt, rotating my shoulders and neck, adjusting my position as I sat back and contemplated life. The ride had mostly been good so far. Some bumps along the way, but mostly good. Right? Wrong. My company was a growing success, but I was stuck in a rut and had been stuck for a while.

The breakdown of my marriage, as painful as it was, showed me it was time to stop pretending that my life was the way I wanted it to be. I imagined myself anxiously walking to the front of the bus. As I cautiously stepped down and onto the shoulder, eyes adjusting to the brightness outside, I noticed a few things. The most obvious? The windows of my bus were not tinted, they were grimed over with detritus from my past. All the lies, the grief and mistakes I thought I'd moved on from were still hanging on like old baggage. I needed to clean that bus. But it was impossible to do that all by myself. There was too much stuff. Counselling had helped me see that I had survived the difficult stuff in my life. Now it was time to tackle the hurts one by one, release the pain, and strip away the barriers to my future.

When I saw it clearly, the whole bus was in rough shape. It needed a complete engine overhaul. The sound I thought was road hiss was the air leaving the tires. All of them were flat and looked like they had been that way for a while. All this time, all this effort, and I hadn't even been moving. Worse, there were other buses passing me by—opportunities I'd been ignoring while I was stuck in my rut of pride and pain, hanging on to my dirty baggage. I had been so comfortable on my dilapidated bus, sitting idly, thinking that I was moving along. I was not living with passion or purpose. I was existing to land the next client, collect the next cheque and go on another family vacation that I did not enjoy because I remained so plugged into work. I needed help not only to deal with my past, but to figure out how to be more present, stop merely existing and start living my life.

This exact point was driven home one day by Shannon, who out of the blue asked me what I did for fun. She probably knew I had no answer—I didn't do anything for fun. I told her I had a business to grow. It certainly was not going to grow itself.

Shannon understood where I was coming from, but said that if I did not have time for fun, I should at least try to create wider circles of influence, get to know people outside of the research space and put my skills to use in other areas. I'd learn stuff that would be useful to me and I'd meet more people who would inspire me. She then handed me a copy of the University of Toronto alumni magazine and pointed to an ad calling for people to apply to become members of the university's Governing Council. I blinked at her. She was one of the few people I'd told that I graduated from U of T with a 1.58 cumulative GPA. Did she not remember? The A on my research course looked like an outlier. Surely the Governing Council was reserved for professors or people who had achieved great success. That was not me.

Shannon took one look at my expression and said, "I bet they will take you."

With many reservations, I decided to take the bet. This was Shannon telling me, after all, and so far she'd always been right. I asked her to write me a reference letter and submitted my application.

I got an interview!

When I walked in, I found that I would be talking with fifty existing members of the council in the same room where I'd written one of my disastrous undergrad exams. My anxiety went into overdrive; maybe they only called me in because they had studied my transcripts and wanted to taunt me. I was embarrassed and uncertain, but took my place and proceeded to respond to question after question under the steady gaze of a hundred eyeballs.

An older gentleman sitting on the left side of the room asked the final question. He wore a tweed jacket and looked as if he smoked cigars, or possibly a pipe. As soon as he opened his mouth, I felt my throat knot.

"When you look back over your life, do you have any regrets?" he asked.

I was perplexed. What kind of question was that? This dude had clearly read my transcript.

When I opened my mouth to respond, the knot in my throat tightened and my eyes started to water. When I say I am a crier, I really mean it. There is nothing easier for me to do. I cry at everything. I do not care who sees me doing it. I just cry. However, this time I wasn't shedding tears because I was sad or embarrassed. I was crying because for the first time in my life I was able to speak the truth about how I felt about the mistakes I had made.

"No," I said as tears trickled down my face. It was so powerful. I was the owner of my mistakes, and I was telling the room that the mistakes didn't own me. The tears turned from trickles to full-blown streams. Speaking the truth in the same room in which I'd had my ass kicked in an exam was almost exhilarating.

I flashed back to taking amphetamines the night before I'd been here the last time. Every time I faced an exam, I promised myself that this would be the last time I'd resort to drugs. Then I would swallow my pills at about nine in the evening and fall asleep. A few hours later, I would wake up to the thundering beat of my own heart, which felt like it would burst from my chest. I would retrieve my textbook and try to consume all the information it contained. I was always able to cram enough to pass, but never enough to do well.

"No," I said again, shaking my head for emphasis, "I do not regret anything I have done in my life."

When I paused, a woman asked me if I would like to take a break. I shook my head again. "Everything I have done in my life has brought me here," I said. "Every mistake, every success, every failure, has brought me to this point. I think I am doing okay, so no, I have no regrets."

I got up, thanked them all and walked out of the room, down the stairs and out the door, crying every step of the way.

When I got in my car, I called Vidal and told him what had happened.

"You cried?" he said at one point. "But wait, you seriously cried?"

I could tell that he was trying not to laugh. He was right. It was really a moment. There was no way that a crying woman was going to become a governor at the University of Toronto. The university had no time for such foolishness.

Late that night, the phone rang. The woman on the other end told me that I was being invited to sit as an alumni member of the Governing Council. I asked her if she was joking, and she insisted that she was not. Still, Vidal and I couldn't help but laugh. Congratulations, Madame Governor, and welcome back to the University of Toronto.

Does any of this sound familiar? There you sit, thinking you are perfectly happy in a situation that seems comfortable. But some part of you knows it's not right for you. Afraid to try something new, you stay put, knowing full well that if you're not moving, you're not growing.

Shannon gave me the kick I needed to fix my bus. It was not good enough to sit back—I needed to be driving. I needed to pay attention when I was running out of gas or when something was about to break, and learn how to ask for help to fix me. Just as I had finally been delegating responsibilities at ReSolve Research, I needed to delegate some of my issues to others and accept that it was okay to let someone else come up with answers that I clearly did not have.

Branching out into other areas of life is as necessary as it is unnerving. Conversing with a new group of people, asking questions and sharing your own story and experiences, enriches not only yourself, but others around you as well. As far as I'm concerned, there was no getting away from occasional flare-ups of the imposter syndrome that tell you that you don't belong in these new places you're exploring. If you venture out of your comfort zone, sometimes you will be the only one who looks like you. The only woman, the only person of colour, the only one with a disability, the only one of a different sexual orientation or the only one wearing religious symbols. It can be scary and lonely, but the world needs us to show up and build relationships.

After the Governing Council, I continued to climb onto other buses. I joined an advisory board at the Canadian Institutes of Health Research—the Institute of Neurosciences, Mental Health and Addiction—at the encouragement of Joyce Gordon, who was then the CEO of Parkinson Society Canada. I also applied for, and won, the Toronto Board of Trade Entrepreneur of the Year Award in 2012. I was urged to go for it by Jenny Gumbs, the past consul general of Grenada in Toronto. I found that saying the first "yes" was often the hardest part. Learning and growing from the experience was the easiest.

I love this quote from Anaïs Nin: "And the day came when the risk to remain tight in a bud was more painful than the risk it took to blossom." You need to gather up your courage in order to get out of your head and out of your own way. It is the only way that you can blossom into your true self. Even so, you need the right conditions to ensure that the delicate petals open fully. And the process doesn't stop with your own flowering. It is important to teach others what you have learned. To reach back as you climb up. Plant other seeds and nurture them too.

On my best days, my past no longer owned me, but it was a critical part of how I'd come to understand my world. I'd had all of these experiences for a reason, and it was time to put the lessons to good use. The first opportunity to do so came when I was asked by the University of Toronto to adjudicate the John H. Moss Scholarship, a competition for students with strong academics and outstanding extracurricular achievements. During the 2013 competition, I received a package with the required documents from each of the student applicants. All of them were impressive, but one, from Samra Zafar, stood out to me. A young Muslim woman, she had had a troubled life and was the victim of a forced marriage and abuse. Now, she wanted something better for herself and her daughters. Her story resonated with me.

The committee members spent the evening of the adjudication interviewing the students. By the end of the night, we agreed that Samra and another student were our top contenders for finalist. Both were equally qualified and could represent the university and the integrity of the award easily, but I felt that Samra's story was so compelling I had to fight for her. She needed someone to be her Carol Greenwood or Don Stuss. While I was waiting for the final discussion, I reread the history of the scholarship and why it was established in 1920: "During the years of the War, no one strove more earnestly or unselfishly than Jack Moss for the success of the cause dear to us all. After the close of active hostilities, he took up with vigour and enthusiasm the equally important task of repairing the ravages of war and securing the fruits of a lasting peace . . . helping our soldier students to regain their place in civil life."

When I made my final plea, I argued that Samra was a true contemporary representation of what the award was meant to do. She took all the pain and hurt in her life, and through her charity work she made a better life for herself, her daughters, and her community. My pleas worked. The committee picked Samra as the 2013 John H. Moss Scholarship award winner. I was so overjoyed, it was as if I had won the award. Even better, the Chair of the selection committee asked me to be the one to call Samra to give her the good news. I do not remember my exact words, but when I talked to her, years later, she did. Apparently I said, "You struggled so much, it was time that you got some recognition. You deserve this more than anyone." She said the words, as much as the award, changed her life.

Samra changed my life too. She taught me that the empathy I had gained because of my own past hurts was a powerful tool to make change for others. All I had to do was use them.

—

These years were a confusing blend of big steps and equally big setbacks on the project of becoming myself. The transformation from a bud (keeping myself and my secrets safely furled inside) to a blossom on full display for the world to see, to praise or criticize, is never easy. One of the biggest and most unnerving steps I took was renaming myself. And my beloved Gramsie was the inspiration. After living with us for quite a few years when I was a child, my mother's mother decided to return home to Grenada. I missed her after she was gone; she had witnessed some of my biggest traumas and hardships, and taught me about the sweetness of humility, the power of gentleness and the boundless possibilities available to you when you have faith. A different personality from Mrs. Caesar, she was not shy about sharing her opinions, but she did it with a kind, loyal and loving determination.

In her early nineties, she became ill, and the circulation in her legs grew limited. I decided to bring her back to Canada to ensure that she received the appropriate medical attention. Within days of hearing the news, I was on a plane from Toronto to Puerto Rico, Puerto Rico to Grenada and back, with Gramsie in tow, all in one weekend. She stayed with us for about a year as I accompanied her to medical appointments and to various tests.

A deliberate, devoted, Seventh-day Adventist, she constantly pressured us to convert so that Vidal and I and the children could be "saved." Every time she tried, I always responded by saying, "I think I am good with God, Gramsie." But she was relentless. According to her, finding Jesus was my only hope of making it into heaven. What made her think that I had not already found Jesus? Was it the constant cussing and my love of alcohol? Each Saturday, Vidal drove her all the way from Whitby to the Malton Seventh-day Adventist Church, near Pearson International Airport—an hour-long trip each way. Vidal thought about joining, and even spoke to me about it a couple of times. When we all accompanied Gramsie to special services, he said that he felt the energy of the church fill him. He loved Gramsie and she, in turn, loved him, but she couldn't get him permanently inside the church either.

One Saturday, Gramsie had to forego her usual service so she and I could attend my cousin's wedding. As we were driving from the church to the reception, she once more told me the story of my birth. Her own mother, Celina Wilson, known as Ma SouSou, had died eight days before I was born. Before her death, Ma SouSou had told my mother that she was having a baby girl and asked that she name her daughter after her. My mother agreed to the letter of the request, but not the spirit, listing Celina as my third name on the birth certificate. After we had parked in the lot of the reception hall, Gramsie was slow to get out of the car. Turning to me, she asked if I would consider taking Celina as my first name. I said yes without even a moment's hesitation. And I went the distance, too, not just casually starting to go by Celina, but, in 2013, legally changing my name to Celina Rayonne Caesar-Chavannes. Rayonne is the bud that will always remain a part of me, but taking Celina as my first name signalled that I was ready to flower.

Maybe Ma SouSou knew my mother was stubborn enough not to let anyone else dictate what to call me and trusted that her daughter would give the name to me when I really needed it. My rebirth as Celina (Caelina, in Latin meaning "heaven or sky") Rayonne (from the French verb *rayonner*, meaning "to shine or glow") was the perfect signal of the energy I wished to radiate, the shining self I wished to be.

Gramsie went back to Grenada not longer after that. Her health problems were worsening, and she decided that she did not want the doctors wasting Canadian tax dollars on an old lady like her. There was no persuading her otherwise. Shortly after returning to Grenada,

Gramsie's condition deteriorated to the point where one of her legs had to be amputated. Vidal flew down to see her in her final days, but I chose not to. I wanted to remember her exactly the way I had loved her over the years; I also couldn't bear to see her confined to a wheelchair and in pain. I knew Vidal would be better at that than me: able to encourage her to drink her energy drinks and slip her some sweets if she wanted them.

On her ninety-seventh birthday, August 9, 2016, I called her and told her I loved her. When I hung up, I told Vidal I thought she was going to die later that day, or maybe the next—she loved her birthdays and wouldn't want to ruin one by dying. She died on August 10, 2016. I also chose not to attend her funeral. If I was going to remember Gramsie, I wanted to remember and cherish her as she was in life. I promised myself again that I would remember her lessons, I would live true to her mother's name and I would make Celina epic.

I had my new name, and I had my renewed resolve not to be brought down by my old griefs and trauma. But I have come to realize that no matter all the bold moves you are making to take the wheel, there are times when the universe decides you are no longer in charge.

I had suffered with the blues after Desiray was born, and after each miscarriage, and now I realized that I was slowly going into a darkness I could not explain and seemingly for no reason. I had worked in the area of neuroscience long enough and administered enough depression scales to know that I would fail one.

At church one Sunday morning, I knelt down and asked the Creator why I felt so out of sorts. As I stayed kneeling, my face in my palms and my eyes closed, I saw a vision of the Creator cradling a stranger who looked old and tired. As I drew closer, I realized that the person was me. It was startling. When I asked what was wrong with her (as if it wasn't me), I heard, "She needs to rest." Nothing more. Nothing less. She needs rest.

I was confused. I did not need rest, my mind insisted. I needed to be needed. I needed to "do" something. What that something was, was unclear, but I was sure that I should be doing something more productive than resting. Still I cried for her. That poor, wrecked, vulnerable version of myself. I felt sorry for her, and maybe a little angry too. How could Celina be epic if she was asleep?

As I type these words now, I wish I had loved her more. I wish I had loved her vulnerability, and her need to take time for herself. To rest, knowing that everything would be okay once she took that time to rest. I wish I saw that she needed to remain in the bud a little longer, instead of trying to force her to blossom. The image of this "resting" Celina plagued my thoughts. Who was she? Why did she need rest? What was happening in her life that rest was required? Yes, my marriage had been shaky, but Vidal and I were working on it. My business was doing very well—I could not bear the thought of slowing down. How could I get to the future I planned if I was sleeping?

But the more I resisted that need for rest, the worse my depression got. In retrospect, I should have given the resting Celina a break instead of fighting her. To be honest, I was ashamed of her. How can you be twice as good as everyone else if you are sleeping?

For months the image haunted me. But instead of heeding the warning and taking the time I needed, I would rouse her from her slumber. Each time, she was reluctant. Each time her Creator would say, "She needs to rest." I was not listening. She did not *want* to rest. She did not *wish* to rest. She *needed* to rest. I ignored it all. I was too busy criticizing myself. I wanted to see myself in the spotlight, taking centre stage in my life.

Why can't we see brilliance in our quietness? Why do we think we're less deserving if we stop every now and then to take time for ourselves? If we take off the superhero cape, will the world stop spinning? It would take me a few more years to appreciate that resting and healing is okay. In fact, it's necessary. But at the time, I was too busy forging my way forward to notice.

nine

"BUT YOU HATE POLITICS!"

FOR ME, FORGING FORWARD meant continuously making upwardly mobile moves. When people notice that I have not one, but two, MBAs—the first in business administration related to healthcare management and the second an executive MBA—they often seem impressed. Me? I feel disappointed. Why does anyone need two MBAs?

In my case, as my company was approaching its tenth anniversary and I was worrying about how to make it even more successful, I convinced myself that taking an executive MBA would be worth it, giving me the opportunity to refresh the knowledge I had gained in my first one. As I type these words, I call bullshit. The only reason I thought of an executive MBA program in the first place was because I had dropped out of the online PhD program in business administration at the University of Liverpool that I'd entered in 2012.

Adding the PhD to the other credentials at the end of my name was supposed to give me the extra leverage I needed to take my company to the next level. Those letters mean that you are an authority; as a Black woman in the male-dominated research world, I still felt I needed all the help I could get. When I started the company, I took steps to make sure my early clients did not know I was a Black woman until the contract was signed and we had started working together. Things were different now. I had strategically raised the profile of my company and hiding was no longer an option. I convinced myself that a PhD would make up for my melanin and the fact that I had boobs. Men rarely seem to have this issue of worrying about their legitimacy. We live in a world where a high-school drama teacher can confidently become prime minister and a reality television star can become president. I could not operate in the blind spot that privilege affords, so I tried to stay one step ahead of the pack.

But within days of starting the PhD program I started doubting myself. I blanked on the simplest concepts. I could not remember the difference between a balance sheet and "What was the other one called again?" I even fumbled over my words, and I am a talker. A few weeks in, and a few thousand dollars spent, I gave up and dropped out of the program. The PhD was supposed to help me find clarity and direction, but it left me feeling confused and lost. Again.

However, I couldn't just sit around brooding on that failure. So, in September 2013, I enrolled in the executive MBA program at the Rotman School of Management at the University of Toronto, which offered me the opportunity to take the one-year course on weekends. Unlike the online PhD program, I couldn't hide behind a screen when my brain, paralyzed by fear, wouldn't cough up the answers to simple questions. I was forced to sit in a classroom and to work on teams with peers who knew who I was and where I lived and expected me to study hard with them and tap my own experience to come up with solutions to the business problems we were set.

And that was the bonus: working with other human beings who weren't my employees or my family. At that point in my life, except for Shannon, I didn't really have friends. Since the betrayal/rescue by my best friend in my early twenties, I had cut off opportunities for real friendships. Sure, I had acquaintances; some of you reading this book may have regarded me as a friend. But what did you truly know about me? My past, my dreams, my failures? I am still particular when I use the word "friend" and I do not use it with just anyone.

At Rotman, I met one person who ended up becoming dear to me: Kyle Holmes. I could tell that most of the other people in our class couldn't understand why I gravitated towards him. He was blunt. He didn't have a filter. Once when he was answering a question from a professor, he called a child a "dud," causing waves of shock to ripple around the room. When I introduced myself to him, I said, "You are an asshole, but I like you." He appreciated hearing the truth about himself, as much as I appreciated saying it. I did not have to pretend with Kyle. We could laugh at silly jokes, and I could reprimand him when he took it too far without him feeling offended. In short, I could tell him to fuck right off without sparking the residual fear that my parents would get the memo.

In December of that year, while teaching the politics component of the program, the professor highlighted the pros and cons of political capital in advancing the objectives of business by helping business leaders push for policy reform, funding opportunities and other supports.

Political capital? It had never occurred to me that it was a thing. I did not know anyone in politics. In my youth, I had volunteered with my family on campaigns for Jean Augustine, the first Black female member of Parliament in Canada, who was also from Grenada. We would head to her riding of Etobicoke-Lakeshore and knock on doors to encourage people to go out and vote. But Ms. Augustine had left politics a while back, and even if she had still been in office, I would never have had the nerve to call her up for a business favour.

As an adult, I didn't follow politics for the simple reason that, though I always voted, the existing political establishment in

Canada left me feeling disenfranchised. The little I saw of politics on television made me resent the divisiveness of the party system. The theatre of the House of Commons frustrated me. What I thought should be a space for respectful dialogue, especially during Question Period, always dissolved into an opportunity for politicians to get clips for their websites and social media feeds. That said, I loved working to develop policy. I had seen the impact good policy has on people while working on the national epidemiology study. At the end of the project, I co-authored the final report, *Mapping Connections*, which detailed the research results and was a roadmap for the various ways government could provide caregivers support to continue to look after their loved ones living with neurological conditions. But I'd never put it together in my head that politics led to being in government and being in government meant the ability to enact public policy.

The professor continued to speak, and the more he did, the more intrigued I became. I had been acting as if I was only a spectator in our democracy, as if the only way I could participate was through voting. I had stood on the sidelines not paying much attention when the opportunity to get more involved was mine for the taking. As a naturally competitive individual, soon I was asking the next question: "How do I get some political capital real fast?"

I had no clue where to begin. My daughters were more politically savvy than I was. Candice, who had been named an Earth Rangers Ambassador after she had raised $1,000 for the Oregon spotted frog, was constantly telling me about the changes the government of the day was implementing to weaken our environmental protections. Desiray came home most days from high school talking about her role in the Model United Nations and Mock Parliament clubs. She talked about world leaders as if they were related to her, effortlessly recalling details about their home countries and the challenges they were facing. Vidal was always following the latest political events, not only in Canada but around the world, and particularly on the continent of Africa. I admired how much they knew, and I realized that I needed to get involved in political life somehow.

Throughout my research career I heard many stories of the lengths people had to go to survive after their own or a partner's diagnosis with a particular neurological disorder or disease. Due to the cost of medication, some people had to move out of their home province to get their drugs covered, since medications not paid for under one provincial formulary might be covered elsewhere. Other couples even filed for divorce so it would be easier for their partner to access services. I'd found the stories heartbreaking, and been frustrated by the lack of direct actions I could take. For years I had been gathering research data related to a host of issues and handing it over to a government relations specialist to figure out the policy implications. If I chose to get involved in politics, I could bring those stories, along with the data to support good policy decisions, to Parliament.

I decided to test the idea with the women in my EMBA course. There were nineteen of them, all highly intelligent, accomplished individuals who seemed to fear nothing. At our end-of-year holiday dinner, in the quaint upstairs dining room of a quiet Toronto restaurant, I broached the subject of possibly getting involved in politics. To be honest, I didn't know what I meant when I said "involved." Maybe I would attend some meetings, or political rallies, or find a way to join an association and provide my insights on policy to my local MP. This is not what my peers thought I meant—the room erupted over the idea of me running for office. One woman, who belonged to the NDP, said that she would gladly help with my campaign and donate; a Conservative Party member said that she would provide advice. Others offered to introduce me to friends who knew the ropes.

Until that point, I had not thought about the political affiliations of any of my classmates, or seriously about my own. I had always voted Liberal, out of blind dedication to what my parents described as Pierre Elliott Trudeau's "invitation to come to Canada." I never went so far as to say I was a Liberal. These women were talking to me as if it was a done deal, as if I knew what the heck I was talking about. They not only thought I should run, they thought I could win.

I then spoke to Kyle, who hated politics as much as I did; if he thought it was a bad idea, he wouldn't hesitate to tell me. But Kyle said he was in—if I was going into politics, he would support me all the way. Next came Shannon, who I'd seen beam like it was Christmas morning every time federal or provincial Budget Day arrived. "Oh my goodness, you would be great at it," she yelled, and then, just as emphatically, said, "but you hate politics!"

"I know," I responded, not realizing that I was foreshadowing my own story.

I spent the rest of the 2013 holiday season googling everything I could about the political parties, how to join them and how to be an active participant. Given my voting record, and from the policy positions I could find online, it seemed to me that the Liberals were the closest political fit, and so I joined the federal party in February 2014.

As soon as I paid my ten bucks and clicked on the box to join, the solicitation emails started to arrive. Lots of them. I did not mind because the solicitations gave me insight into upcoming events and party messaging. Since I had no understanding of how to run for office, I thought I would start by spending some months observing what it was all about. However, on March 8, 2014, International Women's Day, the Liberal Party of Canada started a new campaign designed to get more women to run for politics. Everything in my life changed when I received an email with the subject line "Invite Her to Run." The email went on to ask if I knew a woman who was talented, smart, interested in serving her community, and could contribute to the future of Canada as a political leader.

I pointed to myself, and said, "YES! I know the person. ME!" Then I replied to the email. "Hello Justin," I wrote. "I am interested. Sign me up!" (Yes, I was naïve enough to think that such emails actually went to the leader of the Liberal Party, Justin Trudeau.)

The incumbent MP in Whitby was Jim Flaherty, the minister of finance in Stephen Harper's government. He had represented the riding either provincially or federally since 1995 and he had been Canada's finance minister since 2006. I didn't think I had a chance against him, but I thought if I could win the nomination and run a good campaign, I could bring up some really important issues and gain some political capital. If I lost, which I was sure to do—not only did Flaherty seem unassailable, the riding I lived in was mostly white, conservative, and had never elected a Black person—I would be satisfied that I'd given it a shot and could go on with my life, having at least made some new connections.

I looked up the candidacy requirements and started working to fulfill them. I called the head of the riding association to ask for lists of local Liberals so I could begin canvassing for support. That was my first indication that this might be an even harder slog than I thought. Even though nobody else had expressed interest in running and the association hadn't been terribly active during the Conservative years in power, I sensed some resistance to giving me the list. Don't get me wrong—a handful of local Liberals were eager to help me out. But others felt some trepidation. Most people I approached looked at me like I was a lamb being led to the slaughter. Why would anyone want to run against Jim Flaherty? They had a point.

Then, on March 18, 2014, Flaherty resigned as minister of finance. Tragically, on April 10, before he could move back home, he had a heart attack in his Ottawa apartment and died. The news slammed against my brain so hard it made me dizzy. I actually felt guilty because I thought now I might have a shot at winning the riding.

I asked several people what they thought of me continuing to seek the nomination when the situation had changed so drastically, first among them Vidal and his dad. Both of them said, "Someone is going to have to run, Celina. Would you rather that it was someone without passion, heart and compassion, or would you rather it be you?"

Maybe part of me was looking for an out, since declaring that I would seek the nomination to be the Liberal candidate in the Conservative riding of Whitby had already come at a high personal cost. The national neurological study I was co-chairing was funded to the tune of $15 million by the Harper government—not known to be a generous backer of scientific research. My clients did not want to risk the funding being pulled because of my new partisan affiliation just as we were finalizing the research and asked me to leave the role. Losing this contract was financially devastating. In order to be able to focus on the campaign, I'd also decided I shouldn't take on any new clients. By the time the by-election to fill Flaherty's seat was called, I was already deep into seeking the nomination, and I decided this was no time to let my financial woes stop me.

I pressed forward. When I finally got the list of active members from the association, I visited them one by one to introduce myself and present my case for becoming their elected member of Parliament. I was a political neophyte, perhaps the last person who Liberals so dedicated they'd joined a riding association would vote for. To have a shot at gaining their support, I needed to show them who I was.

One of the more memorable of these visits was to the home of Barb and Wayne, who invited me over early in the morning to sit with them at their kitchen table looking out at their garden, which was just coming into bloom. Barb did her best to make me feel welcome, but Wayne was silent. *This is going to be harder than I thought,* I said to myself. Still, I felt comfortable with them somehow. The expression in Wayne's eyes was kind, and if I was reading him right, he seemed as impressed by my gumption as by my business credentials. Each time I explained my background and experience to the next prospective signatory to my nomination, the more comfortable I felt with my decision to run. After I finished the requirements in my power, I underwent the telephone interview with the Liberal Party of Canada in which my background was probed to make sure I did not have any skeletons in my closet. Even after Flaherty's death, no other person came forward to vie for the chance to run as a Liberal in the by-election, so in June 2014, I was green-lighted to be the federal Liberal candidate for the Town of Whitby.

Although I was acclaimed, there was still a formal nomination meeting and I could not think of a better person to nominate me than Desiray. As she walked to the podium, speech in hand, I was beaming with pride. Friends and family filled the room and Vidal was by my side. I could not believe how many people had shown up. As I got up to speak, I saw the people there who'd signed my nomination papers—Mr. and Mrs. O, and Barb and Wayne. When Mr. O came to the campaign office later to volunteer, I told him that he'd looked so grumpy on nomination night, I'd adapted my entire speech to ensuring he was smiling by the end. He had not been grumpy, he said, he had been a fan from day one! Since the morning I'd sat at Wayne and Barb's breakfast table to make my pitch, I had developed such a great friendship with Wayne that I told him it reminded me of the one between the title characters in the movie

The Intern: he was Robert De Niro and I was Anne Hathaway. We have been calling each other Bob and Anne ever since.

Even though we had to wait for the by-election to be called, from the nomination meeting on, I campaigned non-stop. My Conservative opponent was Pat Perkins. She'd served as the mayor of Whitby for eight years, and before that had been a town councillor for nine. On top of her name recognition, she was campaigning as the heir apparent to Jim Flaherty stressing constantly that she would keep Whitby "Conservative blue."

My learning curve was steep, and I often felt at sea in this new world of politics; everything about me was on display and being tested. I did not mind. My campaign manager wanted to ensure that we won. He had me prepped and ready to take any question I received at the door. He looked for endless ways for me to meet constituents at barbecues, community events and church bazaars. But then he challenged my name, arguing that I needed to get rid of one of my last names because it was too long to fit on a sign. "Choose either Caesar or Chavannes, but not both," he said. I was firm. I told him that all the names stay or I do not run. Out of that argument, someone (it may have been him!) came up with the brilliant idea to use long, skinny, rectangular campaign signs with my first name written vertically, which we ended up calling "Celina sticks." We lined the boulevards with those, while placing the traditional signs, with my first name in big, bold, white letters across the entire width of the placard and my extra long last name in smaller letters underneath, proudly at the intersections and on the lawns of supporters.

We also had help from the top. From the time I was declared the candidate until the election on November 17, 2014, Justin Trudeau came to the riding four times to help rally the vote. Again, because I was new to politics, I thought this was par for the course. But

Trudeau, as the Liberals' new leader, was playing a larger game, going hard in all four ridings in which there were upcoming by-elections in order to test the waters to see just how weary Canadians were of the Harper government. The answer was yes, Canadians were ready for a change, and yes the Liberals, who'd been brought so low in the election that Michael Ignatieff lost to Harper, were making a comeback. The party won three of the four contests.

But not mine. I had learned a lot and we had built an amazing team of volunteers, donors, friends and family from across the Greater Toronto Area. Each person would be in my corner from that moment forward, even in the craziest of political towns— Ottawa. But I was not going there yet. I lost on election night, in more ways than one.

Remember the resting Celina? I would learn to appreciate the message she was sending me at this point, more than ever before.

When all the ballots were counted, with 280 of the 280 polls reporting, Pat Perkins had received 17,033 votes and I had received 14,082—49 percent versus 41 percent. I'd invited Trudeau to come to my house to watch the election results with me and my family, and he'd graciously agreed. Everybody around me, even Trudeau, seemed happy I had done so well; it boded well for my chances in the general election.

But I was crushed. I shouldn't have been. In the previous election in 2011, Jim Flaherty received 37,525 votes (59 percent); the NDP candidate came second, with 14,305 votes; and the Liberal candidate came third, with only 9,066 votes (14 percent). As an unknown, I had taken on an opponent with a significant profile in the community, the former mayor no less, and increased the Liberal share of the vote by almost 30 percent. And I'd done it in the face of the significant fact that the riding had never elected a person of colour. Even in defeat, I had shown that I would be a force to be reckoned with in the upcoming general election in October 2015.

I could rationally concede that the results were way better than anyone had expected, but my mind was clouded with embarrassment and a sense of failure. I felt as if the whole country had seen me lose and that everyone was laughing at the lamb who actually did get slaughtered.

For the first couple of months of 2015, I retreated to my bed. I refused to get out. I rarely showered, washed my hair, brushed my teeth or left the house. My bedroom turned into a battleground, as everything Vidal said to me was wrong or irritated me to no end. If I was not crying, I was sleeping. I ate very little, and when I did, nothing had any flavour. I knew something was deeply wrong but I refused to get the help I needed. I lay in bed, chastising myself for not being able to get up, but I still stayed put.

One day Vidal came into the bedroom. "Babe," he said, "you are going to have to get up at some point." His voice was as gentle as his eyes and I saw that he was hurting as much as I was.

"Do you want to run in the general election, my baby?" he asked.

I nodded.

"Do you want to win the next election?"

I nodded again. As badly as I felt in that moment, I knew I wanted to run and I would be damned if I lost to Pat Perkins again.

Vidal smiled. "Okay, my love. Do you think you can get up?"

I shook my head. I did not have the strength.

Vidal smiled again and kissed me. "Okay, this is what is going to happen. I will help you. I will leave my job, and go canvass for you. We have to start right now. We cannot afford to lose any more canvassing days. So you need to get up. You need to get some help. Okay?"

Tears were streaming down my face and Vidal was holding back some of his own. I could not believe what he had just offered to sacrifice for me and at the same time I did believe it. That is how we operated. When Vidal needed me, I stepped up. When I needed Vidal, he stepped up. By then, he was the vice president academic at a private college and the loss of his income on top of the financial setbacks to my company would put us in a deep hole. But we calculated that we had enough saved in our pensions, RRSPs and the children's education fund to live for a few months. We could figure out how to get the money back later. Right now, we needed to risk it all on the chance to win.

"Don't cry anymore, my baby," Vidal pleaded. "You just need to get up and get some help." When he crawled into the bed with me, all fear disappeared. He was my human weighted blanket, holding me securely, right there for me in the moment I needed him more than ever. We were going into a general election and we were going to do it together.

I found that getting help was the hardest part of the challenges that now faced me. Mental illness clouds the mind so that every thought turns negative. First, I dreaded making the phone call to the doctor. Then my mind raced ahead to dreading the thought of the doctor even finding out about my depression. I imagined the doctor calling friends, and the friends calling friends, until the whole country knew that I was depressed. And then, of course, I would lose the general election. I was so panicked about people finding out about my depression it was difficult to take action.

I eventually reached out to Dr. Jane Philpott, a physician practising in Markham-Stouffville, which was not far from Whitby; she also would be running as a Liberal in the upcoming election. Jane calmed me down and was able to confirm for me that I was in fact suffering depression. She then wrote a prescription and referred me to a psychiatrist in her team. I have always believed that if you do not ask, you do not get. But there was something close to impossible about asking for help when your mind would much rather stay sick. The only thing that got me to the doctor was my promise to Vidal and the fact that we were sacrificing so much.

In the weeks that followed, I got treatment and took my medication. When the cloudiness of my brain lifted, I needed to figure out how to win the upcoming election. The whole campaigning thing was turning into a Pyramid of Champions, with my opponent, Pat Perkins, as the new version of my childhood rival, Alex. But before I could figure out what I needed to do to beat her, I had to stop and have a talk with my old adversary, Ms. Take. I needed to figure out how "I" lost the election—not what other people did, or how circumstances played out, but what role I played in the loss. It sounds a little masochistic, but I sat and reflected and wrote down every wrong turn I made in order to figure out what I could have done better.

That's probably the most important thing to consider when facing adversity or when looking deep into the spiral of your own misfortune. What could I have done differently? I was the only person I could control (at least most of the time). I was the only person who could change the future outcome.

I discovered that the most salient memories for me to replay were the occasions Justin Trudeau came to Whitby to help campaign. During each visit, he took the time to speak with media. I saw myself, each time, standing at his side, subliminally pleading with the reporters not to ask me any questions. I was petrified at the thought of getting an answer wrong, even though I should have been confident in my own ability to intelligently counter any query. For some reason, all four times I was in this situation, I forgot that I was not a complete idiot. I stood beside him, completely mute, and that angered me. Why had I done that? Why was I afraid to answer questions? Why did I let him talk for me?

With a clear head, it did not take me long to realize that I'd tried to run the entire by-election campaign as if I was someone who knew about politics. Talk about imposter syndrome. My ignorance was immense. Desiray, who had been taking Grade 10 civics during the summer of 2014 to get ahead in high school, would come home with her notes and we would study them together. Then she would quiz me on things like the different areas of the House of Commons.

"Mom, now where does the prime minister sit?" she'd ask, showing me the layout.

I would point timidly to a section of the page.

"No, Mom. No. That is the opposition side. The PM sits on the government side."

Candice was charged with helping me remember the names of past prime ministers. She was ruthless. Every mistake I made she had me writing out lines of Canadian political history. (I was never that hard on my children when they did their homework. Where did they learn such behaviour?)

I tried, in vain, to consume as much Canadian politics as possible, like I was back in university cramming for an exam. The more I tried to learn, the more I didn't learn. It also did not help that I had been completing my final assignments for my EMBA, and the last one was due on November 13, four days before the by-election.

I had tried to run my campaign as a seasoned politician, when I should have been running it as the business woman I was. This time I had to show up as myself. I needed to remember who Celina was and gently nudge her to the edge of the deep end, where I would be the one pushing her in, not Dr. Greenwood. I could swim in political waters, but not if I kept pretending to be someone I wasn't. The Celina who could win was the woman who was more than capable of managing complex problems and coming up with creative solutions for her clients. The one who looked up at the night sky and did not see stars, but connected the little bright dots and saw the constellations. If that Celina did not show up and give it her all, the results would be the same.

The next time I was supposed to head to my campaign office before I went out to knock on doors, I put on a long, red, summer dress with a red and white design on the bodice. I made sure my make-up was done properly. When I pushed open the door and made my entrance, the entire room stopped and stared. Clearly, I was not wearing my canvassing clothes.

"Hey, Celina. What's going on?" someone called.

"You look great," another blurted. That comment tickled me. Had I looked like shit when I'd gone canvassing before?

I announced to my volunteers that we were suspending the campaign for the rest of the day, because going forward we needed to do things a little differently. I confessed my fears around politics and told them that for us to have any chance of winning—and for the victory to mean anything if I eventually did win—I needed to run the campaign my way. I was totally on board with the main Liberal message, which was that to have a better, more equitable, more diverse public life, we needed to do politics differently. That suited me. "In order to do politics differently, *we* need to do it differently," I said, "by being ourselves. I know that I can do this, but I need to change the shape of this campaign."

I went to the board and circled the date of the election on the calendar. "October nineteenth. Election Day! What do we have to do to get a win on Election Day?" To make it work in terms I understood and with tactics I'd employed successfully for my clients, we worked backwards from October 19, writing down all of the necessary steps to win.

Next, I changed the usual political titles. I would not act as the candidate but as CEO of the campaign. The Chief Financial Officer would be responsible for fundraising and understanding how much money we needed to raise to achieve our goals, purchase signs and print other materials. The Human Resources Manager would recruit volunteers, learn their skill sets and assign them accordingly. Everyone who came to volunteer would be given a job, even the children. I loved the child volunteers. One of them, Alex, was bilingual, so his job became to tutor me for half an hour every day in French. I decided that fifth graders Evan and Hazel, another couple of kids who knew more about politics than I did, were more than capable of canvassing door to door by themselves. Their parents may have thought I was crazy, but I put them in charge of canvassing their own polls. The Marketing and Communications teams were responsible for deciding which communication materials went to which parts of the riding, once we had divided it up into appropriate sections depending on the demographics. They also decided where to put signs, and which signs to use.

After I was done assigning duties to the core team, I told them that I was confident in the ability of each of them to execute their part of the overall strategy and recruit the right volunteers to help them. I was not going to micromanage, because my job was to be the face of the brand and to go out "selling the product" by knocking on doors. Finally, I vowed that, having made these changes and committed the team to campaign in the best way I knew how, "If we wake up on the morning of October 20 and the results are not what we expected, I will be okay. I will know that we did our best, with what we knew best, and that will be good enough for me."

There were still some dark moments going forward, but none of them were about the campaign. I even took one of them as a kind of compliment: ReSolve Research Solutions, Inc., got audited three times between the by-election and the general election. I had been audited before, of course, but never three times in under a year. Was the Conservative government so threatened by the gains I was making as a candidate in a riding they'd viewed as secure that someone had a word with someone? Who knows? But the last audit happened on October 19, 2015—Election Day.

That night, friends and family piled into the kitchen and living room of our Whitby home to watch the results, as they had done during the by-election. But there was something different about the election results this time around, and not only the fact that Justin Trudeau was not there. During the by-election, as the polls were counted, the results oscillated back and forth between Pat Perkins and me until she was finally declared the winner. This time around, my numbers were ahead of hers in each and every poll. At around ten, I retreated to a private room in the house with Vidal and his dad for the final stretch. As we watched the screen, the lead between me and my opponents began to widen.

"I think we are going to win this," I said. They both looked at me and nodded, though Vidal still looked cautious. He had been through a year of hell, and he certainly did not want to get ahead of himself. Neither did I. I was nervous, too, but at that point my nerves were not about losing. The reality of the situation was setting in. If I was elected as the member of Parliament for Whitby, the real work was about to begin, and I had no idea what that meant. I had campaigned to be the voice of the riding in Ottawa and to advocate for my constituents, but I really had no idea what the job was all about.

And then, there it was, a little after eleven that night—a check mark beside my name on the television screen, declaring that I had been elected. We cheered and we hugged, and then we headed out to celebrate my victory with all the people who had helped make it happen.

—

What was to come over the next few months and years would test who I am. It would require me to tap all the lessons I had learned to that point in my life. I not only entered a world that was foreign to me, it was a world that was not designed for me to be there at all—a place purposefully built by and for white men. To be honest, in that moment, I didn't fully grasp how bumpy the ride was going to get. And I didn't own a seat belt.

I didn't even clue in to the reality of my new circumstance on November 14, 2015, the day of my swearing-in ceremony. I deliberately did not choose to wear a simple modest dress or jacket and skirt combination. I knew that our official pictures would be taken that day and I was not about to blend in with the rest of the class of the 42nd Parliament. I couldn't anyway. I was the only dark chocolate female member of Parliament in the group of 338 people.

I went to the Rideau Centre mall in Ottawa, just east of Parliament Hill, searching for an outfit that would serve notice that I came to slay, not play. In the end, I purchased a black leather Karl Lagerfeld dress, a faux fur black gilet and black leather BCBG ankle-height stiletto boots. I figured that if people were going to talk about me anyway, I might as well give them something to talk about.

The ceremony was held in the Railway Committee Room of Centre Block, the large room where the Official Opposition gathered for weekly caucus meetings. As I placed my hand on the Bible, the Clerk mentioned that every member of Parliament who had preceded me had entered history by taking this oath and then signing their name into the record. As I proceeded to do this, my family members could not help but notice the enormous painting of the Fathers of Confederation hanging above my head. As I stood beaming in front of my guests, who had travelled from Whitby, Toronto and Grenada to be present, I was oblivious to the imagery. But as months turned to years on Parliament Hill, every now and then I thought back to the audacity of that Black woman standing boldly below the Fathers. The confident, defiant person in that leather dress was about to clash with the history of colonialism, institutional sexism, racist immigration policy and present-day structural violence. I would need every ounce of strength, and all the lessons I'd learned from my past, to survive.

ten

GO BIG OR GO HOME

EVERYTHING I DO—EVEN ENTERING POLITICS, where I really
had no reason to think I'd shine—comes from the larger-than-life
expectation I put on myself that my next move will be bigger and
better than my last one. Sometimes I succeed in ways I never imagined possible. Sometimes I don't. But I'm not so much focused on
the outcome—although winning the election was important—as
on enjoying each step along the way. If each step feels dreadful, how
can the destination be amazing? Success itself is not the prize.
Enjoying the moments that allow you to express your passion and
purpose along the way is the real goal.

I recently heard a speech by Dr. Ndifanji Namacha, a medical
doctor and researcher from Blantyre, Malawi, who said that we should
not reach for the stars, we should reach beyond them into the heavens.
She's been doing that herself from a young age, striving to eradicate
malaria in her home country. I could not agree more. You can see the
stars. They are right there in front of you. Reaching for the stars is
achievable. However, reaching for the heavens is something you have
to do with faith. That next step that you enjoy, even when you cannot
see where you are headed, is the "go big" approach that allows you to
reach beyond your fingertips and into your wildest dreams.

Since becoming a member of Parliament had never been one of my wildest dreams, I was confident that the position, in and of itself, was not my destination, but a station in the journey to finding my true purpose. Still, how I used the position—to make a difference, to ensure that those who had previously felt marginalized by the political process could see themselves in it—would matter. Keeping the promise I made to my constituents to stay authentic as I fought for them in Ottawa would matter. Ensuring that I did not become just another name attached to a meaningless title in the history books, occupying space but not standing for anything, would matter. If I could achieve these things that mattered, I hoped that maybe the door to my true destination would open.

The day after the election, I called the Whitby mayor to schedule some meetings. I wanted to get a handle on the needs of the town so I could figure out how I could help the municipality meet them. I also got together with any constituents who messaged me. Since the role of MP came with no job description, in those early days I made it up as I went along, doing what I thought was required. Yes, I wanted to be bold and be noticed (although, given I was the only Black female face in the House of Commons, being noticed was not all that hard), but I also wanted to do an excellent job. I'd promised, based on the Liberal Party's platform and my own convictions, to be open and transparent, and to do politics differently, but I didn't have a roadmap. In the end I decided the best way to go was to hold regular town halls in the riding—I must have held hundreds of them during my four-year mandate—and publish a running tally of the days I was in the House and the days I was away for meetings, who I saw in those meetings and how I voted on every bill. If someone in my riding had a problem—even a problem with me—I wanted to know about it. I wanted to check the box marked "accountability" firmly: as long as I was their MP, my constituents would always know where I was and what I stood for.

I admit I felt some relief when I got the call inviting me for training provided by the House of Commons—although I felt like I was drinking out of a fire hose, at least someone was teaching me about House procedures, administrative duties and everything else a rookie politician needed to know. I also needed to staff an office on the Hill and another in my constituency; since I didn't understand the environment I was now operating in, I needed to find people who were smarter than I was about federal politics. I also felt it important to recruit people from racialized and LGBTQ2+ communities, women and those with visible and invisible disabilities. In Ottawa, I soon hired Alex Howell, who used to work for MP and minister Carolyn Bennett. She definitely knew what I did not know. Christel Ilunga and Kyle Larkin became my go-to team in Whitby. If I had questions, they helped me get the answers. If they had questions, they weren't afraid to ask for answers.

As the day approached when the prime minister would announce his Cabinet, I wasn't exactly daydreaming about becoming a minister. That position was the star most politicians reached for, I knew, but I was too busy learning the ropes. Then I noticed how often my name came up when pundits discussed potential picks; some of them had taken note of how involved the PM had been in the Whitby by-election and had apparently heard me mentioned as being in the running to become minister of Something. They planted a seed. The more I thought about it, the more excited I became. I turned my ringer volume to high and kept it constantly plugged in so I would not miss "the call."

Then, the day before the presentation of Cabinet, I read a newspaper column that joked that some rookie MPs were probably still waiting by their phones, though everyone else knew that the final decisions had been made weeks before. I was that rookie MP. I kept waiting by my phone until the moment I saw the new ministers walking along the driveway of Rideau Hall on the morning of November 5, poppies on their left lapels, smiling and waving as they headed for their swearing-in. Admittedly, I was gutted, even though I shouldn't have expected anything. And when the Liberal Party declared that this new Cabinet "looked like Canada," I was truly disappointed, publicly pointing out that it didn't look like Canada to me. There were a number of communities missing from it, including anyone from the Black community. That was the authentic Celina speaking, for sure; I didn't know that a first-time MP didn't usually launch her career in Ottawa by criticizing her party.

No matter my outspokenness, I soon received a call from Katie Telford, who, along with Gerald Butts, was one of Justin's key PMO staffers, to tell me that the prime minister had selected me as his parliamentary secretary. She explained that he was flying back from COP 21, his first United Nations Climate Change Conference, held in Paris that year, or he would have made the call himself. I was happy he'd chosen me, and I immediately began thinking about what the role would entail and how I could add value. I wanted to make some things clear, though, and decided that I'd speak to them at my first meeting with the prime minister after the election, in December 2015.

When we sat down together in his office in Centre Block, the prime minister and Katie Telford greeted me with some small talk about the recent election and plans for my appointment as his parliamentary secretary. It was a nice way to break the ice. I was nervous, conscious that I was maybe the only MP who hadn't spent time touring the nation's capital, and yet here I was sitting and chatting with the prime minister as his chosen parliamentary secretary.

But I could not let my purpose be lost to my general giddiness. I needed to let him know that I was not about to be a token in government. "Let me tell you something," I said, when I finally had the nerve to cut through the pleasantries. "If I have been appointed as your parliamentary secretary to fill some gender or racial gap you have in your government, I do not want the job. I am perfectly happy being the member of Parliament for Whitby."

Trudeau insisted that obviously this was not the case. I was there on merit. Besides, we'd formed such a great relationship during the by-election that I was the natural choice. We chatted a little more, and then he asked me if I "trusted his judgement."

Why would he ask me that? I had been married to Vidal for almost twenty years, and had moments when I didn't trust *his* judgement. Why would I trust someone I didn't really know? I was not at all surprised when the Black girl in me popped up and said, "Nuh-o."

I don't think the prime minister was prepared for that answer, and I certainly was unprepared for the level of tension in the room when I responded just as bluntly when he asked me why I felt that way: "Because you rewarded your friends and people who helped with your leadership campaign with ministerial positions." I thought, as the first parliamentary secretary to this PM, he needed me to tell him the truth, to be his eyes and ears when things were going awry, and this was something I had heard other Liberals say. I got the distinct impression from the look on their faces that neither he nor Katie Telford wanted such plain talk from me, but it turned out I did not care. I was not going to nod my head and just go along. Telling the whole truth might not work in my favour, but my lies had landed me in enough trouble in the past that I was most definitely always going to tell the truth here. Parliament was no place for a Black woman to be caught lying.

Somehow we got past that moment and I had achieved my aim, which was to deliver the message that I would not settle for being a token. At the end of our discussion, the prime minister asked me if there was anything I wanted. I was mad at myself for not coming prepared with a list of priorities. That hadn't even occurred to me. Half-joking I told him I had two items on my bucket list. I said I'd crossed off the first—shaking Prince's hand. The other item was to meet President Obama. As soon as I said this, the prime minister slapped his hand on the table in front of us and said, "Done!"

Done? Umm, what did he mean? What kind of done? Was the meeting done? Was I going to get to meet Obama?

I couldn't ask what he meant because he'd already left the room.

Now that I'd told my boss that I wasn't about to be a token, I was determined that no one else assumed I was only in the role for my beautiful Black face. There was work to be done. Once again, I looked around to see if there was a list of duties a PM's parliamentary secretary was expected to fulfill tucked away somewhere. No such luck. Off the top, I decided to take meetings with any and all groups who came to Ottawa asking to meet with me as a parliamentary secretary or MP, and attend every event I was invited to. I operated on the principle that I was supposed to help the people coming in to see me, from the International Association of Fire Fighters to the Canadian Nuclear Safety Commission. Politics done differently, right? I later found out that many veteran MPs rarely went to events. While I sometimes attended six or seven an evening, others would attend six or seven a year.

I prepared for meetings by reading copious amounts of notes and briefings in my rented Ottawa condo—did I mention that this was the first time I'd ever lived on my own and I secretly loved it? Although I am not a morning person, I got up early to read news from left- and right-leaning papers, pundits' columns and social media feeds. If I got called upon in Question Period or by the media to respond to issues on behalf of the prime minister, I did not want to be caught off guard, and I also wanted insights into what our opposition was thinking. To fulfill my role with a bilingual prime minister in a bilingual capital, I worked on my French with a tutor three times a week, and in between sessions, I practised using apps and reading briefings in French and listening to as much French as possible.

I had to keep on my toes because I wasn't the only parliamentary secretary to the prime minister. He'd appointed Adam Vaughan, a progressive MP from Toronto, as his parliamentary secretary on intergovernmental affairs. And because the PM was also the youth minister, he had a parliamentary secretary on that file, too—Peter Schiefke from Quebec. Remember my competition with Alex, back in grade school? Here, too, I felt compelled to work extra hard to ensure that I was better able to answer questions on behalf of the prime minister than my two male counterparts. Not, as it turned out, that I ever answered any questions. My liaison in the PMO soon made it plain that it wasn't part of my job—even during Friday sittings of the House, when very few members were there and other parliamentary secretaries answered on behalf of their ministers, who at the end of the week were often headed off to their ridings or attending to other duties. I wasn't sure what to think about this, or that fact that Peter sometimes answered a question on the youth brief for the PM. Other parliamentary secretaries were coming to me to ask how to do their jobs, upset about the variance in job descriptions and responsibilities from department to department. They must have figured that I was in a position to tell them. What did I know?

I was uneasy about it all, but I told myself the PM, and members of his team, were busy and just hadn't had the time yet to bring me up to speed. I'd observed that very few ministers had the close relationship the finance minister, Bill Morneau, had with his parliamentary secretary; I'd seen them dining together through the window of the ground floor bar at the Château Laurier hotel, and Morneau had also invited him to his home. But Morneau was a straight shooter who knew how to organize and delegate. He might have been a first-time politician, but he came from a business milieu, as I did, and he treated his parliamentary secretary the way he would have treated a trusted business colleague.

Though I wasn't allowed to speak in Question Period, I was still required to attend the mandatory one-hour pre–Question Period prep every week. That started to play on my mind. Why the charade?

On January 29, 2016, while sitting in the Cabinet room for one of these prep sessions, I started to feel faint and put my head down on the table to catch my breath. When I lifted my head, I saw stars floating around the room. I remember thinking about the cartoons I'd watched as a child, when Bugs Bunny would hit Daffy Duck over the head and stars would appear. I lifted my hand to touch one of the stars, when the reality of what I was about to do hit me.

I did not bother to excuse myself. I simply moved my chair back, stood up, and headed straight to the nurse's office. Soon an ambulance was called to the back entrance of Parliament, which took me to the emergency department at an Ottawa hospital. That's when I began to feel both guilty and embarrassed for missing the session. Why was I sitting on a hospital gurney when I should be in my assigned seat in the House of Commons? Here was resting Celina back again, making excuses for not being able to do her job. How was I going to prove that I was a competent politician, maybe even a future Cabinet minister, when I could not handle the first few months? I felt myself spinning and all I wanted was to go home to Vidal.

I checked myself out of emergency and got on a train back to Whitby. I spent the entire train ride sobbing, with my make-up streaming down my face and my head turned towards the window so no one would see me, wiping the snot and the tears on my sleeve. At some point, I pulled out my computer and typed an email to Katie Telford and Gerald Butts resigning as Trudeau's parliamentary secretary. I appreciated the job, I wrote, but I couldn't ignore any longer the nagging feeling that I was, indeed, only a token. I called Vidal *after* I clicked send so he wouldn't talk me out of it, but hung up before he answered. I couldn't bear the weariness and panic I knew I would hear in his voice: he'd sacrificed so much to help me get to Ottawa. Instead, I called my father-in-law and then my best friend, Kyle, from business school. I was certain that they would understand why I had to resign. Both were equally concerned and both of them told me that, in the state I was in, I should not have sent the note to the PMO.

The panic kept heightening. This felt a lot worse than my most recent episode of depression. Vidal picked me up at the Oshawa Via station and wanted to take me straight to the emergency, but the thought of spending hours in a sea of sick people in the feigned sterility of a hospital ward made my panic intensify. Seeing the state I was in, he agreed to take me home so I could get some sleep. We'd assess how I was feeling in the morning.

But there was nothing encouraging to assess. I remembered a conversation I had with Don Stuss, shortly after I had been elected. We met for lunch in Whitby to catch up on old times, and update each other on current happenings. When I told him about my depression, he wrote his cell number on a piece of paper and told me to call him if I was ever in trouble. At the time, I wondered what kind of trouble I would be in that would require me to call Don Stuss instead of my husband. But on January 30, I knew exactly what kind of trouble he meant and I called him. He told me not to worry, that he would handle it and ensure that I received the best treatment. Within the hour, I was at Sunnybrook Hospital in Toronto, under an alias, waiting in the emergency room for six hours beside a man who needed more help than I did and a woman who needed more help than he did. When I finally saw a doctor, there were no beds available, though the doctor told me I needed in-patient care.

After several hours of examination and treatment, I went back home. I was crumbling in front of my family, crying uncontrollably and completely inconsolable. My children and Vidal looked at me with pity. Everybody did. I looked at myself that way. How could this be happening? I was stronger than this.

Where was the savvy business woman? Where was the mom who raised three children, ensuring that they all could read before the age of five? Where was the woman who was asked to join the Governing Council at the University of Toronto, despite her undergraduate 1.58 GPA? Where was the fearless leader who spoke at national and international conferences about the inclusion of marginalized populations in clinical research? Where had she gone? Who was this crying, blubbering person? Everything I knew about me was lost in a sea of despair and darkness. It was like I was being sucked into a dark hole, fast and furiously swallowed up. My mind wandered to my childhood and the beatings I'd endured. I recalled the disconnection, the sadness and frustration I felt after Desiray's birth, the periods of darkness that followed the two miscarriages and the loss of the by-election. It seemed like I re-experienced every bit of pain and hurt in my entire life in that single moment. I felt as if I'd made so many mistakes and this was my penance. It was Judgement Day and I did not have the strength to plead my case. I stayed in that state of guilt and despair for four solid days, even as I drove back and forth between Whitby and Toronto for psychiatric treatment.

After those crisis days passed and I was able to function again, I entered a see-saw period in which my doctors tried medications for mood, motivation and to help with sleeping. Some made me gain weight, others made me nauseous, others simply did not work. There was no panacea to be found, and I was still feeling extremely guilty about how January had ended, so I picked up the pace again and, by mid-February, was working twice as hard, twice as fast and twice as long. I likely should have taken it easy, given that my erratic behaviour persisted. I fought constantly with Vidal, sent angry emails to colleagues and had to leave social gatherings early.

I had never received a reply to my resignation email, and the parliamentary secretary role was becoming even more challenging—not only because of my distress. I asked for and finally got a meeting with Gerry Butts to express my concerns. I told him that I was troubled by the lack of coordination between my office and the PMO. I never knew what the prime minister was doing, and therefore had no idea what gaps I should be filling. When I complained about this to my veteran staff they reassured me that the disconnect was the result of the newness of the administration. We had upwards of 180 members in our majority government, and we had hit the ground running. It sounded reasonable, but I did not believe it to be true. Sooner or later, either the PMO or the PM had to allow me to do the job properly. When I expressed these frustrations to Gerry, he seemed to understand.

After the meeting, I sent an email thanking him. I said that the last thing I wanted to do was add to anyone's burdens, acknowledging the sheer volume of work that the team in the PMO had been faced with over the first couple of months of governing. I reiterated that I wanted to be respected as Trudeau's parliamentary secretary not to soothe my ego, but because I believed I could contribute in a meaningful way. I liked Gerry, and being able to discuss the situation with him had given me a little boost.

Even so, I knew that a list of duties would not be coming, and might never exist, and I went ahead and prepared a framework

outlining the responsibilities I believed fit the role. I included specific tasks with full descriptions, objectives and timelines. It seemed
to me that a big missing piece I could handle was to act as a caucus
liaison with backbench members who were feeling excluded. I had
witnessed more tensions brewing among caucus members, who'd
felt spurned by the Cabinet selection process and/or who felt alienated from the PMO. I also thought that I could act as a liaison with
the other parliamentary secretaries, holding meetings with them to
understand their needs and to ensure that they had adequate support. Most importantly, I suggested that it would be useful, too, for
me to engage in community outreach to ensure that the needs of
various community organizations and cultural groups were being
adequately addressed. I had seen too many politicians show up at
cultural events, profess their solidarity and then disappear, only to
show up again at the same event the following year and do the same
thing all over again. I found this kind of performative allyship nau-
seating. If our government was to be different, we needed to engage
differently, and that meant going to celebrations, yes, but also listening to and acting on community concerns. How else were we to
integrate diverse cultural perspectives into new policy and ensure
that communities saw themselves reflected in government legislation. To make the point, I told the prime minister that I would not
attend Ottawa's Black History Month event that year if he did not
sit down with Black politicians from across the country and listen
to their concerns. When he asked if I meant he had to cancel the
event if such a meeting did not happen, I responded, "No." Of
course, he could have the celebration without the meeting, but if
there was no meeting I was not going to attend the celebration; that
would send a loud enough message.

Lastly, I could take on community meetings that the PM could
not attend. The goal, I wrote, was not to speak on his behalf (unless

he asked me to), but rather to act as a conduit for information and projects that should be reported back to the PM and his team.

By the end of February, I was waiting around for another meeting in order to review my framework. I felt that the process of reaching agreement about the framework was almost as important as acting on it. With other parliamentary secretaries coming to me with concerns about what was expected of them, I felt like they were depending on me to lead the way, and I was ready to be the leader they were looking for.

I sent another couple of emails asking when a meeting would happen, then wrote again to say that if everyone in the PMO liked what was in the framework, they could simply give me the go-ahead. But I needed some sort of endorsement. I thought back to ReSolve Research Solutions and how detrimental it would have been to move forward blindly or without team support on major projects. It just did not make any sense to me. I had been on the job long enough by then, and had listened to the concerns of enough members of caucus, to know that each element of the framework was necessary. I patiently waited for some kind of a response—either no, or yes, or maybe. At some point, I went ahead and implemented some of the elements on my own. If necessary, I would ask for forgiveness later.

Around the same time, I received a call from the Prime Minister's Office inviting me to join the Canadian delegation that would accompany Trudeau to Washington in early March on his first official visit to the United States. No need for an evening gown: I was told I would not be attending the state dinner. But I would be invited to meet the president during the welcoming event on the White House South Lawn and to attend a lunch with Senator John Kerry. Right. This is what the prime minister had meant when he said, "Done!"

Wow! It was really happening. I had been practising what I would say when I met President Obama steadily ever since I'd watched him being sworn into office in early 2009: "Hello, Mr. President. It is an honour to meet you." Each time, I teared up before I got to the end. He was the personification of every dream of greatness told to little Black girls or little Black boys—living proof that we could be anything. Now the parliamentary secretary to the prime minister of Canada was going to meet President Barack Obama. Little me from Grenada. ME. Talk about tears.

It was cold and dreary when we flew out of Ottawa on the morning of March 9, but it was glorious weather when we landed in Washington. The sun was shining as brightly as it had the day after President Obama won the 2008 election, when it seemed to me as if a whole new version of the sun had risen. I put on a bright fuchsia dress, made by one of my favourite Grenadian designers, and headed to the White House. As I walked along the path to the South Lawn, I looked up at the balcony—that's where Olivia Pope and Fitz, from the television show *Scandal*, always stood when they were stealing a few moments with each other. I might have mumbled that out loud and I definitely pointed to the balcony. The White House staff accompanying me likely wondered if Canada had legalized marijuana early.

I located other members of my group by the yellow pins on their lapels that indicated that we were allowed to stand in front of the "golden rope" erected on the lawn. I checked out three different spots along the rope before settling in directly behind the place tags on the ground that marked where Michelle Obama and Sophie Grégoire-Trudeau would stand. I dug my heels into the soft earth of the lawn so that no one could push me out of my spot, and waited.

When the top-level delegation of Canadian ministers and government officials arrived, they stood directly in front of the glorious golden rope group, obstructing my view. By the time the president and first lady, the prime minister and Madame Grégoire-Trudeau arrived, I could hardly see a thing. The four shook hands and chatted and smiled with the top-level folks, ignoring all of us "golden ropers," and then the president and prime minister walked directly to the stage. I was devastated. *Really, B?* (I say B with all kinds of respect on it.) *How you gonna play me like that? Walk directly to the stage, huh?*

Well, at least I was there, and so I took some selfies with the first lady and Madame Grégoire-Trudeau in the background. I got some shots of the PM at the microphone and some pictures of the president too. People started texting me to let me know that they could see me in my fuchsia dress on television. I continued to take pictures until someone behind me said, "Celina, here he is!"

Here who is?

I fumbled my phone into my pocket and lifted my head just in time to see President Obama a couple feet away from me. What in God's name was happening? The moment I had been waiting for had arrived and I almost missed it because I had been so busy taking pictures and acting the fool. When the president finally stood in front of me, I couldn't get a word out of my mouth. I had to thank the prime minister for saving my bacon, as I felt him place his hand on my back and introduce me as Celina Caesar-Chavannes, his parliamentary secretary.

I got it out at last. "Hello, Mr. President. It is such an honour to meet you."

Then the president said, "Is he doing a good job?" *He* was asking *me* about the prime minister. I was not prepared for conversation—I had only practised saying hello! When I remained silent, he added, "If he isn't, you let me know." At last I was able to mumble something in response—I don't know what—and he walked away. I thought I was going to pass out on the South Lawn. I kicked myself. I should have said, "Yes! Please give me your number and I will call to let you know if he is doing a good job." I got my phone out again to take some more pictures, but the euphoria of the moment was interrupted by a text from Vidal: "Put your phone away. You are still on TV!" I put it away, composed myself and beamed.

That evening my brother Ryan texted me to ask why I'd dissed the president when I met him. What? I hadn't dissed him. Are you crazy? But, when I watched the coverage, I noticed that at the end of our interaction, the president had gone in to give me a hug and I'd stepped back. I could not believe it. I really had dissed the president. Then I remembered that I'd noticed Prime Minister Trudeau's official photographer trying to capture a picture of us and I'd stepped back to ensure I was facing into the lens. My vanity cost me a hug from Obama!

As I stood on the South Lawn beaming in the wake of meeting the president, yet trying my best to be dignified in case the cameras were still on me, my phone buzzed furiously. I stealthily pulled it out again and read a message from Susan Smith, a principal at Bluesky Strategy Group and co-founder of Canada 2020, a progressive think tank, asking if I was going to the event with Michelle Obama and Sophie Grégoire-Trudeau. "No," I texted back, jokingly requesting to be her plus one. She replied, "Get in a cab and meet me here." She did not have to ask twice.

When I arrived, Susan took me to sit with some remarkable women, including Vicki Heyman, the wife of the US ambassador to Canada, Zita Cobb, owner of the Fogo Island Inn in Newfoundland, and many others. While waiting for the guests of honour to arrive, I basically burbled to these impressive women about how I'd crossed the last item off my bucket list when I met the president. One of them asked me, "Now that you have completed your list, what are you going to do—add more items to it?" The question took me aback. What *was* I going to do now that my list was complete? I thought for a moment and then replied, "I don't want to add anyone else. I guess I want to be the person that someone else puts on their bucket list and wishes to meet." That might have sounded like ego talking to the person who asked, but what I meant was that I wanted to be the kind of person someone else *could* look up to, a role model they could aspire to surpass by becoming their most authentic self. The same journey I was on.

After Mrs. Obama and Mrs. Grégoire-Trudeau arrived and made their remarks, I was standing around with all the bigwig ladies I'd just met as the two guests of honour came to greet them. I watched, amazed, as my new acquaintances chatted with Michelle Obama as if they were old friends, and realized that most of them were old friends! While I hadn't been invited to this gathering, still I mustered my courage and stepped to the front of the group, extending my hand to Michelle Obama. "Hello, Mrs. Obama," I said. "It is such an honour to meet you."

Well, I kid you not. This magnificent, tall, gorgeous woman stepped back on one foot (shod in a black kitten-heeled shoe), checked me out from top to bottom, then said, as she pointed at me with her perfectly manicured finger, "Huh! I remember you. My husband was giving you some love this morning." I froze, unsure if she was joking or not. I didn't want to wait until girlfriend pulled off her earrings and slid off her heels to find out. Michelle is from Chicago, and while I would usually never bet against myself, she could whoop my ass, and, out of respect, I would have to let her. I looked down at my outstretched, unmanicured fingers, politely shook her hand, and retreated out of sight.

I laughed at myself all the way to the next event. I couldn't believe that I'd just had a moment with Michelle Obama. You might assume it was painful. I beg to differ. It was epic, and left me fanta-sizing about how she might bring it up with President Obama later that evening. (I know, I know, but fantasy by its nature is not real-ity, so here goes.)

MO: Hey Barack.

BO: Yes, darling.

MO: Do you remember that lady in the stunning fuchsia dress from this morning? At the South Lawn event with Justin and Sophie and the other Canadians.

BO: Absolutely! That was a fun moment.

MO: [muttering] Fun my ass.

BO: Pardon me? What did you say, my love?

MO: I just said that she looked like she had a little sass!

BO: Yes, she did. You know she's a member of the Canadian Parliament, appointed by Justin as his parliamentary secretary.

MO: [muttering, again] Really? I wish I knew that before I gave her the once over.

BO: Sorry, darling, I missed what you just said.

MO: I was just thinking that we really should invite her and her family over.

BO: That is a great idea. Let me make some calls.

You can expect that Michelle Obama and I will laugh about this story at some point. And when we do, I will also tell her that I learned another life lesson from those beautifully manicured hands of hers, an extension of the one I tried to give Desiray when I explained how unrealistic the notion of work/life balance is. Since I met Mrs. Obama, I always take the time to manicure my nails. Each time, this simple act of grooming provides me with fifteen minutes to half an hour of me-time. A few moments to nurture and take care of me. The more coats you add, the longer you have to yourself. Short of holding a glass of wine, there is not much you can do with your nails wet; in effect, you have given yourself permission to refuse all demands from others, tend to yourself and take a moment to blossom. With a little bottle of nail polish, I could signal to everyone around me that the do-not-disturb sign has been hung. Thank you, Mrs. Obama.

As incredible as the trip was, in big ways and small, it was also a bitter reality check. Though he did introduce me to the president, the prime minister did not say one word to me the entire time. I had not been asked to take any meetings or assigned any duties. I felt out of place and useless; it seemed as if the only reason I was in Washington was so Trudeau could fulfill his promise to me. Thrilled as I'd been to meet the president, I felt guilty about the cost incurred by Canadian taxpayers to satisfy a whim I'd expressed for lack of anything else to say in my one meeting with the prime minister.

And there were so many awkward, uncomfortable moments on the trip. Everywhere we went in Washington, we travelled by motorcade. In one instance, the minister of fisheries, Hunter Tootoo, was directed to the minivan I was riding in. I was in there by myself, with lots of room, so I certainly did not mind. But at the next stop a staffer opened the door, ushered the minister out and profusely apologized for putting him in "that" vehicle. Why was the van so terrible for him, but perfectly acceptable for me? I know that the staffer's job was to maintain protocol, and I guess protocol meant that a minister wasn't supposed to be riding with a mere parliamentary secretary. But it felt bad to be treated as though I was a contaminant of some kind.

Worse was taking my lonely van ride in the motorcade to a speech Trudeau was giving at a university the day after the state dinner. When we arrived, I got out of the van and, since I didn't know where I was going, I followed the other members of the delegation into the venue's elevator with the prime minister and his retinue. Suddenly they were all looking at me as if I was a complete stranger. Finally, Gerry Butts said, kindly, "Celina, you're not supposed to be here," and held the door as I got off. I didn't have the nerve to ask where I was actually supposed to be. The lump that formed in my throat kept growing as I found a set of stairs to take me to the main auditorium, but I somehow managed not to cry. After the speech, the motorcade left for the next event without me. In some respect, I was relieved. I needed some time alone after the embarrassment of the elevator. Although I could have taken the bus, I walked back to the hotel, stopping at a Payless to buy two pairs of shoes. Trivial, I know, but satisfying.

I guess my place in the scheme of things should have been clear to me on the flight down to Washington: I was the only elected official seated in the back section of the plane, on my own in a row facing a walled-off section reserved for the prime minister, the ministers and senior staff. The media were back there too, but I was carefully separated from them as well. On the flight home, Trudeau came out to chat with junior staffers who were sitting on the opposite side of the plane from me. I sat up straight and leaned a little forward so it would have been easy for him to make eye contact—I was alone again in an island of empty seats so it wouldn't have been hard to spot me—but no such luck. His jokes were reserved for the staffers, his waves for the media.

It was the first instance in my time in government that I truly felt like a Black woman. Clearly, I have been Black and female all my life, but isolated in my space on the plane, I experienced a familiar, yet unfamiliar feeling—if that makes any sense. I felt my posture weaken and the shape of my face change in a way I remembered from my childhood. It had been the way my father's expression and bearing had changed the night he came home from his job and vowed that he would start his own business rather than put up with more racism at work. His face had looked so drawn its flesh seemed sunken. I hated seeing him like that. Now here was my face forming those same contours, my body disappearing into the seat. I shook myself, trying to dismiss the feeling. *Stop being so sensitive, Celina. You're not being treated this way because you're a Black woman, but because you're the new kid on the block.* Thinking this did not stop the tears from falling, but I had to believe it was true, and for maybe a little while longer I did.

A week after the state visit, on March 18, 2016, I woke up in my Ottawa condo to my phone buzzing. This is not uncommon. My phone buzzes. A lot. But normally not *that* early in the morning.

In a daze, I rolled over and picked it up. I could hardly focus on the names of the people who were emailing and texting. I squinted. "Congratulations," one message said. "Front page and above the fold, well done," said another. "Is that you?" another asked.

In that moment, I realized that an interview I'd done with Jane Taber of the *Globe and Mail*, part of a series of profiles she was doing of new Liberal MPs, had landed on the front page. I'd expected the article to be on page five or six of the lifestyles section, not the front page. I texted Jane to be sure. "Is your article on the front page?" She texted back that yes, it was.

Huh. As I was recovering from the plane ride home from Washington, I felt like the timing of the article was perfect. It outlined my life struggles on the way to becoming the parliamentary secretary to the prime minister, showing me what I already knew but kept forgetting: how much I had sacrificed to get to that point, that I had every right to be in the position and that I did not steal the job or take it from someone else. No one flew across the country to meet with me or considered asking me to join the Liberal team. I worked my ass off to get there.

It also reminded me that to whom much is given, much is expected. So many people had helped me get to Ottawa, it was not good enough that I just *be* there, struggling to stay on my feet. I needed to share the experience with others—the good, the bad and the ugly. I had not been elected to sit on the sidelines, but to enter the political arena and assert myself on behalf of others.

At the end of that month, on Youth Day on the Hill, I offered Kyra, a seventeen-year-old young woman from Goderich, Ontario, the opportunity to shadow me for the morning. We met at 7:30 a.m., and together decided to skip the day's opening remarks and go on our own little adventure. We went to the House of Commons, took pictures in the PM's and the Speaker's chairs and toured the government lobby. I then accompanied her to the third floor of Centre Block to see the Prime Minister's Office. Even though I had been in Ottawa since November, attended Question Period prep every day, and clearly stood out in the crowd of MPs, a guard stopped us as we walked towards the office to ask why I was there. The unfamiliar familiar feeling started up in my gut, but I calmly told him that I was parliamentary secretary to the PM and was taking my young friend on a Youth Day tour. He took a closer look, and this time he seemed to recognize me. He let us pass.

Kyra took pictures of everything around her, thrilled to be there. As we were about to leave, the PM's executive assistant, Tommy Desfossés, surprised us by allowing Kyra to venture into the PM's office, sit in his desk chair, and have her picture taken there. I was not only happy for her, but felt that I was finally doing what I was supposed to do with my access—encourage young women with political aspirations. If we want to change politics by adding women, they might as well get a picture of themselves in the chair. Kyra now has that picture. Maybe one day she will also have the job.

Despite my increased profile after the newspaper article, my role as parliamentary secretary to the prime minister was continuing to cause me grief. Or, rather, my non-role.

I was still going back and forth with members of the senior team in the PMO on the framework I'd come up with. I puttered along until mid-April when, again, I decided that I had had enough. I'd had one five-minute meeting with the prime minister since our introductory session. To be effective as his parliamentary secretary, I needed to be on the same page as he was. I was not. I fully understood that I would never get the full attention of the PM, who was extremely busy. I'd only asked for fifteen minutes a month, with an agenda sent to him in advance, to ensure that we were in tune. Apparently, that was too much. I hadn't yet been asked to attend any events on his behalf, something I could have easily done to lighten his load. I was continuing to work with other parliamentary secretaries to ensure they had better relationships with their ministers, knowing full well that the relationship I had with mine was not the greatest.

I loved my work as the MP for Whitby. We'd taken over some tough immigration cases left unfinished by the previous member, in which people were about to be deported and families torn apart, often completing them with positive results. I didn't need a symbolic role as the Black woman who sat at the right hand of the PM. It was barely symbolic by this point! It also bothered me that I was earning an extra $16,000 in salary. Since I was basically doing nothing much to justify the title, I felt it was a waste of taxpayers' money. My psychiatrist and I were still adjusting my medication and even though he warned me that all the tweaks could make me irritable and that

I shouldn't fire off any more resignation letters, I was growing angry again. I sent an email to Katie Telford and Gerald Butts.

I'll quote it in full to show how much I was at my wit's end: "We need to have a meeting to discuss my role going forward. The way I am being treated by the PMO is absolutely disrespectful, and dare I say racist and sexist. This situation is absolutely terrible. I am blatantly treated differently than other PSs. If I have done something wrong, this is not high school, talk to me about it. Don't try to punish me, by not including me. This situation needs immediate attention."

I hit send and regretted it immediately. I followed it with an immediate apology to Gerry and Katie, and sent another directly to the prime minister. What the fuck was happening to me? I felt like I was always looking over my shoulder and that my senses were always tingling about various injustices. I now realize I had named what was happening in the email, but at the time I immediately blamed myself for using the word "racism" so carelessly. Surely I had to endure a lot more of such treatment before I could show that the pattern of racism existed?

Isn't that what we are supposed to do? Pile up irrefutable evidence of bad behaviour against us before redemption is granted? Cradle the burden of racism in our arms until it is bold enough to rear its ugly head so blatantly no one can ignore it? Microaggressions, such as I was experiencing, did not count. They were too subtle to prove that they had even happened, let alone that they'd had an effect on the recipient. Wasn't that correct?

I thought I had stayed immune to racism's effects for so long—all the way through school and as an entrepreneur. Why was my immune system so compromised now? Maybe the state of my mental health had weakened my system like kryptonite. On the other hand, maybe racism had caused my disease, and anxiety and depression were the symptoms. Or maybe it wasn't racism at all.

I knew one thing for sure, whatever "it" was, it was not only driving me crazy, it felt like "it" was killing me.

I lay low for the next couple of months, concentrating on doing what I had to do and trying not to obsess about how I could be doing things better.

In August 2016, I met with the prime minister to speak with him about the importance of Canada recognizing the United Nations' International Decade for People of African Descent (2015–2024), which was adopted by the General Assembly on December 23, 2013. It was a recognition of the need to promote and protect the human rights of people of African descent along with their full and equal participation in all aspects of society. This was, and still is, a tremendously important resolution, but ultimately its significance will be determined by whether it engenders positive policy and programming that leads to tangible improvement in people's lives. I told the prime minister I had gathered with a group of federal and provincial Black political leaders a week earlier in Toronto with the goal of formalizing a plan to help members of our community. As a country we finally had to come to grips with systemic racism; we believed a national recognition of the resolution could provide a framework for that to happen, especially in the areas of justice, recognition and development. Given the issues supercharging the activism of groups like Black Lives Matter, it was crucial that the federal government and its members respected and recognized the contributions of Black communities to Canada.

After hearing from many experts, our group of Black politicians had decided to move forward with three main initiatives shaped by equity-based analysis, rather than the gender-based analysis that the Trudeau Liberal government relied on in its focus on the rights of women and girls. First was a push to have provincial and federal governments recognize the Decade and undertake efforts to promote recognition, justice and community development. Second, we wanted to advocate for an apology from the federal government to Black communities in Canada for historical incidents of racism and segregation whose long shadows were still reinforcing systemic racism and oppression. Lastly, we wanted to encourage more government procurement opportunities for Black-owned small- and medium-sized businesses. The prime minister seemed eager to learn more and do more in this territory, and I grew excited by the possibilities. It seemed like I had finally found a place where we could work together.

In September, when the PM couldn't attend the opening ceremonies of the National Museum of African American History and Culture in Washington, I was asked, for the first time, to attend an international event on his behalf. The next, and final, time I was asked to represent him was at the inauguration ceremony of the Republic of Ghana's new president, Nana Akufo-Addo, in early January 2017. I wondered then whether I was only being asked to attend Black events on his behalf, and once again I had to dismiss the uneasy feeling that thought gave me. *Just be grateful that you have the job and you are at the table?* Isn't that what I was supposed to do?

I kept being surprised by how daunted I felt not only by the political games on Parliament Hill, but by the actual space. Each time I ran into a woman of colour or a Black staffer, they told me that they, too, struggled with feeling excluded or being met with sexist, racist or microaggressive behaviour. I hated that they felt this way. Soon, every time I passed a young woman in the hallway, I would slip her a note with my personal cell phone number on it and invite her to call me. If I was having such a hard time adjusting to life on the Hill, knowing full well that I could not be fired by anyone but the electorate, how were these women dealing with it all? I would see them with their big, super curly Afros, or dreads or braids, and their extra-dark velvety skin, and reach out to them to let them know they had an ally. On Sunday nights we arranged phone calls or Google hangouts so we could discuss what had happened during the past week in a safe and protected space. We strategized together on how to fill in the gaps we saw in how the government was rolling out policy, especially when the development of those policies excluded the voices of Black women. We laughed over some episodes and cried over others and, most of all, we had each other's backs. The sisterhood we built in those calls and meetings has been long-lasting.

But I did not always succeed in protecting my young mentees, who included my own staff members. When my Whitby office manager, Stacey Berry, and I attended a meeting with an Ontario provincial minister and the CEO of a multi-billion-dollar corporation, she felt the same ice-cold reception first hand that I had experienced in many such meetings. As usual, we got there early enough to find our seats and say our hellos to the other people in the room, most of them men. Some refused to look at us as we greeted them and others ignored our presence completely. We, nonetheless, remained pleasant.

When the minister and the CEO arrived, the men in the room gathered around. As we approached to say our own hellos, they closed ranks so we could not join the circle and tightening up so much that neither the minister nor the CEO could even see us. Stacey's face fell. I couldn't tell if she was about to cry out of her own hurt or from mortification that she hadn't protected me from such a snub. She was about to shoulder a path into the circle, when I gently placed my hand on her arm and told her that we were going to sit back down. "I know you're upset," I said. "I am, too. But you need to remember one important thing. This meeting can't start without us." I smiled. "Whether they choose to acknowledge us now or later, they need us."

When the minister finally was able to break through the circle of men, he came to greet me warmly. When he introduced me to the CEO by name and included my titles, I could see the other men's expressions change. Suddenly they were all interested in engaging, but I had no energy for them now. Instead I asked the minister and CEO, "Shall we start?"

This was me calling on the lessons in patience and forbearance I had learned in the years I was running my business. More than once I had arrived for a meeting with a new client only to be ignored. I would sit in the lobby and quietly wait. I was being paid for my time, after all. Also, in those early years, I knew my clients weren't expecting someone who looked like me. Remember, I deliberately hadn't put my image on any of our printed promotional materials or on our website, so I wouldn't be prejudged for my gender or race. Once, a client only briefly glanced at me when I arrived for our meeting, then told me to wait my turn. I went back to reception and sat down. When he burst back into the lobby complaining that the person he was supposed to meet was late, I spoke up. "No, I'm not. You told me that you didn't have the time for me. Do you have time now?" The look on his face was priceless. He clearly was not expecting a well-dressed, young Black woman to be the owner of a research management company.

When we hold positions that traditionally have not been occupied by people who look like us, and enter spaces where we have been historically few in number, the people who inhabit those realms often don't even see us. In business, I had to learn how to occupy such spaces with poise and confidence, and I did so by channelling the three-year-old me, the one who walked around naked singing at the top of her lungs. To her boldness, I added a couple of lessons my friend Shannon had taught me when I was struggling with my marriage. She told me that the ability to look at yourself in the mirror, without the filters, the clothing, make-up or accessories, and to appreciate what is there—not criticize all the lumps and bumps, the parts that are too big or too small—boosts your confidence, and she was right. But it takes practice. Even now, every time I step out of the shower, I take the time to look at myself in a full-length mirror and appreciate me. We often turn to others to validate us in their space, instead of doing it for ourselves in our own space. Especially in our own skin.

Shannon also taught me I needed to value myself in other ways. One day at work, she actually asked me what underwear I was wearing. (Yes, really.) I did not need to look. I bought them in jumbo packs at Walmart. You know the kind in the plastic Ziploc bags that are folded and taped together so the manufacturer can squeeze more in?

"Throw those away!" she said in disgust. "From now on, you purchase yourself some matching sets. You are worth the investment, aren't you?"

She was right. Why would I take the time to admire all the chocolatey goodness the good Lord had blessed me with and then put on some dingy underwear? I admit I took a deep breath at the prices, but I started to purchase matching sets. Then I gave Vidal the assignment of buying them for me, once a month, as part of our "getting back together strategy." Pleasing Vidal was part of the plan, but I was also wearing them to please me. To reinforce that I was worth the investment.

As I managed to deal with some of the situations politics handed me, I slowly realized that I'd had ten years of practice in how to be in spaces that had excluded people who looked like me before I ever ended up in politics. Although I was having a difficult time, I had built myself a foundation to stand on. I just needed to get my footing back.

Also, if I was going to be different in politics, as I vowed I would be to every voter I'd met on every doorstep, I could not be a fraud. I really couldn't pretend my way through this. I needed to be candid about the good times and the not so good times—as transparent as I was about my voting record and how I spent my time. It was not enough to post pictures on social media and have Sunday meetings with Black Hill staffers. I needed to use the opportunity politics afforded me to do some good.

On World Suicide Prevention Day in September 2016, a terrible storm was brewing in Ontario. I posted on Facebook that although stormy weather was coming, just like it does from time to time in our lives, the storm would eventually roll away and everything would be okay. A few days later, a reporter from Huffington Post got in touch to ask if I would write a blog expanding on my post. I decided it was time to describe my depression in 2014 and my crisis in January. I never would have imagined the impact the post would have as it went viral. The more I was asked about my depression, the more I spoke about it openly, and the more openly I spoke about it, the more I would run into people who were grateful that I did.

After talking about depression during a keynote speech at a Mississauga hotel, an elderly Black woman, dressed in a staff uniform, approached me with tears in her eyes. I started to panic. All Black children are taught to revere our elders, but elder Black women have a very special place in my heart. I thought she was crying because she was disappointed that I had revealed my struggles, that I had allowed myself to appear weak in front of a room full of people. Speaking about mental health in the Black community was still taboo, and I wanted that to change. We could not continue to teach our children to be twice as good, study twice as hard, and practise twice as long, without understanding that it was not a sustainable way to live your life. I did not want the next generation to suffer in silence. But she wasn't coming to chastise me. When she reached me, she took my hands in hers and said, "Thank you." Her eyes were soft, and seemed almost solid black, the whites dark and rusty-red from tears. I could see the hard work, pain and struggle in every line of her face. Still holding on to my hands, she told me, "Every day, for years, I would wake up with the sun and stare out the window until the moon appeared. I did not go anywhere. I lost my good job. I stayed a prisoner in my home and in my mind. I did not know what was wrong with me. I stayed there, watching the sun and the moon for years. Thank you for talking." Now my tears fell too, and we hugged for what seemed like an eternity in the back hallway of that west-end hotel. When I'd shared my story, I'd shown her she was not alone, that it was okay to not be okay.

Later, however, I received a private message from another woman who had heard the speech. She told me she thought it was great that I felt comfortable enough to tell my story, but she feared that if she told hers, she would lose her job or lose her children or both. I knew then that it wasn't enough to speak up about my own experiences. Many other stories needed to be heard, many other situations needed to be talked about and a multitude of voices needed to be amplified.

During the following weeks, I spent time opening up to my caucus colleagues about these issues and talking about what we, as a government, could do. I felt comfortable speaking there because everyone in the room was sworn to secrecy. When discussing another piece of legislation earlier that year, I told my colleagues about my experiences at Sunnybrook. We needed to do more. I went to Jane Philpott, who was the minister of health, and asked her what support she needed to get mental health funding into the next federal budget. She told me I needed to speak up for it. "I cannot be the only one who asks," she said.

"How much do you need?"

"Three billion dollars," she said.

"Come on, Jane! Let's be bold and ask for five billion. That way every young person across the country who needs help can get help."

At our next caucus meeting, I stood up, along with other colleagues, and asked for $5 billion towards mental health. The 2017 federal budget included $5 billion earmarked for mental health funding as part of the provincial-territorial health transfer. Although some provincial leaders were hesitant about receiving earmarked funds related to services that were outside of the federal jurisdiction, all the provinces eventually signed on and used the funds to increase access to services for youth under the age of twenty-five.

All right. With that one win, I'd proved to myself that I was more than capable of making change through politics. It was time to stop playing small and safe. It was time to decide if I was truly ready to go big and start being 100 percent Celina. And if I was going to be 100 percent Celina, I needed to use all the tools in my toolbox, including my perceived character flaws of being impulsive, impatient and naïve. I vowed to stop trying to cuss less and restrain my quick temper. In some way, these flaws were my superpowers, though I knew I would have to strike a careful balance between using them too much and not using them at all. But to be authentic in politics, I couldn't pretend anymore that I'd become some careful, subdued, agreeable version of myself. Otherwise, I would never find the courage I needed to speak up and clap back, finding the resilience to weather the storm and the wisdom to know what to do when using my powers got me in trouble. As it would.

eleven

IN CHARGE OF MYSELF

IN DISCUSSING HOW A person can be happy in their career in an essay called "How Will You Measure Your Life," Clayton M. Christensen, a professor at Harvard Business School, wrote that "the most powerful motivator isn't money; it's the opportunity to learn, grow in responsibilities, contribute to others and be recognized for achievements." I was finally starting to remember that how I measured my life, especially my life in politics, had nothing to do with how the PMO or the prime minister treated me or whether they recognized my work. During the first year of my mandate, I kept waiting for someone else to define my purpose, to "give" me the opportunity to learn, grow, contribute and be recognized. But I was the only person who had control over that. And increasingly I began to take back that control. I needed to remember how and why I got into politics, and the answer to both questions was the people.

When in November 2016 Donald Trump was elected to the office that Barack Obama had held, I knew I couldn't stay on even in the minimal role I was playing as parliamentary secretary to the PM. I wrote a letter to Trudeau on the weekend after the US election telling him that I knew that diplomacy had to continue between our two countries, but that going forward, he couldn't rely on me to play a US-facing role: I didn't have the diplomatic capacity to risk being put in front of that man. I had a bigger thing to ask him too. I reminded him that I had a Black son, who he had met at my house the night of the by-election. I told him that yes, we were in Canada, and yes, we had our own problems with racism, but my children and I, and all of Canada, needed him to stand up against the hateful rhetoric that would, without a doubt, spill over the border and affect our lives too. I knew I was putting him on the spot. Even if he was underutilizing me, he couldn't be seen to just drop me, given that I was the only Black female face in his government. I knew that I would still be valuable in helping with the recognition of the UN Decade for People of African Descent. I'd also heard that he and the strategists in the PMO were planning a mini-shuffle of Cabinet, and thought there might be another place in government for me.

Rumours of a shuffle grew louder in December 2016, at which time I asked the PMO whether it would be useful, given that I had built relationships with the other parliamentary secretaries, for me to prepare a report for him on their various talents, abilities and matches and mismatches with their ministers. I suggested it could better inform his thinking when it came to finding new roles for people. I actually created an Excel spreadsheet in which I described each parliamentary secretary's relationship with their minister and recommended whether they should be moved or stay put or even become a minister themselves. I have no idea whether anyone in a position of power consulted my spreadsheet, but some of the moves that were made in January 2017 mirrored my recommendations. Including one for me: I became the parliamentary secretary for the minister of international development and La Francophonie. I was never replaced as parliamentary secretary to the PM—the role was dropped altogether.

I was ecstatic, though I was careful not to show just how happy I was to my new minister, Marie-Claude Bibeau, whose previous parliamentary secretary, Karina Gould, had just joined her in Cabinet as the minister of democratic institutions—becoming, at twenty-nine, the youngest female minister in Canadian history (and in 2018, the first sitting Cabinet minister to have a baby while in office). I made sure to remind Madame Bibeau that I was the person who had helped build momentum over mental health funding in caucus, and was a total neophyte in the area of international development: there was no way I was gunning for her job. At last, I was learning a thing or two about how the political game was played.

And with this portfolio I could be really useful. After being quickly brought up to speed on various files, I began representing the government of Canada, and our newly released Feminist International Assistance Policy, with unapologetic enthusiasm all over the world. The focus of my work was on improving the lives of girls and women, most of whom looked like me, many of whom lived in places like the one in which I'd been born, and who were struggling with all kinds of disadvantages that Canadian funding and support could help address. I had been a baby left behind when my parents seized the opportunity to come to Canada to make a better economic life for us; if that had never happened, I might have lived a life just like theirs, and that fuelled my enthusiasm for the work. I found myself sharing hugs and stories and tears everywhere I travelled—and my jewellery, too, which I found myself handing to the young women I met.

The development story is the greatest story Canada never tells. We have people across our country and around the world doing amazing work in difficult situations. Then, when disaster strikes, they double down and do more. I was proud that our feminist policy was complementing their work and that women and girls were at the centre of the programs we funded—a direct result of the government listening to recommendations from national and international stakeholders as to what would make the most impact in terms of raising people out of poverty and leaving no one behind. They already knew what we were just putting into practice. Placing women and girls in the centre of policy is not just the right thing to do, it's the economically smart thing to do. According to a 2015 McKinsey Global Institute report entitled, "How advancing women's equality can add $12 trillion to global growth," when women and girls are given the tools to reach their full potential and succeed, their efforts can add anywhere from $12 to $28 trillion to our global GDP. It was not about empowering them—women are born empowered— but about leveraging what they had in order to improve their lives. Our funding was tied to programs that involved women and girls in the decision-making, execution and the evaluation of the projects we backed. I also loved that in my new role, everything I spoke about and supported from the stage at national and international events was in opposition to the rhetoric and acts of Trump's new adminis- tration, busy cutting funding to any NGO or government who wouldn't get behind its anti-abortion stance. For the first time in my political life, I felt like the entire government of Canada was standing on the stages with me, boldly promoting women's rights as human rights. When people pushed back against the policy in certain juris- dictions around the world, I stood up and spoke even stronger.

But I was also, always, honest about the state of affairs in Canada as well. The national shame of missing and murdered Indigenous women and girls was a salient example, but other countries also knew that debates were happening in Canada that would result in one province, Quebec, passing a law forbidding public employees from wearing religious artifacts to work. We had as much work to do as a country as others did, and I was glad to be a part of the inter- national conversation about these issues.

—

But, oh, it was a learning curve.

One of the trips I took was to Japan to attend the fiftieth anniversary meeting of the Asian Development Bank. I had never been anywhere in Asia and I was warned in my briefings that "cultural differences" meant that being a Black woman might not work in my favour and the meetings might not be as warm and receptive as I hoped. None of that dampened my excitement over the trip. Just as I had done when I was running my own company and had to make a business trip somewhere beyond our normal reach, I decided to bring my two daughters with me (we didn't really have the money to spare, but I didn't want them to miss such an opportunity).

At the airport we were greeted by a liaison officer from Japan's Ministry of Finance and a representative from the Canadian embassy. After we cleared customs, we were off on a whirlwind, four-day trip in which I had several meetings in Yokohama and Tokyo with government representatives from Fiji, Bhutan, Samoa and other countries in the region. The two most important items on my agenda, though, were bilateral meetings with Takehiko Nakao, the president of the Asia Development Bank in Yokohama, and Katsunobu Katō, the Japanese minister of women's empowerment and minister of state for gender equality in Tokyo.

Before I met with Mr. Nakao, I got together with David Murchison, Canada's executive director for the Asian Development Bank (ADB), along with other members of the Canadian delegation (which included some people from Global Affairs and some who worked for the bank), at the Intercontinental Hotel. We discussed Canada's financial commitment to the ADB as part of the Canadian government's larger pledge of $2 billion in the global fight against climate change. In the middle of the session, I received a text from my daughters letting me know that they were heading to a nearby mall and then on to other tourist destinations. I texted back that they should have fun and be safe, but after I put away my phone, I must have seemed distracted because a member of the delegation asked, "Is everything all right?"

"Oh, yes. For sure!" I exclaimed. "I was just wondering whether I gave my daughters enough money for the day. I left them with seventy thousand yen." I looked around to see everyone looking back at me with surprise—or was it pity? "That's over eight hundred dollars!" one of the women finally said, clearly trying not to laugh. I shook my head, pulled out my phone, and texted the girls to tell them not to spend all the money. Interesting how I didn't hear back from them on that one. They were usually so good at replying to their mother.

As we left our session and headed to the main ballroom of the hotel, I noticed a big display of copies of a book called *Banking on the Future of Asia and the Pacific: 50 Years of the Asian Development Bank*. I grabbed one and placed it in my purse. In breaks throughout the day, I scanned the contents, hoping to gain a better understanding of the bank. I also made sure to read the foreword, written by Mr. Nakao, and I watched videos on YouTube of talks he'd given. It was easy to see his understanding and passion for the region and its people, and also how proud he was of this historical account of the bank he governed.

My fifteen-minute meeting with him was scheduled from 5:25 to 5:40 p.m. When I got to the door of the room, I saw two rows of five to eight chairs set up facing each other dead centre in the intimidatingly large space. At the top of the two rows were two chairs where Mr. Nakao and I would sit, with the Canadian delegates on my side and the Japanese delegates on his. This was the meeting where I would announce Canada's $200 million commitment towards the second phase of the Canadian Climate Fund for the Private Sector in Asia, which I would follow up the next day with a speech to a larger crowd. The investment was intended to build on the success of the initial Canadian Climate Fund, which had allowed the bank to test innovative approaches to climate finance. We knew that governments could not fund climate action alone. We needed the private sector to make investments as well as share their knowledge and expertise if we were to have a shot at achieving the climate goals we committed to at COP 21.

I took a deep breath, and headed straight for Mr. Nakao, about to offer him the firm handshake we politicians and businesspeople are taught to give. Before our hands met, he briskly reminded me that he only had fifteen minutes for the meeting.

Totally okay by me, I did not say. *I only planned to be here for fifteen minutes myself. I am just as hungry as you are and cannot wait to eat something at the reception when this meeting is over.* I thought this without rolling my eyes, which at the time seemed a small, but necessary, victory.

After we took our seats, I covered the usual talking points about Canada's relationship with the bank and Mr. Nakao responded with the usual appreciation for the bank's relationship with Canada. Yawn! I hated this type of formulaic to-and-fro, so bureaucratic and banal. Eventually, Mr. Nakao went to hand me a copy of the bank's history, signalling the end of the meeting. I held my hand up in protest. "No thanks," I said. Time stopped. The faces of the Japanese delegation expressed pure disappointment at my rudeness. The faces of the Canadian delegation showed pure horror. There wasn't a non-bulging eye in the room.

I slowly leaned over to unzip my bag and pulled out my copy of the book. "No thank you," I repeated. "I have my own copy. Will you sign it for me?"

The collective sigh of relief must have been felt clear across Yokohama. Mr. Nakao beamed at me and graciously signed the book.

Impression made! #BlackGirlMagic! He and I chatted as if we were old friends for another ten to fifteen minutes, well past our time allowance. After we were done, we walked together to the reception.

The meeting with Minister Katsunobu Katō was so important I was briefed at breakfast by the ambassador himself, Ian Burney. Katō was known to be a close ally of the prime minister of Japan, Shinzō Abe, and the pressure was on me to ensure the encounter went well. This time I did not have a book to pull out of my bag, but I did my homework as best I could.

Again, the Japanese sat on one side of the table and the Canadians on the other. Minister Katō and I were placed across from each other, with small versions of our respective country flags in front of us. Katō made his opening remarks—about the value his government placed on Japan's relationship with Canada—and I returned his pleasantries. Good grief. How could I get to the real conversation, the one when we finally put away the talking points, bypassed the bureaucratic ping-pong and connect as people? The light bulb went off. We *were* just people. I pushed my notes to the side. Out of the corner of my eye, I could see the ambassador shuffle in his seat a little. Was he nervous? I hope not.

"Mr. Katō," I said, smiling at him. "You have four daughters, right?"

He responded that yes he did.

"Well, my two daughters are running around Tokyo right now, spending way too much money because I incorrectly calculated the exchange. When we really think about it, everything that we are doing in this room is about them, isn't it?"

He leaned forward. "Please, let your daughters stay and spend as much money as possible!" Then he laughed, and the meeting finally started.

In such moments, I remembered that the cornerstone of our democracy is our humanity. No matter our political affiliation or influence, we are just people who happen to work in politics. Our diplomats handle so much of the load of our relationships with other countries every single day. The best impact a visiting politician like me could make, I thought, was building personal, human, connections, and that rarely came in a briefing package.

At last I was learning to trust that I could be as "politically" savvy in politics as I had been in business. One of the lessons I'd learned is to pay attention to people and appreciate the differences that make every one of us unique. For instance, anyone who paid attention to me at a social gathering might not realize I am not too fond of crowds, and would much prefer to sip my wine, leaning in a corner, and watch others interact. But I consider myself a trained extrovert who can put on the smiles when I need to survive a reception or "meet and greet."

I had studied Mr. Nakao and Mr. Katō in order to be effective in my job, for sure, but I also did it because I was impressed by them, and was interested in how they'd succeeded in their respective fields. I wanted to get a sense of what made them tick. I study myself just as much as I study other people. The way I speak, my hand movements, the way I walk into a room, the way I stand in a room, the way I sit in certain situations versus others, the way I smile, the way I nod, if and when to furrow my brow and whether or not I allow my heels to click, clack on the floor. I have taken the time to study which of my movements make people nervous and which make them feel comfortable. Depending on the mood and the matter of the situation, I adjust.

The management of one's presence in the world is an art. Figuring out your strengths and weaknesses, your abilities, style and values helps you identify what type of contribution you can make to the world. I know that I am valuable to the organizations and the spaces that I occupy, even though I suffer through periods of self-doubt. The point of learning the ways your behaviour affects others is not to become a sort of master manipulator in order to get your own way. Taking the time to truly understand yourself and why you behave the way you do opens the door to understanding, kindness, empathy and compassion towards others. And so often the effort to make lasting, beneficial change in this world rests on treating yourself and others with kindness and respect.

Not that any of this is easy. While I was finding firmer footing with every success in my new brief in International Development, I continued to face a barrage of microaggressions on the Hill, and beyond, that made me question whether I would ever belong there. They ranged from being asked why I was walking down a particular hall, to being warned by a woman in the bathroom not to steal the wallet she had left on the ledge by the door, to being denied access to a government buildings, including my own office. Even on my travels to places where the racial mix was much different than Canada's, I was used to people not seeing me. Once, while travelling as the head of delegation to an international conference, I arrived early for a meeting with the vice president of another country. "Who is the head of delegation?" the vice president's staffer asked my team. They pointed at me. The staffer looked right through me and asked, again, "Who is the head of delegation? The parliamentary secretary?"

I sighed the kind of sigh that makes you remember you have clavicles. "I am the head of delegation and the parliamentary secretary. Is the vice president ready to start?" There was no point in dwelling on it. I needed to be professional and keep things moving along.

When one of my Liberal colleagues told me while we were

waiting for the Parliament Hill bus that he would give anything to run his fingers through my hair, I told him, very seriously, that "touching my hair would be the worst fucking mistake you could ever make in your goddamn life." He decided he would walk, and I got on the bus.

Situations like this were a weekly occurrence, and though they made me uncomfortable, I was able to use my voice to deal with them. But on March 22, 2017, when a PhD student named Judy, who came to the Hill as part of the University of Toronto's Women in House delegation, had her hair searched by security without explicit consent, I was both hurt and furious. The Women in House program is designed to give women from diverse backgrounds the opportunity to come to the Parliament and shadow an MP, and Judy and another woman from U of T were joining me. When neither of my guests showed up in the reception room where we were to meet, I asked other members of the program if they had seen them. Yes, they had. One of the two missing women had had an issue gaining entrance to the building and both of them were still at security.

I headed straight for the checkpoint, where I found two Black women looking distraught. Judy had her hair in large, long braids, some of them tied up in a bun. She was in the middle of explaining to the security guard who'd insisted on searching her hair how inappropriate it was for someone to do such a thing, especially without warning. It was a devastating and embarrassing experience for her, and equally for me. I work in the House, but the House belongs to her. It belongs to the people of Canada. One of the security guards was extremely apologetic, but the guard who had done the search was not. One ironic aspect of this terrible situation: Judy was completing her PhD in the area of profiling and cultural search procedures. I couldn't make this stuff up even if I tried.

This incident brought home to me that it was all very well to travel the world speaking boldly about women's rights as human rights, but what was I going to do here in Canada? The issue of mental health was something everyone of all backgrounds could get on board with, even if some stigma still existed. Tackling subjects related to equity and justice, racism and intersectionality, especially in caucus, was much tougher. I wanted my colleagues to really understand why experiencing microaggressions is like a death by a thousand cuts—how what is said, and how it is said, impacts people. I wanted what happened to Judy never to happen again, and for that to be the outcome, my colleagues had to understand that a trespass had been committed by a security guard who insisted that she was just doing her job.

Although the government House leader and Speaker of the House were informed of the event, and vowed to make necessary changes, I worried about the incident to the end of that sitting, and on through the summer break while I was at work back in my constituency. I was part of a Liberal government that had sold itself as better than what came before, as the voice of sunshine and progress and open dialogue, as the face of Canada. Though I supported what we were striving for, when it came to these kinds of issues, I didn't feel much sun, light or air. I'd tried hard to dismiss my own uneasy feelings about the ways I was being treated as a Black woman in Ottawa and get on with it, which is certainly what some in the Black community thought you should do when you joined this club: don't get identified as *that* kind of representative of the community—the one who can't have a conversation without talking about racism—or they'll pigeonhole you and, worse, never invite the rest of us in. A Black woman in politics was supposed to be nice, sit nice, dress nice, remain humble, and be glad that she was "allowed" a seat at the table. But I was already failing at all that.

At the end of the summer of 2017, I reached the watershed moment where I finally realized that if I didn't step up, no one else was going to. Every summer we had a fall caucus retreat. This year, the women's caucus was being held the day before the retreat started, which really pissed me off, because it meant I had to miss my children's first day back at school. Also, what was with a supposedly feminist government that didn't put the women's caucus meeting on the main agenda?

And then, when I got to the meeting and heard Maryam Monsef, the minister for women and gender equality, speak, she told us that her primary focus for the following sitting was going to be on promoting the interests of Muslim women. I shook my head in disbelief. While travelling through Canada earlier in the year, she said, she'd heard stories that Muslim women were being denied job opportunities and access to services because of the way they dressed or the names on their résumés. That was true, of course. I knew the prejudice faced by Muslim women. I had heard the stories about them being overlooked from business colleagues. However, this minister's job was to ensure equity for all women, especially those belonging to equity-seeking groups. Her ministry's mission was to investigate and develop legislation and policies to mitigate the disadvantages all marginalized women faced, especially women of colour, and yet here she was announcing that she'd chosen to prioritize one group. After she came off the stage, I asked her if I'd heard her correctly when she said that she was going to focus "primarily" on Muslim women. She told me I had. When I asked what her rationale was, she replied that she needed to act because Muslims in Canada were being targeted with violence, and she reminded me of the Quebec City mosque shooting in January 2017. As if I needed reminding—the whole country had been shocked. She also insisted that she needed to act because Muslim women, in particular, were denied employment and opportunities because they wore a hijab.

"So are Muslim women who are denied opportunities for employment more important than Black girls who are removed from school because their hair is too puffy?" I asked.

She did not respond.

I continued. "Well, if you are going to be involved in putting forward initiatives for one equity-seeking group, don't you need to also understand what other groups are facing and put forward the most comprehensive policy?"

Was it possible that the minister, along with so many others, didn't understand what *all* women face on a day-to-day basis, especially Black women? It's true that in the mainstream, conversation about everything from body shaming to sexual assault was mostly limited to the experiences of white women. Progressive people agreed that talking about a woman's baby bump or other body parts was unacceptable. The rest of us were still pretty invisible in the discourse. Do a quick Google image search for "professional hair" and you come up with pictures of white women with straight hair in the latest styles. Search "unprofessional hair" and the results are largely photos of Black women with braids and Afros. I decided that it was not enough to defend Judy and her dreadlocks at the security desk. I needed to defend us all.

Before Question Period begins every day, MPs have an opportunity to make a statement about a topic of their choice. Right after that women's caucus meeting I requested a time slot in which I would speak about issues affecting Black women. I only had a minute allotted to me and I had to get it right. I began to write, and rewrite, practising in front of the mirror and with my family in order to perfect my words. Then I realized it wasn't enough to make the speech, I also needed to make a statement and I decided to braid my hair so my words would have maximum impact. But there was a little wrinkle. The date I'd been given was Monday, September 18. We'd only get back from the UK, where we were delivering Desiray to her first year of law studies at the University of Leicester, on the Sunday before I had to get back to Ottawa. It would be next to impossible to get an appointment on a Sunday night to get my hair braided. Then I got lucky: a friend's stylist was willing to do my hair. We drove straight from the airport to the appointment.

As I stood on the platform waiting for the train the next morning, I was nervous. Had an MP ever worn braids in the House of Commons? I felt like all eyes were on me. Why did I always have to go overboard? My phone vibrated and I checked my texts to see that the chief government whip was wondering if I could postpone my speech until the Wednesday session. What could I say? *Sorry. No. I braided my hair for this speech and I need to get it over with today so that people do not ask questions about my braids, touch my hair, or stare at me for the whole of the next two days wondering what is up with me.* Of course, I couldn't say that, so I agreed to wait.

Around the same time, the minister of environment, Catherine McKenna, was in the news because a Conservative MP had called her "climate Barbie" on social media. Catherine, like me and other female members, had dealt with different types of body shaming since we got to Ottawa, and we were all reaching the point where we'd had enough. I decided I had to take the advice I'd given Maryam Monsef. Even though my one-minute speech was designed to raise awareness on issues related to Black identity, I felt it wasn't enough to speak solely about Black hair, when I knew that all women and girls were shamed because of their appearance. When Wednesday finally arrived, I'd rewritten my speech one more time and I was ready.

When it was my turn to speak, I rose. "Mr. Speaker," I said, "this week I have my hair in braids, much like I had throughout my childhood. However, Mr. Speaker, it has come to my attention that there are young girls here in Canada, and other parts of the world, who are removed from school, or shamed, because of their hairstyle. Mr. Speaker, body shaming of a woman, in any form, from the top of her head to the soles of her feet is wrong. Irrespective of her hairstyle, the size of her thighs, the size of her hips, the size of her baby bump, the size of her breasts or the size of her lips. What makes us unique makes us beautiful. So Mr. Speaker, I will continue to rock these braids for three reasons. One, because—and you have to agree—they are dope! Two, in solidarity with women who have been shamed based on any part of their appearance. And third, and most importantly, in solidarity with the young girls and women who look like me and those who don't. I want them to know that their braids, dreads, super curly Afro puffs, weaves, hijabs, headscarves, and all other varieties of hairstyles, belong in schools, the work place, the boardroom and yes, even here, on Parliament Hill. Thank you Mr. Speaker."

At the end, my voice cracked with emotion. I was speaking up for myself as well as speaking up for others. When I started in politics, I wore my hair long and straight. When I first decided to cut it into a short bob, my staff told me I shouldn't do it. They stressed that I needed to wear my hair exactly the same way for the next four years: "That is how it's done. You want people to know who you are and changing your hairstyle confuses people." I corrected them. That is how it had to be done in a system that was largely inhabited by white men. I was not a white man, so those rules didn't apply to me. By the time I left Ottawa, I had worn it in a different style pretty much every week. I'd cut it into a short bob again, had it shaved on one side, shaved it completely off, wore it natural and every other style in between just to prove the point. To some men in the House, and even to some of the women, the issue I was addressing in my speech may have sounded trivial, but the overwhelming national and international response confirmed that it wasn't. And soon, Oprah's magazine, O, was calling, wanting to feature me in an upcoming issue about people who were standing up and making a difference.

While being interviewed by David Letterman on his Netflix show, *My Next Guest Needs No Introduction*, President Obama said: "Part of the ability to lead doesn't have to do with legislation, it doesn't have to do with regulations, it has to do with shaping attitude, shaping culture [and] increasing awareness." His words described the purpose I'd finally found in politics. I could review acts of legislation and vote on them with the 337 other people present, and did, but the ability to speak up about issues that brought pain to people was not just my responsibility, it had become my motivation and my calling. I'd found the perfect intersection of my past pain and present purpose. Politics gave me the platform to amplify the voices of the quiet little Black girls who felt and saw injustices and could not say anything. It gave me the platform to speak to young students who were struggling to connect with their immigrant parents, while carving out a space for themselves in the world. And it gave me an opportunity to tell women that I saw their pain and hurt, as well as their beauty and strength.

The problem was that for most of my time in office so far, I'd felt like one of the turtles riding the East Australian Current in *Finding Nemo*. I was trying to keep up with the flow and move with the others in Parliament. I was meeting with my constituents in the riding and those who came to my office in Ottawa, and had been paying attention to the situations in their lives that were causing them grief and anxiety. But if I wanted to understand the root cause of at least some of the problems they were having, and help them, I could not do it if I was rushing by, trying to stay with the pack. If I was passionate about the people I served, I needed to take the time to really listen. I would need to step fully out of the rushing current and form my own space.

As I started to speak out on issues, I felt as if I had stuck one foot outside the current into the calm waters where I was meant to be. But I couldn't stay straddled in this position for very long, one foot in, one foot out. It was painful. Even with what seemed to me like the half-assed way I'd been going about things, I faced an onslaught of negative messages from social media and received death threats against me and my children. I was being sued by a constituent who felt her immigration case was not proceeding fast enough and going through mediation with a staff member who wanted closure after she quit working for me. I realized that there was no turning back now, no path of least resistance. It was my responsibility to shape attitudes with my words, shape culture with my actions and increase awareness through my representation. And if representation truly mattered, I needed to represent something that mattered to me, and that was my community. Politics afforded me the opportunity to reconcile my pain with my purpose, realize my worth and build back my self-esteem. I wanted to help others do the same.

twelve

BLACK COFFEE, NO SUGAR, NO CREAM

IN JANUARY 2018, I SPENT weeks working on a letter, to be published in the Huffington Post on the eve of Black History Month, paying tribute to all the Black women who had been calling out injustice and standing up for issues long before I came on the scene. I wrote it out of love and respect, but also out of some guilt that a person like me, coming so late to the political struggle, was attracting attention because of my position on Parliament Hill. I want to quote it in full here, still out of love and respect, and because it marked such an important moment of understanding for me.

"A Love Letter to Black Women"

Dear Sisters,

I know that it has been a while since I spoke to you. I seem to have just popped on the scene. Over the last twenty or so years, I have been busy raising a family and growing a business, and we have lost touch. I have not been to the barbecues, community meetings or get-togethers in my "busy-ness." Now, I know what you are thinking, "Well, Celina. We have all been busy, and yet some of us still attended the community meetings and gatherings." Yes, I know. And that is why we (I) owe you a debt of gratitude. You stayed connected, where I did not. You sacrificed your energy, time and spirit, and we (I) owe you.

That is why I am writing. To tell you that even though we may have been distant, and I may seem far away, I love you and #ISeeYou. I have tried to reach out through my posts and blogs and speeches and the work I do, behind the scenes, related to policy. I have tried to break the status quo and talk about mental health issues, microaggressions, and the fact that body shaming includes our hair, the size of our thighs, the size of our hips and the size of our lips.

I may not be doing everything you want, as fast as you want. I am trying my best. It is no excuse, but from time to time, my depression and anxiety get the best of me, as I try to navigate this political beast that is very new territory for me. But the outreach was my way of saying that I see you, and through this position, I see you clearer than ever.

I see you Elders. You paved the way. You have lessons to teach and skills to pass down, if only we would listen. Your wisdom runs deep, because it is connected to this land, our homelands, and the motherland. #ISeeYou

I see you Moms. Single or otherwise. Holding it down for your children. Trying to protect them from the streets, and the institutions that keep them down and funnel them into prisons and foster care. I see you praying to God HE doesn't get stopped and carded, and SHE doesn't have somebody put her hair in elastic bands because it is too puffy. Both actions, damaging to their little souls. I pray too. #ISeeYou

I see you Wifey. Loving so deeply and strongly that it hurts. Because you have a partner that you want to inspire, protect and support, yet want to show the door every given day, and Sunday. (I have one at home too. Love him fiercely one minute then want to throw him out the next. Yet when I look into his eyes, all I see is love and my #rideordie). #ISeeYou

I see you Corporate. Holding it down. Producing the results. Bringing the strategy to management, then to fruition, all while being second guessed, passed over for promotion, and silenced when you face aggressive behaviour. I know what that is like. #ISeeYou

I see you Entrepreneur. Trying to make a dollar out of fifteen cents. Trying to get your hustle going. Putting it out there in the hopes that it will be successful and brilliant and everything you imagined. Hoping that they do not steal your idea(s), or pass your brilliance off as their own. Trying to get loans that may never come through, investors that cannot see your vision and naysayers trying to hold you down. #ISeeYou

I see you Activist and Protester. Yes, I am speaking to you @BLM_TO and others like you. You. Doing what this democracy affords you the freedom to do, yet you are met with hate and resistance. You with your brilliant minds and passionate hearts, who know your history, have done your research, who occupy and protest not just for the Black community, but for Indigenous rights, LGBTQ2 rights, and simply put, human rights. #ISeeYou

I see you Journalists, Policy Advisors and News Anchors/Bloggers/ Deliverers. We do not always see eye to eye. Do we have to? You need to hold my feet to the fire. You need to keep me accountable. That is your job. That is your calling. Don't water it down or go easy on me because we are sisters. Go hard, because you want me to produce the best policy for everyone, and I want YOU to be the best damn person in your field. #ISeeYou

I see you Book Store Owner, Historian, Educator and Author. I see you documenting and preserving our history and telling the stories of our present. It is a story that is erased from the consciousness of the world, and your work will be your legacy. It is important. Our people are storytellers and you are the keepers of this beautiful gift. #ISeeYou

I see You. Grinding every day, no matter the occupation or task. Hustling and grinding. Grinding and hustling. Being twice as good, twice as fast, twice as everything, because that is what we were taught. That is the only way we can succeed. I also see that it comes at a cost. The wear and tear. The exhaustion. The mental drain. I see that you are tired. And yet still you rise.

My sisters, in the face of all this you rise, and I see you. I see your brilliance and courage and unconditional love.

I see you with your black velvet, dark chocolate, jamocha almond, caramel latte (with a sprinkle of freckle) and all shades of skin in between, that, when it is kissed by the light, makes your melanin shine brighter than the sun. #ISeeYou

I see you when you walk into a room and the air has no choice but to gravitate to you, as you suck the oxygen out of the space. #ISeeYou

I see you with your curves and shape. The ones that have a price tag now, but yours have been divinely bestowed, rightfully placed, blessed and cursed at the same time. #ISeeYou

I see you saying that everything is going to be all right. I see you supporting me, even in our distance. I see you praying for me and keeping me in your thoughts.

I see you. I thank you. I love you. And this Black History Month, it is my privilege to honour you.

Love and Hugs,

Celina
@MPCelina

The irony was that my love letter appeared the day after I received another overt and painful personal lesson in invisibility. On January 30, the prime minister had gathered select Cabinet ministers and Black community leaders to stand behind him in the foyer of the House of Commons as he announced that Canada would recognize the United Nations International Decade for People of African Descent and also committed his government to creating a better future for Black Canadians. At his side stood Ahmed Hussen, the first Somali-Canadian to be elected to the House and the first to become a Cabinet minister, having been put in charge of Immigration, Refugees and Citizenship early in 2017. Though I had been the one to flag this opportunity, and moral obligation, for the prime minister twice in 2016, I had heard nothing from him or anyone in the PMO since, which was awkward given that I heard regularly from the community members the government was consulting. They knew more about what my party was planning than I did.

It had gotten so awkward that in June 2017 I'd sent yet another fruitless email to Gerald Butts, along with a handwritten note to the prime minister, to remind them that, as a Black female, I brought a unique perspective to this issue. I also mentioned that they needed to reach out to more than one organization in order to consult Black communities. In my email I specifically mentioned an instance in which I'd found out about a meeting that had happened a few weeks earlier from community members who wondered why I wasn't there, just so that Gerry would know that some solidarity existed among the people trying to move the agenda of recognition, justice and development for Black people forward. I reassured him that I knew the issue was bigger than me and that I wasn't going to make a huge fuss about being excluded. Ahmed was more than capable of championing the road to official recognition of the Decade, I wrote, but surely the input of a Black woman should be pertinent too.

I did not receive a response (a familiar pattern). On the morning of January 30, I put on a mint green dress with a gigantic bow at the neck, designed to make me hard to miss, and stood at the back of the crowd that gathered in the foyer as the prime minister announced that Canada would be among the first countries to recognize the Decade. I was thrilled for my community and for Canada, but as usual I couldn't stop the tears from running down my face. Adam Vaughan had come to stand beside me and handed me some Kleenex. He knew all too well what had happened and had always been an ally.

I wiped my eyes and then I smiled like everyone else. There was no point in crying over being excluded from this one battle when there was much more war to fight.

The Huffington Post piece came out the next day, February 1, at the beginning of Black History Month. (It was also posted to ByBlacks.com, an online magazine started by Camille and Roger Dundas of Whitby, which highlights Black businesses and stories of success in Black communities, and was printed in *Share Newspaper*, a Toronto-based Black community newspaper.) I had chosen to write to Black women specifically, and not to male community activists like my own husband, because I knew that they faced the completely undermining combination of both racism *and* sexism—or "misogynoir," a term coined by queer Black feminist Moya Bailey. Members of my own government had schooled me in the term even as it pledged feminism and diversity as strengths.

On the same day, the government announced that it was going to spend the month highlighting Black women—a fitting and long overdue honour. Our stories of strength, courage and vision were celebrated with hundreds of events throughout the country; more than fifty MPs held such events in their region. In the House of Commons, members made seventeen special statements to call out amazing Black women. The day also saw Canada Post issuing stamps honouring Lincoln Alexander and Kathleen (Kay) Livingstone, two prominent Black Canadians who shattered barriers for all people of colour in Canada. On February 12, Black Canadians representing dozens of communities across the country came to Parliament Hill to meet with MPs from all political parties to discuss their pertinent issues and ask for government attention, funding, and support. This annual day of action had begun in 2016, with a meeting I'd suggested between Black elected officials and the prime minister. A first.

—

In his book, *Faces at the Bottom of the Well: The Permanence of Racism*, Derrick Bell, the first tenured Black professor at Harvard Law School, wrote about Dr. Martin Luther King Jr.'s struggle to remain committed to the "courageous struggle whatever the circumstances or the odds." He went on to say that "part of that struggle was the need to speak the truth as he [Dr. King] viewed it even when that truth alienated rather than unified, upset minds rather than calmed hearts, and subjected the speaker to general censure rather than acclaim." During the early months of 2018, I would live this reality, after I called out a prominent opposition politician for his actions only to have my own colleagues, media and members of the public express their disappointment in me for doing so. I knew full well that I couldn't take a shot at shattering the status quo if I was afraid to get cut. The glass was going to fall somewhere and if I was the one closest to it, I could expect to bleed. And bleed I did.

In late February, our government released its 2018 federal budget. For the first time in the country's 151 years of existence, a federal budget included an allocation designed to help create equity in Black communities. I was surprised to see $19 million dedicated to Black youth and mental health, $23 million to develop an anti-racism plan and $6.7 million for the creation of a centre for collection of disaggregated racial and gender data that would help the government create equitable policy. I was surprised by these details because I had not been involved in any conversations about this budget allocation. I had also objected to the lack of broad consultation with Black communities and the relatively minimal number of dollars. At the Black caucus meeting that followed the budget announcement, my colleagues told me that I should get on board because at last we were putting money behind such pledges. I could promote that, I agreed, even though I wished that the budget allocation was a lot higher.

In response to the funding, the former Conservative leadership candidate and sitting MP Maxime Bernier tweeted, "I thought the ultimate goal of fighting discrimination was to create a colour-blind society where everyone is treated the same. Not to set some Canadians apart as being 'racialized.' What's the purpose of this awful jargon? To create more division for the Liberals to exploit?"

I could not believe it.

I responded with a quote retweet that ended with an invitation to the man to straighten out his head. "@MaximeBernier do some research, or a Google search, as to why stating colour blindness as a defence actually contributes to racism. Please check your privilege and be quiet. Since our gvt't likes research, here is some evidence: theguardian.com/commentisfree/ . . ."

Twitter erupted. It seemed like everyone and their dog was upset, not with Bernier, but with me for calling out his privilege. Soon Rebel Media, a right-wing Canadian online publication, said I "might" be the "most racist MP" in Canada, a weirdly soft word choice for Ezra Levant's outfit. Nonetheless, it was enough to activate their hordes of social media bottom-feeding trolls. There was no way they were going to let a Black female MP tell a privileged white male MP the truth. In their twisted view of the universe, I was not supposed to be challenging the views of prominent male members of Parliament. I was supposed to be grateful I had the job, and just sit back and stay quiet.

I actually could not understand why so many people were angry with me and so few were calling out Maxime Bernier, a failed contender for the leadership of the Conservative Party of Canada, when he described a long-overdue investment in an underserved community as divisive. Well, I *could* understand it: he'd blown a dog whistle designed to be heard by his right-wing base. Still, he'd been elected to serve in Canada's Parliament: How did he get away with such irresponsible views? Didn't the very nature of the job require him to understand that many equity-seeking groups need government assistance and resources to help create equitable communities? I hadn't been paying much attention to the race to replace Stephen Harper, I have to admit. I didn't know Bernier was one of those guys who wanted to be in government in order to tell us we need as little in the way of government as possible—even as taxpayers paid him a salary to look out for them.

The more I reflected on this last question, the angrier I got. Bernier was being described as the victim of my angry Black womanness. Pundits opined about white privilege and their disappointment in me for pointing it out. I was being depicted as the culprit in this exchange for speaking out against his narrow-minded, unjust attitude. I could not look at my social media without scrolling through hundreds and hundreds of offensive messages. I won't repeat any of them here because I don't wish to give them any further space, but they made me sick and scared and worried for my family and my country. I had predicted that Trump's election would embolden haters everywhere, and the prediction had come true. It was horrible to be the target of such a gaslighting attack. In an attempt to create some breathing room for myself, I tweeted another message to Bernier, saying that it hadn't been cool for me to tell him to be quiet and inviting him to have a chat with me. But since I wouldn't apologize for telling him to check his privilege, he refused and the controversy roared on.

I needed to put my business hat on and figure out what I needed to do to get back on the right side of this issue in the minds of Canadians. The first step was not to back down. On March 7, 2018, I was supposed to deliver an International Women's Day speech at a "Women Who Lead" event at Toronto's Empire Club on behalf of Maryam Monsef, the minister of women and gender equality. The job was straightforward: all I had to do was to read the words written for and vetted by her. But, given everything that was going on, I was a bag of nerves at the thought of standing up in front of a largely white crowd of business people. Vidal came with me and tried to keep me calm, but as predicted, he and I were the only Black couple there. During the private reception before the event, I was a little reassured when many people from different sectors, ages and backgrounds approached me to offer their congratulations for standing up to Bernier. And the one Brown person in attendance, who turned out to be the event sponsor, Chandran Fernando, founder of Matrix360, a talent management and workplace strategy firm for equity and diversity in the real estate industry, came up to me, grinning. "You gave it to Maxime Bernier!" he said, and gave me a big hug. The hug was just what I needed to melt the nerves away.

As I stepped on stage, I realized that if I did not talk about body shaming, microaggressions or the obvious workings of racism here, I was doing a disservice to the community I represented. Not just the Black community, but all the racialized and marginalized communities across the country: women, people of colour, including Black and Indigenous folks, persons with disabilities, religious minorities, those with different sexual orientation. Everyone with an intersecting identity needed their voices amplified.

We often hear in Canada that "diversity is our strength," but is it? Diversity is ubiquitous; it is all around us. *Inclusion* is a choice. Inclusion is what will make our country stronger, but achieving inclusion requires consistent and deliberate work. As the anti-Black racism protests of 2020 brought home so urgently, rolling across the whole globe in response to the modern-day lynching of George Floyd, and in Toronto, the untimely death of Regis Korchinski-Paquet, who fell to her death from her apartment balcony after the police came to do a mental-health check, we have such a long way to go.

Although the spaces we occupy are diverse, they are not truly inclusive. Imagine the rewards that will follow from building a country in which each person has the opportunity to bring 100 percent of their authentic selves to their lives and work. Imagine the cultural wealth, the literal wealth, and the innovation flowing free in such a place. Much as all my new critics liked to deny it, we needed—we *need*—systemic change in order to ensure our institutions are barrier-free. Systemic racism flows from policies that reinforce the inequities between us—policies created in the context of systemic racism in the first place: one reinforces the other. That's why we have to keep the pressure up on our lawmakers at every level of government; they're the ones who set the frame and the laws that can dismantle racist policies. But there are some smaller changes that would help mitigate the microaggressions people face on a day-to-day basis. For example, in most workspaces and restaurants, people are still required to choose between a male and a female washroom. Do we really care about the gender assignment of washrooms? In my humble opinion, use whichever toilet you want, just remember to wash your hands.

When Black women and girls are ostracized and criticized for the ways we wear our natural hair, it makes me wonder just how interested we are in being inclusive. I wonder the same thing when I think about the laws we now have in this country that discriminate against public employees who wear religious paraphernalia. We have deteriorating or non-existent infrastructure in Indigenous communities, which inhibits people from reaching their maximum potential while living on and off the land they have occupied for centuries. All these things make it plain that we are *supposed* to choose a washroom carefully, straighten our hair so we don't upset anyone, and take off our religious items when we go to our public-facing job in case they offend the narrow-minded; if our community does not have clean running water we're supposed to just move to the city.

Every time someone is faced with the demand to lose a piece of themselves in order to accommodate those with the power to enforce that demand, our businesses, schools and communities—our whole country—loses. We lose the benefit of 100 percent of that person's contribution. Instead, they give us 90 percent, then 80 percent, then 70 percent and on down, until they are so weathered by the daily context within which they exist, they have no choice but to step away. These are awkward conversations to have, but they need to be had. Loudly, and in public.

As I delivered the minister's speech about all the ways our government was trying to enact policies and legislation to improve the lives of girls and women at home and abroad, and asking all the people in the room to reflect on what their own feminism looked like, the usual butterflies in my stomach once again turned into cheerleaders. I needed to include my own call to action. Since I was already in boiling water with the Bernier situation, what did I have to lose? At the end of the minister's speech, I added this: "I cannot leave this stage without acknowledging that over the past few days it has been particularly challenging for myself in the role I have. I have heard individuals say that I might be a one-term MP because I continue to speak up about issues. And I accept that. I accept it because my feminism requires me to be bold. It requires me to have uncomfortable conversations and to speak my truth. It requires me to smash and challenge the status quo.

"But my feminism isn't for everybody. Not everyone likes black coffee, no sugar, no cream." Here I heard the sound of one person clapping, and glanced down to see that the applause was coming not from Vidal, who was being circumspect, but from my new ally Chandran Fernando.

"So I implore you," I continued, "I implore you to be bold in your definition of your feminism. We have an army of young girls and boys here in Canada who are expecting no less from you."

I was never so glad to be done a speech, and never so glad to have strayed from the script.

After the speech, I headed straight to the airport to fly to Nova Scotia to attend, with Finance Minister Bill Morneau, the unveiling of Canada's new ten-dollar bill honouring Viola Desmond, a civil rights activist from the province. I hoped that my colleagues and I in the party's Black caucus had played a small part in the choice. We'd been sitting together at dinner a couple years earlier during a party retreat in Saguenay, Quebec, when Morneau came over and sat down with us. When he realized we were having a meeting, he asked if he could stay. When we agreed, he told us that they were about to select a woman to feature on the ten-dollar bill and asked for our suggestions. We all told him that Viola Desmond should be the one. As he got up to leave, I pulled him aside and made one final plea from the only Black woman present. In the end, many thousands of Canadians weighed in on the choice, but I was proud that our Black caucus (a parliamentary group that hadn't existed before the 2015 election) had played its part.

The edition of O, The Oprah Magazine that singled me out for speaking up against body shaming was released the following week, but even the magic of Oprah Winfrey couldn't tame the controversy still raging around me.

As the Bernier feud attracted national media attention, a prominent Ottawa journalist, Robert Fife, claimed on a CPAC show that systemic racism did not exist in Canada because high-school students of different races hung out together all the time. In response, on March 24, 2018, another Canadian journalist who wrote for Buzzfeed, Ishmael N. Daro, tweeted, "Robert Fife, the Ottawa bureau chief of the nation's paper of record, does not seem to know what systemic racism even means. He thinks it's about whether teenagers of different backgrounds hang out together."

I quote retweeted Daro along with a response on Twitter at 12:02 a.m. on March 26: "To suggest that systemic racism does not exist, makes me question your ability to investigate stories of the Canadian experience without bias." I mean, really: how could Robert Fife accurately report stories of marginalized Canadians and Canadians of colour for the *Globe and Mail* if he doubted the existence of racism?

Later that night, Brian Lilley, another Canadian journalist, posted that, "Liberal MP sees racism everywhere. Is @MPCelina going too far in attacking @RobertFife? Read and RT bit.ly/2IQVD69 #cdnpoli."

Had I attacked Robert Fife? In my opinion, I'd just asked a legitimate question about Fife's ability to accurately report on the lived experiences of people of colour in Canada. Secondly, do I see racism everywhere? Not necessarily, but you better believe I am going to call out bullshit when I read, see, or hear it. Lilley's tweet started another Twitter firestorm. At 9:19 the next evening, having stared at way too much of that firestorm sitting alone in my Ottawa condo, I sent out this message: "So tired of being attacked as a racist b/c I question racism or speak up against it. The label does not belong to me. I will not sit & let others say what they wish, because they feel they can get away with it, or others are too cowardly to object. I will speak up #NotToday."

I *was* tired, and I also felt myself spiralling into the dark place I never wanted to go again. I put my phone down and decided that it was best to stay away from social media for the rest of the night, if not the rest of my life.

At seven the next morning a knock at my door woke me up. I was so groggy I felt almost drunk. I peered through the peephole and there was Vidal, my rock and the love of my life. I burst into tears as I fell into his arms. "What are you doing here?" I asked.

"I left Whitby at three-thirty to be here for you." Vidal knew that his wife was about to spiral and that he needed to catch her when she fell. He carried me into the bedroom, lay down with me and allowed me to cry. He said nothing. He did not ask me to stop or take it easy. He knew that I needed to let it out. All of it. The frustration and anger and exhaustion. I cried until there was nothing left. Then he got me up and led me to the shower. "You need to get ready now, my baby, and go to work," he whispered. When I was dressed and ready, he walked me to my first meeting; only his love and support kept me upright. I thought I could handle everything that was being thrown at me, but by that point I felt as if I had no fight left.

Since I had put away my phone, I didn't know that others had picked up my fight. Andray Domise, a community activist who writes for *Maclean's*, had been chatting with Vidal as Vidal headed for Ottawa, and decided to send a message of support via social media. At 8:28 a.m., Adam Vaughan tweeted a thread of solidarity, including #HereForCelina in every one. "Before anyone wants to discount racism," he wrote in his first tweet, "check the attacks attached to Celina's posts." He then composed an alphabet of individual tweets, outlining the reasons why Fife's comments were incorrect. Under Lilley's post, he described how systemic racism exists in Canada. He included personal stories to drive home his points, along with quotes from various thought leaders. Soon others started adding their thoughts, using the hashtag.

Vidal was waiting for me when I finished my scheduled morning meetings, and told me that I was trending on social media. My stomach instantly sank. I stopped walking. "Why?" I asked, as I trembled with fear. I was staying away from my phone on purpose. I wanted the whole thing to go away.

"No, no, babe. It's a good thing. People are supporting you. Adam and Andray started a hashtag, #HereForCelina, and it's trending in Canada."

I fumbled to pull out my phone. Hundreds of messages from Canadians and people around the world appeared on my social media pages; there were texts and emails. I trembled even more as the tears rolled. "I am not crazy. I am not wrong. I am on the right side of history." I think I even said that out loud.

Later that afternoon, prominent members of the Black community called to tell me that, in addition to posting messages with #HereForCelina on social media, they had started a letter-writing campaign to the PM, his Cabinet ministers and all Liberal members of Parliament asking them to support me. They had had enough. As one of them said, "You have put yourself out there long enough. Others need to get on board. Canadians are supporting you. American journalists are supporting you. Your caucus needs to do their part."

They were right: only Adam and a couple of others had supported me publicly through the weeks after the Bernier exchange. Bernier had attacked the Liberal's budget, giving them a perfect opportunity to show their mettle and their commitment to diversity. Yet during our Ontario caucus meetings, some members indicated that talking about gender, race and intersectionality did not resonate when they knocked on doors in their constituencies. One of them said that people in his suburban riding asked him, instead, "What are you Liberals doing for our white sons?"

I was not expecting much support from them in tackling issues specific to the Black community, but it did not take long for the letter-writing campaign to bear fruit. That evening, at about six, I received a call from Mike Power, who had been my liaison in the PMO when I was the PM's parliamentary secretary, asking me if I was okay and whether I needed anything. He indicated that the prime minister wanted to meet with me before our national caucus meeting the next day. My blood started to boil. Really? *Now* they were asking if I was okay? When #HereForCelina had gone viral?

Where had the PM, the PMO and Liberals been for the last three weeks? Where were their tweets or support during that period?

As annoyed as I was, I remained calm. There was no point in turning into the "Mad Black Woman" and giving them any more ammunition to use against me. Staring at Vidal, I told Mike that yes, I was okay and, in fact, I had everything I needed (right there in the presence of my husband), and agreed to meet with the prime minister. The fact that he wanted to meet before national caucus meant that he really didn't want to talk. My Ontario caucus ran from eight to ten o'clock and national caucus, which he attended, started at ten. When exactly were we supposed to have this conversation?

Vidal and I decided to go out for dinner that night to Whalesbone on Elgin, my favourite local restaurant. I knew everyone in the place, as I ate there by myself at least three or four times a week when I was in Ottawa. We toasted how the day had turned out, laughed and counted our blessings. Everything was better when we were together. Even though he was carrying a full load at home—looking after the children during the week, finishing his doctoral studies and working as the dean of the Police Education and Innovation Centre in Durham—he'd flown to me in the night like my superman. After dinner, we went back to my apartment and I was able to sleep in his arms for a few hours before he got in the car and headed back home.

The next morning, I left Ontario caucus ten minutes early and made the five-minute walk to Parliament Hill to see the PM. We had maybe three minutes together, which, at this point, was about as much as I could handle and felt like more of my time than he deserved.

As frustrated, outraged and demoralized as I was by the entire Bernier/media episode, I was more frustrated, outraged and demoralized by the lack of response from my own political party. Even if they wanted to keep their distance from me—the woman who had raised the topic of white privilege—someone should have defended our budget's investment in the Black community. It would have signalled that it wasn't only "the Black woman" who was offended and rejected Bernier's views, but that the entire government was. If they even briefly glanced at the comments bombarding my feeds, they would have seen that they were under assault too.

Before Black community members started to write letters, no one from the party or the PMO had called me to see how I was doing or if I needed support. I knew that at different times they had reached out to other members, Iqra Khalid for one, who were experiencing issues and threats, but not to me. I mentioned before that one of the rules I try to live by is "If you don't ask, you don't get." And it's true, I didn't ask for their help. I accept full responsibility for this. But when did I have the time to ask? Why did I even need to ask when I was dealing with a public outpouring of hate visible on the internet, trying to insulate my family from it all and continue to handle my job?

In my most cynical heart of hearts, I figured that the party hadn't extended a lifeline to me because someone somewhere had done the political calculus, and figured that their majority was secure in the next election (though no one in politics is able to foretell the shit that's going to come down in the future!). As a consequence, they decided they didn't need to defend the apparently controversial MP of a riding they didn't need to win. And, given that I didn't hold my tongue when it came to Liberal failings either, maybe they wouldn't mind if I didn't come back to the House of Commons.

Still, all the vitriol was also affecting my role as parliamentary secretary to the international development minister and the organizations that counted on me to support their work. Whenever I posted about a development organization or project, the trolls and bots would flood their timelines with racist and sexist comments too. No matter what they thought of me, shouldn't the party have wanted to shut that down as fast as possible? It felt like I was the only one worried about how the fire I was drawing on a regular basis was affecting the ministry. When, in September 2018, I received a call from the PMO extending my term with International Development, they seemed completely surprised when I said no.

I easily resisted attempts by a few people in the PMO to persuade me to stay, but then Jane Philpott called. I was tickled. Jane, who had been shuffled from one increasingly difficult ministry to another in Cabinet, was often the person the Liberals called upon when they needed a tricky situation handled. I loved Jane. She was not only a colleague, but a confidante. Smart, empathetic and humble—she was everything you would want in a minister of the Crown. "Jane, don't you have anything better to do than call me?" I said, when I picked up, and laughed. "Quit doing their dirty work. You know why I am saying no." She could not disagree, given that she knew what I had been going through. I told her, though, that she could tell the PMO they didn't have to worry about one thing, at least—I was not going to disclose my frustrations and why I was leaving.

On the morning in September 2018 when the new list of parliamentary secretaries was released with my name not on it, the prime minister asked to meet with me in my riding after he made a funding announcement at Ontario Tech University in Oshawa. He asked me why I resigned, and, as usual, I was blunt: "I resigned because you did not value me enough to give me a simple phone call or ask a member of your team to find out if I was okay." One phone call from anyone in the PMO at the height of the Bernier controversy—it didn't have to be him—to say that they saw me. A call to say that they understood that the community I represented in Whitby was 70 percent white and to offer their help to fix this attempt to mischaracterize me as a racist. A call to say that they wanted to support a member of the team who was facing the full force of political backlash, a backlash that was spilling over onto the ministry I was supposed to serve. A call to say that they valued the work I was doing.

The prime minister responded that no one called because I did not ask for help. Then he said that I was such a strong, independent woman, he didn't think I needed it.

Right. A strong Black woman like me, with a big mouth like mine, wouldn't possibly need help; we were all so fierce and scary.

At that point, it became abundantly clear that the awareness I was trying to bring to the rest of the country about microagressions and racism had not registered with my own organization or its leader. The prime minister's experience, largely shaped by his privilege, blinded him to how completely inappropriate his comment was. (When the whole controversy over his dressing up in blackface emerged in the 2019 election campaign, I thought I should have seen that one coming.) I didn't even try to correct him.

After this encounter, I decided I needed to give an interview to someone I trusted about why I'd left the role with International Development. That person was Charelle Evelyn, the managing editor of the *Hill Times*. When I first saw her in the press gallery, I thought I was seeing things. People of colour were so rare in the gallery that spotting a Black woman had me looking around to see if anyone else saw her too. Maryam Monsef caught my eye, pointed to the gallery and smiled, confirming that, in fact, Charelle was real. I was careful in the interview to keep my promise to Jane, dropping only hints as to why I'd turned down the offer to stay on. In her piece, Charelle wrote that my decision to leave had been "brewing for some time" and quoted me saying that I found it difficult to leave because it was a job that I "thoroughly enjoyed." I described my resignation as the "smartest, most strategic decision for me and my family at this time," but I did mention that the "constant need to analyze and second-guess oneself gets exhausting." Anyone reading closely, and with some knowledge of me, would know that I was referring to the microaggression and racism I experienced within my own party.

But a bigger seed of doubt had been planted by my most recent interaction with the prime minister. I'd left the role of parliamentary secretary, but did I actually want to stay on in politics or with the Liberal Party? I was unsure. The past three years had been amazing in terms of the work I was able to accomplish, but my desire to do the job right meant I continually had to challenge attitudes in my own party. Fighting the opposition was one thing, but fighting Liberals was something I did not want to have to do.

On November 14, 2018, I noticed that my schedule for the day included a lunch with an elder Black woman, a former politician I'd met only once before. She'd requested a chat. The next election was a little less than a year away and I was excited about meeting her and receiving the wisdom she would surely impart to a younger Black female politician who had made some noise on behalf of the community and, as a result, had been publicly tossed and turned in the political arena.

We met at a coffee shop in Whitby. After the necessary pleasantries were out of the way, she leaned in and I did too. But what she had in mind wasn't a cozy session in which she would praise me for my accomplishments as a newbie politician and encourage me to keep the faith. No, her message was that if I wanted to remain a member of the Liberal Party of Canada and run in the 2019 election, I needed to "figure out what type of Liberal I was going to be." I was shocked.

She went on to explain. My rebuke of Bernier, she said, was actually a "mark" against me, because in that kind of situation, where the issue was racism, the old adage that "all publicity is good publicity" did not apply to me. That was not all. The first mark against me, she said, was criticizing the prime minister when he'd said that the 2015 Cabinet looked like Canada.

I felt like I'd entered the Upside-Down-from-*Stranger Things* version of Sally Walker's office. I needed to straighten her out. I told her that I had been right to criticize the Cabinet because it did *not* look like Canada, and I would do the same again. I wanted to ask her if she had nothing better to do for the past three years than to tally up the "marks" against me. I restrained myself, but she had even more digs to get in before she gave me the bill for lunch.

She told me that my impact in government had been minimal at best, that I could have had greater impact if I had been friendlier with people in the Prime Minister's Office, and that I would regret the bridges I had burned. Fuck me. I just wanted to get out of there. But I stayed put. No matter how painful it may be to listen to your elders, you do. Patiently and respectfully. More or less.

"I may not have had the impact you had when you were minister of . . . what were you minister of again?" I finally said. I went on before she could answer. "But rest assured that if even one person feels less alone, more resilient or walks with their Afro puffs a little higher because of what I have done while I was here, it has been more than worth it. And I know for sure that more than one person feels this way, and that is all that matters."

I paid that bill, then made sure that no one in my office submitted it as a reimbursable expense. I did not want any more Canadian tax dollars spent on this former politician. I did not want me, or anyone else, to owe her anything.

After that lunch, I wrote the following on Facebook:

Today I had a conversation with someone I truly respect. However, I left the conversation feeling hurt and misunderstood, and I wanted to share some of my thoughts.

When we use the hashtag #AddWomenChangePolitics, it means that when you add women, things will change. However, this can only be true if the women you add are willing to be the change they wish to see; otherwise you have #AddWomenMaintainTheStatusQuo.

I recognize, quite clearly, that I am not your typical politician. I speak my mind (sometimes to my own detriment—human beings do that from time to time), I am transparent (my constituents get what they see) and I am willing to have the uncomfortable conversations that many will shy away from. I am not afraid, and I will not be held hostage by votes.

I also recognize that I represent the Liberals. However, I was not elected by the Liberal Party of Canada. I was elected by the people of Whitby, and it is to the people of Whitby that my allegiance lies. Clearly, based on the conversation I had today, some do not like that, and I am totally cool with it.

At the end of the day, I am here to serve the various communities I represent, which are all contained within Whitby. Women, men, people of all ages, dispositions, races, religions and ethnicities, marginalized populations, people who feel disenfranchised by the political process, etc. They all live in Whitby, and as such, I represent each with passion and vigour.

I do things differently. Sometimes it is not about right or wrong, correct or incorrect, it is just different. I will leave you with this. On David Letterman's Netflix show, *My Next Guest Needs No Introduction*, Barack Obama says that, "Part of the ability to lead doesn't have to do with legislation or regulations, it has to do with shaping attitude, shaping culture [and] increasing awareness." I hope that my contributions to politics, thus far, have helped to move the needle in that direction.

If we want politics to change, we may have to change how we do politics.

Love and hugs,

C.

Nina Simone's song "You've Got to Learn" will be playing during this scene in the Netflix biopic of my life. I'd learned to show a happy face and to pocket my pride, but I'd also learned "to leave the table when love's no longer being served."

I was at a point in my life where I finally understood how valuable I was. Not just to the Liberal Party and politics, but to my community and family. If you do not understand how valuable you are, you will always accept what is given to you. One of the first rules of business is that you should never accept the first offer. It is a hard lesson to learn because most of us are grateful to have received any offer at all. In the workplace, however, the first offer is usually the lowball one—the place the employer starts so that when you counter, you will reach a mutually amenable deal. But how do you know what to offer as a counter? We (meaning women in particular) are often humble people who find quantifying our skills and experience—our worth—daunting. But you need to make the effort. And you need to ask, of any situation in your life, are you getting as much out as you are putting in? Are you getting more? Are you getting less? Friends, lovers, community service, even reading this book—is it worth your time?

If you are not getting as much out of any of them as you are putting in, it may be time to walk away. This is one of the hardest lessons I've learned. But, once I was able to understand my worth, and the value I bring to other people, it became easier to love myself more, create and nurture lasting and loving relationships, and also to walk away when love was no longer being served.

thirteen

AN INDEPENDENT WOMAN

AS I WRITE THIS, TRYING to identify the patterns in what was a chaotic and overwhelming period of my life, it may sound like I had perfect insight at all times about what was happening to me in Ottawa.

Not at all. In the moment, any flashes of clarity were quickly clouded by the insidious nature of acts of racism, sexism, microaggression and other forms of discrimination. They creep into the crevices of your mind in a way that makes you feel like you are going crazy. Somehow, as it had with Bernier, the onus of the act falls on the victim, while the culprit slides away. *Did that just happen? Did anyone else hear what that person said to me?*

I had never felt so much like a "woman," a "Black person" and a "Black woman" until I entered politics. I tried to address this, even to make light of it, in speeches, where I'd look down at my chest and exclaim in mock-surprise, "Oh my, I have boobs!" I'd hold out my hands, and stare at them, saying, "Oh my, I am Black too." But I found it hard to articulate the reasons for the deep, underlying discomfort I felt for most of those four years I was in Ottawa. I've recounted some of the events that felt like explicit assaults, but it was so much more than that.

In an issue of *Variety* published in April 2019, I read an open letter to the CBS television network from Whitney Davis, a Black former executive at the company who at first had pursued a journalistic and then a creative role at the network, but ended up working as its director of entertainment diversity and inclusion. The final episode that sparked her resignation was a large-scale investigation into the company culture that had allowed the former CEO, Leslie Moonves, to get away with sexual harassment and exploitation of female employees for years. Two outside law firms were hired to interview hundreds of staff, Davis among them, and they had given her the impression that their exploration of the company's toxic culture would be wide-ranging. She cooperated fully, happy that at last there was a safe place in which she could detail the casually accepted racism that, in particular, permeated the creative side of the business. She hoped for real change, and when real change was denied—Moonves was let go, but none of the other toxic cultural issues were addressed—she got out of there. But leaving wasn't enough; she felt she had to go public with her own experiences because that might be the only way to pressure CBS to address what she called its "white problem."

The examples in her open letter were so familiar to me I felt myself inadvertently nodding at each one. Even the denial of her experiences by the culprits she called out was familiar to me. Davis's letter helped me name for myself the ways in which the mind games caused by racism are both powerful and debilitating. Her truth allowed me to come to terms with my own.

Despite its lip service to the value of diversity and the diverse viewership it counted on for its success, CBS was not a diverse workplace. Neither was our federal bureaucracy. I could understand the lack of diversity in the House. Becoming an MP required a person to agree to run, seek the nomination, be the candidate and

224 · CAN YOU HEAR ME NOW?

then win the election. There were a lot of factors that were outside of one's control.

But hiring within the federal system was a much more straight-forward, manageable process. Though I knew there were more than enough qualified Black people to fill these positions, when I looked across the federal departments for Black faces, I saw none in the senior positions of deputy minister or assistant deputy minister. In fact, since confederation there had only ever been one Black ADM and four Black heads of mission; the first Black woman was appointed to that role in 2018. Additionally, although there is no tally of the number of Black-owned businesses with procurement opportunities with the Government of Canada, I would bet that those numbers are negligible too. Was it only me, or did the government that touted diversity as a strength have a "white problem"?

Davis described how when she and another young Black woman held the two lowliest positions in the CBS newsroom, their white colleagues couldn't keep their names straight. She wrote it off to the fact that she and the other Black woman were not important enough for anyone to take the trouble to remember. She figured it was more about status than race, and it likely happened to young white people in junior positions too. But when she and her boss were the only two Black people working at the executive level in the entertain-ment division—their brief: diversity and inclusion issues and talent-spotting to try to rectify the "white problem"—other executives still couldn't tell them apart.

I, too, had run into people who could not remember if I was me or some other political Black woman. I got mixed up with Mitzie Hunter, for instance, who was the only other dark-skinned woman in Canadian politics during my mandate. The context should have been a clue: she was an Ontario MPP (provincial not federal) rep-resenting Scarborough-Guildwood (not Whitby) who worked in

Toronto (not Ottawa). Not to mention we looked nothing alike. Still, colleagues greeted me as Mitzie on multiple occasions. One man addressed me two or three separate times as Mitzie, even though I corrected each of his mistakes. Once a Liberal colleague tagged me in a photo on social media at an event "we" had attended. I wouldn't have given it much thought, except I did not attend the event. It was Mitzie, not me! Davis wrote, "I don't think most people understand just how demeaning these daily micro-aggressions are. Or maybe they do and don't care." I could not agree with her more.

I want to include one more example from Davis, who described what happened after a senior producer used the "n" word in front of her. When she reported it to her boss, he told her she needed to grow a "thicker skin." Thicker skin? We are Black women. We were born with thick skin.

Our strong reaction to such slurs, and to other racist, sexist and homophobic behaviour towards us and others has nothing to do with the thinness of our skin and everything to do with how the system treats us and dismisses us. Do people think that the Black women who succeed against the odds and ascend to the heights could possibly have thin skin? From the day we're born, our mothers tell us that we have to be twice as good as the other children. My mother in particular was relentless on this subject. We have to work twice as hard and be twice as smart. Everything we do needs to be doubled because we have two strikes against us already: we are girls and we are Black. We can't afford to be thin-skinned. This is the reality of growing up Black.

In sharing her experience, Davis helped make real all the things I still worried were figments of my imagination. Her story spoke to me, and let me know that my experiences were not made up, but accurate reflections of my time in politics. These are not experiences shared by a few, but by many people of colour. Those in power and authority, who are usually white and male, can make us feel that the way we are experiencing their oppression is invalid. They can make us feel that we are too sensitive—that we are just taking "things" the wrong way. We are supposed to get over it, move on and stop making such a big fuss. But we are not the problem. We really aren't.

There are a few more twists and turns in my political journey still to share. Just as I was wrapping up work on this book, teasing out the final thoughts I had to share, I came across a graphic that struck me dumb. It was called "The 'Problem' Woman of Colour in the Workplace," and it described the beginning, middle and the end of my life as an MP so clearly it took my breath away. What I experienced is actually so commonplace, an artist was able to make a step-by-step roadmap out of it. (The version I saw was adapted by a Quebec NGO, the Centre for Community Organizations, with permission from the original source, a US-based human rights organization called Safehouse Progressive Alliance for Nonviolence.)

In it, a woman of colour lands in a workplace where the leadership is white. Everyone is pleased with themselves over her hiring and the woman herself feels "welcomed, needed, and happy." Then a phase called "reality" sets in as she begins to see and then to point out failings and issues inside the organization. She's careful to "work within the organization's structures and policies" even as she "pushes for accountability." After all, she wants to keep her job and keep doing the work she was hired to do.

No, none of those things are happening here, the leaders respond, and even if they are, surely he's the one with the insight to fix them. How can they be asked to correct something they can't perceive? They look around for support that they are blameless and in that effort "People of Colour are pitted against one another."

Next comes the retaliation phase in which the organization decides that really the only problem they have is her. The organization "targets her" but claims they are doing so because "she is not qualified or 'not a good fit.'"

Exit, woman of colour.

I wish I'd seen that graphic before I waded into January 2019. It might have made what followed a little more comprehensible and, because of that, a little less painful to live through.

I was completely surprised when the Speaker of the House asked me to deliver one of the toasts at his annual Robbie Burns dinner at the end of January. I wasn't Scottish. I had no romantic attachment to Canada's colonial history. I wasn't much of a fan of Burns, a white man who was a womanizer and got away with things that most people of colour, especially Black men, would not be able to get away with and keep walking around with their skins intact. But my audience would be Cabinet ministers, MPs from across all parties, and some of the Ottawa elite, and I couldn't resist the opportunity.

When I got up to deliver the ritual toast called "the Reply to the Laddies" (after Jane Philpott had toasted the poet himself and Rob Nicholson had finished his address to "the Lassies"), in true Celina fashion, I spoke about white privilege, race and the toll of being a woman of colour in politics. At the time, I didn't know the story behind Jody Wilson-Raybould's recent move to Veterans Affairs, just that both she and Jane Philpott had new portfolios. But, after detailing all of the women Robbie had slept with and all of the children they bore as a result, I made a crack about the shuffling of two prominent women ministers. "All of his penile philanthropy leads me to believe that Burns may not have just been his last name, but also the feeling you got when you lay with him," I said, then joked that Jane, on account of her medical practice, must know all about that feeling, and might have also felt a bit of a burn at being moved three times over the course of three years into increasingly difficult portfolios. "Speaking of Jody Wilson-Raybould," I continued, "if Robbie Burns was a member of our government, she would have been asked to remove him from our Parliament, not just our caucus. . . . If she didn't succeed, she would have been fired. And if she succeeded in removing Robbie Burns from Parliament, well, she would have been fired. You can't have an Indian doing that to the white man." That was close to the bone, but the PMO had always been eager to point out that Wilson-Raybould was the first Indigenous woman to hold the position of minister of justice, yet had just moved her to Veterans Affairs in what everybody viewed as a demotion, replacing her at Justice with a white man.

I realized there was a lot more behind her move than I'd guessed when, after my speech, the press started to hound me for details they assumed I had to know—forgetting what else they knew about me, which is that I had resigned as a parliamentary secretary four months earlier and likely wasn't in good standing with the PMO. On the scent of the SNC-Lavalin story, they dissected my speech for clues, and even criticized me for withholding the truth when I told them I had no idea what they were talking about. To me, it was just another day in the life of a woman of colour. You do something wrong and you are reprimanded. You do something right and you are reprimanded. I did not know about the issues with Jody and the prime minister. Until that point, I'd barely spoken with her. In my speech, I'd simply stated the truth as I knew it, not knowing how true it was.

Within weeks, the story broke that Wilson-Raybould was moved from the post she'd held for three years because she refused to intervene in a criminal case involving the Quebec-based global engineering firm SNC-Lavalin. In a statement, she indicated that she had come under "consistent and sustained" pressure—including veiled threats—from the PMO, the Privy Council Office and the finance minister's office to halt the criminal prosecution and that she was moved from her portfolio when she did not agree to do so.

After she went public, the *Globe and Mail* reported that some Liberal colleagues were displeased with Jody for her lack of discretion and had anonymously attacked her character, painting her as someone who was not a team player. That angered and appalled me. In those few weeks of the SNC-Lavalin scandal, I posted messages on Twitter like little breadcrumbs, leaving a record of events. On February 10, I tweeted, "As someone on the inside, who knows @Puglaas, I can tell you that she is fierce, smart and unapologetic. When women speak up and out, they are always going to be labelled. Go ahead. Label away. We are not going anywhere. #IAmWithHer #StandUp #ISeeYou."

In the era of #MeToo and #TimesUp, the Liberal Party had positioned itself as the party that would "believe her." Liberals liked to portray themselves as the ones who stood by women when they disclosed interactions with others that caused them to feel pressured or uncomfortable or victimized. I believed in that principle, just as much as I believed Jody. So it was easy for me to publicly support her when other members of the party were turning away. I found it interesting that the party would "believe women" when it was convenient for them and leave them when it wasn't.

By this point, I knew that I would not—should not—run again, but the guilt of leaving a job I was good at, and people I cared about, made the decision torturous. Even though, at my regular riding town halls, we argued about various issues colourfully, I knew that the people of Whitby respected me as their representative and I respected them. They appreciated me as a straight-shooting MP who didn't bullshit or play favourites. Everybody who came into my office was sure to get the truth from me. I was not going to shoo them away, saying that I would "take their concern under consideration." There was nothing to consider. Either I was going to do something about it or I wasn't. Still, even when I wasn't going to take on their issues, I tried to make sure that a constituent or stakeholder never left my office feeling badly. I would take the time to map out ways to make their idea better, present some other options for their consideration, and leave the door open for future meetings. But I also made it clear that I would not sit still for abuse because I was afraid to lose their vote. You could not come into my office or approach my staff in a hostile or belligerent manner. You would be shown the door or hear a dial tone. The fact that a voter was paying my salary with their taxes did not give them the right to treat me or my people with disrespect. I loved each and every member of my team and I panicked at the thought that some of them might no longer have a job.

I told my husband and a couple of close associates first. They supported my decision not to run, but when I added that I was considering sitting as an Independent MP for the rest of my term, they thought that would be a bad look for the party. With much hesitation, I agreed; I supported many of the government's overarching policies and initiatives, and I did not want to undermine those if I could help it. My Ottawa staff advised that I should do the PMO and the chief government whip the courtesy of informing them of my decision before I made it public. Again, I agreed, and on the morning of February 12, 2019, I sent a note to each man's office.

I was startled to receive an immediate call from the PMO to say that the prime minister wanted to speak with me later that day. As if I had not learned anything over the past three years, I thought he might want to say that he was truly sorry to hear that I was not running again, and ask me to reconsider. But February 12 was also the day Jody Wilson-Raybould resigned from Cabinet. When Trudeau called at nine-thirty that night, it was to tell me that he wanted me to wait to make my announcement because the news that I was leaving his caucus and politics would adversely affect him—he "could not have two powerful women of colour announce they are leaving at the same time."

I responded as carefully as I was able. I said, "I hope you can appreciate, not today, or tomorrow or a year from now, the impact that the past year has had on my family. Again, not today or tomorrow, but at some point."

With those words, the prime minister lost it. "Oh my God, Celina. Oh my God. I can't believe that you are telling *me* to understand!" He insisted I should appreciate *him* for supporting me in the by-election. He pretty much yelled that he was tired of people reminding him of his privilege, and ranted on about how he and his family had also been affected. I had put my phone on speaker, as I usually did when I was having work conversations at home. Vidal was within earshot, and as Trudeau spoke, he could see me growing tense, and he was too. I started to pace the living room, the only safe space for me to move in the house we'd just moved into. (We were in the middle of major renovations, the floors torn up and walls knocked down, fixtures sheeted in plastic.) The more Justin spoke the angrier I got. I started to pace up the stairs, through the construction zone, back down the stairs and into the living room, again and again.

The manner in which he was speaking to me took me back to my childhood, when my mother would correct me forcefully for behaviour I didn't think was wrong and I would take it because I had no other choice. I let him rant away. But when he was done speaking, I made him understand that I was not a child he could correct, or even the Celina he had "helped" in the by-election. I was not taking this from him. "Motherfucker, who the fuck do you think you are speaking to?" I slammed the words in his ear so hard, I am sure that everyone in the room with him heard me.

Good grief. I've heard that people who swear are very smart. By the end of my monologue, I'd dropped the f-bomb enough times to make me a fucking genius. Why should I be grateful? I'd worked my ass off in his government for three years. I hadn't even raised the issue of his privilege with him, though now I pointed out that I was well aware that his family had paid a price for his political ambitions, but his had RCMP protection, whereas mine had none, even though both families had received death threats.

The next thing I heard from him was a tearful apology.

I had no time for it. "Are you done?" I asked. He mumbled something inaudible. "Good!" I responded, and hung up the phone. Vidal and I stared at each other for a moment in shock. Did I just use a dictionary full of expletives with the leader of a G7 country and then hang up on him? Better fuckin' believe I did. But Vidal knew that we needed to be calm and think about the situation. He said, "You are not going to like what I have to say, but I think you should honour his request, and wait to make the announcement." Vidal slept on the couch that night.

That phone conversation played and replayed in my mind for days afterward. I wondered if Scott Brison, the former president of the treasury board who had stepped down and out of politics a week earlier, had received a similar berating. From the way he'd looked in the news coverage of his resignation, I bet he hadn't.

Still, I wavered between Vidal's advice and my pride. In the end, I gave the prime minister a pass, deciding that I would postpone my announcement until March 2. I sent him a note to that effect the next morning. When I hadn't heard back from the PMO the following day—at least acknowledging my decision to postpone, if not expressing any appreciation for it—I left another breadcrumb on Twitter. "T-14 When you ask someone to do you a favour, and that favour is completed, be grateful and say thank you."

Within two hours, Brett Thalmann, the director of administration and special projects within the PMO, emailed. "Hey Celina, I wanted to make sure you knew that the PM did see your email from yesterday and appreciated it very much. Thank you for agreeing to delay the announcement. I was also hoping we could meet next week when you are back in Ottawa as I would like to get your advice on a few things. Can you let me know what times would work for you? I'd be happy to come to your office or we can meet at PMO. Whatever your preference is. Thanks again and I look forward to catching up with you in person."

I wrote back: "With all due respect, Brett, fuck right off." I had been giving the PMO advice for years, and nobody listened. Why the hell did they want to talk to me now? To tell me how to slam the door on my own ass as I left?

Bits of the PM's rant kept coming back to me. Even when you feel you are fully justified in losing your temper, somehow it seems necessary to replay the scene in your head, looking for where it could have gone differently. Now I remembered the long minutes he'd spent telling me about the work he had done for the Black community, including on the federal recognition of the International Decade for People of African Descent. He'd at last explained why I had not been included in the planning for marking the Decade. During the meeting in 2016 in which I'd flagged the Decade for him, I'd mentioned that I did not want to be "central" going forward. By excluding me, he insisted he had been respecting my wishes.

He was correct, sort of. What I had told him was that I did not want to be the one person in government speaking "for" Black communities. Communities have been speaking for themselves for years. When he'd asked me for my thoughts about how to proceed,

I advised him that the government should consult the community broadly—elders who had been doing this work for a long time, but also young people who needed to be engaged. He could establish community consultations, but he also needed to reach marginalized Black Canadians either by telephone or with an online survey. On February 15, I tweeted "Not central ≠ Excluded." Only he would know what I meant, if he happened to look, but Twitter had turned into my version of keeping a public record. I needed the record to show that Trudeau had made the decision to exclude me. I hadn't excluded myself.

On the evening of February 16, I received a phone message from a Liberal MP, panicked about a tweet he'd sent out that had called me a "penis." (Of all the words to use, *this* was the best he could come up with?) He called again on Sunday morning, and this time he got me. He wanted to apologize, he said. The tweet wasn't his fault. A friend of his had taken his phone and sent it. Really?

After he hung up, I posted, "All of a sudden everyone wants to have a conversation?? Calling me at 9:30pm on a Tuesday evening or 10:30am on a Sunday morning to play me like a fool is not a winning strategy. I. Am. Not. A. Pawn. In. Your. Game. Come correct or don't come at all. #NotToday."

My husband was not having it, either, and tweeted, "@MPCelina you have just proven that you are not a pawn, you are the Queen." We were both so tired of all the games and so relieved that I'd made the decision to leave politics. In one sentence, my husband promoted me from pawn to queen, enabling me to make any move I wanted.

I went to the next national caucus meeting on February 20, 2019, the following week intending to tell my colleagues that I wouldn't be running in the next election and that I had been thinking of withdrawing from the party to sit as an Independent as a head's up, and out of respect for them. I stood in line waiting for my turn at the microphone, listening to all the expressions of solidarity and support being extended to the prime minister over the SNC-Lavalin affair by the other MPs—it was now so bad his principal secretary, Gerald Butts, had been forced to resign a week earlier. My frustration must have been showing on my face because Frank Baylis, a first-time MP I respected who had also been an entrepreneur in the medical field, pulled me out of the queue to talk with me. Although he did not know about the phone call, he knew I was upset and unsure about staying on in politics, and I am sure he read my face in the way most Black men can when a Black woman is angry. He told me not to let the actions of the prime minister get to me. He reminded me that in caucus my role had always been to try to pull the team forward towards a goal, and I shouldn't stop now. I trusted Frank. A natural leader, he was so thoughtful that every conversation we had made me think more deeply myself. If he advised that I needed to calm down before I spoke, he was probably right.

I got back in line and when it was my turn, I told my colleagues that while I wasn't going to run again, I would stay a Liberal because the people in this room had taught me grace. I would stay a Liberal for the greater good of the team and for the grace that they showed me, which had allowed me to be bold and to speak up. More importantly, I would stay for the 37 million Canadians who sent us to Parliament to serve them.

During the remainder of the caucus meeting, I thought long and hard about grace, and about the ability to forgive and have compassion. I reviewed the events of the past few weeks, especially the pressure the SNC-Lavalin scandal had put on everyone in the room. When the meeting was done, I went to stand in another line, this one made up of MPs wishing for a moment of the PM's time. I waited patiently as other members shook his hand, gave him hugs and in other ways showed him that they were on his side. As I watched, I couldn't help but wonder if he had ever spoken to any of them the way he'd spoken to me. I also wondered if any of them had ever had cause to cuss him out in the epic fashion I had.

Finally, the others were gone and it was my turn. I knew the conversation would be awkward, but during the caucus meeting, the prime minister had talked about the importance of togetherness, of respect and of the value he placed on the team. Other MPs had spoken eloquently on these subjects too. I was sure that he, too, would want to put the telephone call behind us and move on.

"I know that our last conversation was not the greatest—"

The look on his face stopped me before I could finish the sentence. It told me that he had no time for me because he was angry. All the talk about team and togetherness applied to everyone but me. I did not know how to carry on in the face of that so I turned and left the room. It struck me forcibly as I walked away that this man held power and I did not know whether he intended to use it against me. What exactly did he mean when he'd said my decision to not run again would have "impact"? I was so disillusioned I felt sick.

I retreated to my desk in the chamber. On Wednesdays ahead of Question Period, the doors to the House of Commons didn't open until two o'clock, and the space was quiet. I needed that quiet to meditate and centre myself again. When Question Period started— the cameras rolling, media and spectators in their galleries—a figure crouched just behind me and whispered in my ear, "I am sorry. I should not have responded to you in that way after caucus."

Did he mean to make it right with these words? Why couldn't he at least say them to my face? Three years of dismissal, offensive behaviour and disregard worked against me even believing him. The tears I had been holding in since the end of the caucus meeting started to stream out. I left the chamber, found a quiet room, and collapsed.

Jane Philpott and Mark Holland, who represented the riding of Ajax, next door to my own, found me. Mark blurted that he wanted to help because I was not in "good shape."

Poor man. I yelled at him. "This is not about my depression," I said. "I am not crazy. You can't continue to treat me like this and then call me crazy. Jane, please tell him I am not crazy!" She did just that. She'd been standing up to the prime minister herself, in solidarity with Jody.

But I also realized that we were all accomplices in the prime minister's behaviour. Despite what I'd been thinking about grace and my previous wash of fellow feeling for my colleagues, we had all seen him verbally admonish MPs who expressed ideas in caucus that ran counter to his own. We'd made excuses for him or said nothing. When other Liberals felt that to best represent the people in their ridings they needed to vote against the government and then were removed from their duties in committee, we said nothing. When colleagues said that they were experiencing intimidation from fellow colleagues, we said nothing.

I thought about all the times I should have stood up for my colleagues, but didn't. It turned out I did not have enough strength to fight for my colleagues on the inside and for the Canadians I promised to fight for who lived outside the political bubble. I had to choose my battles, and fighting Liberals to save Liberals was not mine. I would need to forgive myself for this.

On the monitors in the room, we saw that, in the chamber, Jody Wilson-Raybould was standing on a point of order to explain why she had abstained from a vote calling for a public inquiry into the SNC-Lavalin affair. She indicated that she abstained because the vote had to do with her personally, and that she hoped that at some point she would have the opportunity to speak her truth. I drew strength from her words.

—

When I went home to Whitby that weekend, I plugged into the true source of my energy. I went to a couple of scheduled events in the riding, but spent the majority of my time with friends and my family. On Monday morning, February 25, I felt ready to return to work.

I caught the 7:15 train for Ottawa. I sat with an older couple who were just returning from a trip to the Galápagos Islands and a woman who owned a company in Belleville. We laughed together for the whole four-hour journey, exchanging stories about travelling and life. I told the couple they should write a travel blog and they told me I had to take a trip to Madagascar. I was sad to see them go when they got off in Smiths Falls.

In Ottawa, I dropped off my suitcase and looked at the schedule. I had Question Period, a couple of meetings and then a panel for CARICOM's Day on the Hill, to discuss the legacy of Caribbean-Canada relations. I scanned the panel details for the questions the moderator would ask so I could prepare my thoughts. It was then that I noticed that the prime minister was going to attend. I immediately felt sick and rushed to the bathroom. After I rinsed my mouth, I texted my assistant to ask her to confirm that the PM really was attending. She did, and he was. I then called the organizer, Sherry Tross, the high commissioner of St. Kitts and Nevis, and asked her for more specific details. We had votes scheduled that evening, so there was a chance I would miss the PM. No, she said, even if I left early, the PM and I would cross paths on the stage. I thanked her and hung up, my chest even tighter and my stomach now in knots. I put my coat on, grabbed my bag and walked to West Block. I thought I would sit in the chamber for a while before Question Period, but as I took my place, I was immediately overwhelmed. I felt just like I had the previous Wednesday. I texted Jane Philpott and she met me in the government lobby, adjacent to the

House. She took one look at me and told me to head back home. I was on the 2:30 p.m. train.

The next day, I scheduled a video call with my psychiatrist. I knew if I waited too long to talk with him, I would go into that dark place I wanted with all my heart to avoid. In advance of the call, I'd provided him with a breakdown of all that had happened to that point. I had also taken the time to call some of the white male colleagues who had decided not to run in the next election and asked them what it had been like for them to break the news to the prime minister. All of them said that he had treated them well. One went so far as to say that the "easiest part of the entire decision was talking with the PM."

I asked my psychiatrist why he thought there was such a difference in the way the PM had reacted to me. Maybe, my psychiatrist said, the prime minister felt that a white man leaving politics was part of the regular course of things, whereas a Black woman leaving reflected badly on him as a leader. Thinking back, that is more or less what Trudeau had said to me. But my psychiatrist didn't think the prime minister was driven by political considerations—which is how the PM had framed it to me. He called it discrimination. That was powerful to hear. He also suggested that I should think about why the PM had knelt behind me to whisper his second apology. Could it be that in his eyes I now had enough power that he was afraid to look me in the face? That all the hard experiences I had been through had made me strong? He advised me not to have any communication or contact with the prime minister except in public places when I couldn't avoid it, and he told me I should stop thinking I could "fix" the relationship by trying to be reasonable. There was nothing reasonable about the situation I was in.

When I got off the call, I felt better. He'd confirmed everything I was feeling and reassured me that I wasn't "crazy" to feel it.

Echoing what Serena Williams said in her recent Nike commercial, which I'd watched on the train ride home and tweeted about as soon as I finished it: "We feel crazy, second guess ourself, underestimating our power, and make changes to satisfy the fragile ego. Show them crazy. #mood." I was tired of appeasing fragile male egos in politics. Racism and sexism undeniably exist on Parliament Hill.

Though I'd left my trail of breadcrumbs on Twitter, I had not told anyone save for my closest circle about my recent interactions with the prime minister, and I announced my resignation publicly on March 02, 2019 as promised without mentioning the PM's reaction. Little did I know that Jane Philpott, one of Justin Trudeau's most trusted ministers, would announce her resignation from Cabinet on March 4, 2019, citing a lack of confidence in the prime minister's handling of the SNC-Lavalin affair. So, three days after Jane's resignation, during what was supposed to be a speech of contrition to the country over the scandal, the prime minister said, "I believe real leadership is about listening, learning and compassion. . . . Central to my leadership is fostering an environment where my ministers, caucus and staff feel comfortable coming to me when they have concerns."

I could not believe those words were coming out of his mouth.

He went on to say that Jody Wilson-Raybould had never come to see him about her concerns about the SNC case. I went from incredulous to furious. If I were her, I would not have taken my concerns to the prime minister either. At that point, I felt I owed it to the electorate and my colleagues to correct the portrait he was painting of his leadership style. So I tweeted about the differences between how I was treated and how he claimed to treat his caucus and staff, and then I told my story to Laura Stone of the *Globe and Mail*.

The Ontario caucus met next on the morning of March 20, 2019, and the session was painful to sit through. My colleagues were focused on their disappointment with Jane's actions and they let her have it to the point of reducing her to tears. Most of them seemed to believe that the right thing for Jane to have done was to put her party above her principles. What happened to the idea that we were elected because we said we would do politics differently?

Every now and again, somebody would lump me into their tirade of disappointment. The charge against me was that when I called out the prime minister in public, I'd gone against the entire caucus. They did not want me there, any more than they wanted Jane. I realized in that moment that I didn't care what they thought. I still believed that the Liberal Party comes closest among all the federal parties to putting forth policies in the best interests of the people I was fighting to serve, but I could no longer be part of the herd mentality that party politics induces.

After Ontario caucus, I went directly to the Speaker's office and asked for a new seat assignment away from the government benches. I stayed there, keeping a low profile, until just before the afternoon Question Period session was to begin.

At two, I took a seat at my new desk in the far southwest corner of the House of Commons. I was shivering, not from cold but from nerves. It is one thing to know what to do and another thing to do it. And maybe sitting by myself in a far corner was just a little too close to my childhood of being seen and not heard when the adults gathered, careful not to draw any of the kind of attention that would lead to trouble. I kept my head down and tried not to make eye contact with anyone. I hoped that if I made myself as small as possible, for a little while nobody would notice that I had made the decision to leave the Liberal caucus and sit as an Independent MP.

Of course, members of the opposition soon clocked where I was sitting, but when they came over to offer their support, I shooed them away. I did not want to be alone, but I was not one of them.

The press gallery noticed too, and out of the corner of my eye I saw reporters staring down at me with interest from the balcony above. The news would be out soon.

Then Frank Baylis sat down beside me. "I am not going to let you sit here by yourself," he said. "You don't deserve this. You did so much for us and for Canadians. We needed to fight for you and we didn't. I will stay with you." Now I wanted to cry, but I had no energy left to make tears.

As I continued to sit in my corner, through that afternoon and evening marathon of votes on the 2019 budget, I had time to try to get used to my new situation and to reflect on how it had come to this. At least I hadn't waited to be kicked out of the party (which would happen to Jody and Jane two weeks later). I had deliberately taken my fate into my own hands, having realized how untenable it was for me to try to continue to speak up for my community, and myself, in this party.

As the news spread, messages started to come in on social media. One of them, from a constituent of mine called MJ, read: "I did not vote for you to be an Independent. Disappointed that you did not stick in the Liberal party. . . . Sorry times."

I tried not to respond, but the temptation was too great. "Sorry about that MJ. I appreciate the note."

The reply was instantaneous. "Well I am liberal in my way of approaching the world. So loyalty and sticking in the party would have been what I would have done. Can I share an example to give you food for thought: I am a catholic and of course right now the church has tremendous issues and changes to make. I am not leaving my way of faith over these changes. My hope is to make changes from within. I wish you the best but disappointed."

There was much to unpack in those few short lines. First of all, I'd had to stop going to my Catholic church in Whitby myself when

I stood up, with my Liberal colleagues, for a woman's right to choose, and also made clear that I was pro LGBTQ2+ and a supporter of medical assistance in dying. When the other parishioners protested my presence, and the presence of my family, I had to weigh my devotion to a religion that could not deal with all of me. MJ's chastisement actually reaffirmed my decision to sit as an Independent member. Sticking with the party for the sake of sticking with the party was not my way of doing business. It was absolutely not the way I wanted to represent the people who'd elected me. I'd had to choose whether to subordinate my values and principles to the party or do what I believed was right. Put that way, the choice was straightforward.

My decision to leave was about politics, but it was also about whether I thought it was worth it to try to keep navigating spaces that are not accustomed to including people like me. To survive in such places, we need to carve out our own niches, because we do not fit into the pre-designed and pre-defined boxes. We disrupt the narrative that underpins the rules by which we play. That takes work and, even when it totally wears you out, it still needs to be done. You need to be relentlessly strategic and smart, because you are so often working against the way "things have always been done."

I had worked diligently to advance issues that are often whispered about but not acted upon: mental illness, microaggressions, racism, equity and justice. I did not do this to be "a voice" for anyone— everyone has their own voice—but because I was conscientious about amplifying the voices of those who are often excluded from the political process—people who aren't dyed Liberal red or Tory blue or NDP orange or any other political colour. I was not going to dismiss the people who elected me to appease a party that disrespected me. If I'd stayed on as a Liberal, I would have had to settle. I would not have been able to look my children in the eye or carry on confidently acting according to my beliefs. MJ, who had reached out to remind me that it was important to be loyal, had reminded me, instead, that I should never settle.

My actions—in particular the interview I did with the *Globe and Mail* in which I spoke out about the PM's behaviour towards me—hurt many of my colleagues and supporters. That was not my intention. But my honesty shouldn't have surprised anyone. From day one in Ottawa, I rarely acted as a bobblehead who read the party lines verbatim. I used my own research and experience to complement the messaging, and came up with my own words as they pertained to the issue and to the people of Whitby. Why would I drink the party Kool-Aid when the world was flowing with great wine?

I was the exact opposite of the "Liberal" MJ identified with. Whether in a place of employment, a classroom, a community or a relationship, I believe we should never be expected to accept bad behaviour or stay put when we know we should leave.

I had embarked on a mission to be different in politics and do politics differently. Taking my place as an Independent was the realization of that mission—and marked my final realization that I have been independent all my life.

There is no time. Like the present. I changed this phrase and added the period in between because the past and future don't exist—we only have now. We only have the present.

As much as I have tried to live in the present, it does not come easy. I often find myself holding on to past hurts and thinking about next steps, all the while neglecting the present moment.

At the beginning of my political journey, I was challenged by the burden of responsibility. It was lonely. Very little in the space reflected who I was, or the contribution of people who looked like me to this country. I walked through hallways under the frozen glares of white men, most of whom seemed disgruntled to see me. A history of structural violence was baked right into Parliament's stones; the halls and offices and meeting rooms, even the House—our national symbol of democracy—made me feel strange and uneasy. Maybe in 2020 with people, including me and my children, having taken to the streets in spite of a global Covid-19 pandemic in order to protest anti-Black racism, we've moved the needle enough so that it isn't just the BIPOC community who understands what I mean.

There is a history of policy enacted and implemented by the Parliament of Canada that has made life difficult for people of colour, that has supported the creation of social institutions that prevented some of our citizens from meeting their basic needs, let alone fulfilling their dreams. I felt that history. I was acutely aware that the space was not made for me as I signed my name into history under the ornately framed picture of the Fathers of Confederation on the day of my swearing-in. I knew even then that it was going to be a long four years.

Then, after writing my first blog in the Huffington Post about my mental health issues, I started to realize that my burden was lessened whenever I used my voice to speak about uncomfortable issues. The heaviness was still there, but I started to understand that the burden of responsibility I was feeling was not a burden at all—it was an opportunity for me to embrace the present and use my position to stir the pot. I loved using my voice to speak about micro-aggressions, body shaming and systemic racism. It was my responsibility, I realized, to bring to the forefront of mainstream politics the whispered conversations people of colour, and in particular Black women, had at water coolers every day. I love my community, and I loved the ability to share their stories in a way that could take the burden off them, to help to create better schools, communities, work spaces and political institutions where we, too, can be comfortable. The community of women who walked with me and those that came before me had paved a way into that space. We are not going to create or build sustainable change for equity-seeking groups if we are constantly afraid to speak the truth. Most importantly, we cannot get to a place of reconciliation if we shy away from speaking truth to power.

CONCLUSION

SOMETIMES I WONDER WHAT WOULD have happened if I had kept my big mouth closed, settled politely into politics, and rode that wave all the way to the lifetime pension? Would I have minded people calling me "the Honourable Celina Caesar-Chavannes" for the rest of my life? Absolutely not. Would I mind that I would have had to call myself dishonourable because I had not stayed true to myself? Absolutely.

It was the right decision, but, still, I felt enormous sadness in the months that followed my decision to leave. Not regret—I still have no time for regrets. If I had never stood for office, I might not have learned how important it is to operate from a place of unapologetic authenticity. Politics led me to a place where I could at last use my voice. It reintroduced me to the three-year-old Celina who did not know what fear was. She loved herself, sang at the top of her lungs and didn't care what anyone said about her, her body or her voice, which cracked more often than it held a note.

But the challenge I knew I now faced was how to live like that for the rest of my life.

That's what I've been doing since leaving politics—digging into transforming myself from a fairly selfish, competitive and money-conscious entrepreneur into a person who cares more about people than titles, more about impact than rhetoric, and more about using my voice for good, and not about spewing pre-written platitudes from unfamiliar pulpits. How do I continue to act on what I learned?

How do you live your best life when you are unsure about what to do next? It's quite possible that I still don't know.

In August 2019, with just a few months to go before the fall election and the end of my tenure, I spent the day packing up my constituency office with the help of my staff. Just as I walked in the door at home, Stacey Berry, my trusted office manager, called. She had something to tell me, she said, and it had to be in person. This was odd, because during all the hours we spent packing up four years of our political lives, we'd spoken of all sorts of issues—except what was keeping me up at night: the thought of her and my other Whitby staff no longer having jobs.

When the people who worked for me in Ottawa found out in March that I was not seeking re-election, they'd easily moved on to other positions. My interns were all returning to school in September. Ang, who came out of retirement to join me in Whitby, could easily return to retirement. But the future prospects for Stacey and my immigration specialist, Christel Ilunga, were not clear. I'd hired Christel right after the 2015 election, and she had stayed by my side through the thick of it. After months of trying to find the right person to fill the job of constituency manager, I'd taken the advice of Margarett Best, a former minister with the government of Ontario, who had hired Stacey while she was in office, and given Stacey a chance. She was brilliant and detail-oriented, and knew exactly how to look after my interests and the work of the constituency. With Christel and Stacey in Whitby, I had never had to worry about a thing. I told her to come right over, and when she got to the house, we settled down in the front sitting room, full of late afternoon light. Maybe she had come up with a wonderful plan that would soon have us working together again. I wanted that too. But, no, what she wanted to deliver face-to-face was an answer she had heard to a prayer she had made for me.

"Your crown has been bought and paid for," she told me, quoting Maya Angelou, who herself was paying tribute to words by James Baldwin. "Put it on your head and wear it. You did your job, and you did it well. Now put your crown on and wear it proudly. What happens next will come. You do not have to chase it. You do not need to ask for it. You deserve it. Just be patient."

No surprise to those of you who have come this far with me: I burst into tears. I don't know if I was crying because of her telling me to wear my crown or at the thought of having to sit patiently until "the next thing" arrived. I am a go-getter. A doer. How could I stay resigned to doing nothing but wait for a revelation with a crown atop my head?

"So how long do you think I will have to wait?" I asked.

We both burst out laughing. There she was, eloquently, earnestly, relaying the message she received on my behalf from her God, and I was asking about the timeline. But she forgave me: Stacey knew how hard it was to put "Celina" and "patience" in the same sentence.

I needed a drink after that and immediately opened a bottle of champagne. Why? Why the fuck not? This was the end of something, and the beginning of something else, and even if I did put on my crown and wait, who knew when the answer would come and what it would be. I pulled some seasoned salmon out of the fridge and told Stacey to call Christel. If this was the end, we were all going to celebrate together. After Christel got there, we laughed, talked, cried, drank—well, Christel doesn't drink, but at least there was salmon for her to eat—for hours. To say that I love these two women is an understatement. They started as employees and became family, and now we were at the end of our road together. I had vowed long ago never to regret anything, but this came pretty damn close.

—

So here I was: forty-six years old, a mother of three, unemployed, Black and female. Don't get me wrong. I was content with my decision to leave politics, but in order to figure out what came next, I needed to take time to reflect.

One of the things I had to reflect on was how beautiful but rare those late summer hours of laughter and reminiscing with Stacey and Christel were. In my life to that point, and especially while I was in politics, I rarely called up girlfriends and asked for their help or got together to laugh, drink and eat, taking a time out from our struggles. Now the fact that I had never reached out to anyone struck me as sad. I had been so busy running through life that I hadn't taken the time to gather a village of such friends around me. Just as organizations select a board of directors to act as a sounding board and provide strategic direction, we, too, need a team of advisors to get us through the tough, the good—well, any kind of times. I had assumed that being independent meant being alone. But independence isn't synonymous with loneliness. I realized that in the times when I felt most lonely, I shouldn't have made so much effort to "protect my independence." I should have pulled those that I loved closer to me.

Maybe I had been too embarrassed to admit I needed help or arrogant enough to believe I could handle it best by myself. My inability to reach out might also have been related to the guilt and shame I felt for having never been part of any activist movement—I did wonder what right I had to ask the community to help me. For so long I had kept to myself to protect my secrets and my traumas; I know I feared that connecting with anyone on more than a superficial level would potentially expose me. The truth of it is that I could have connected more, across the board, in politics. There was actually no point in hiding my secrets. The effort just closed me off from others.

So, although I did have a lot of support—so clear during the #HereForCelina moment—I still felt alone. I let the idea of being the "only Black female member of Parliament" get in my head and form a protective barrier. While I *was* the only Black female in federal politics at the time, I was not the only Black female experiencing loneliness at work. There are countless "only" ones in the world, and if I'd sought them out, their experience could have helped to guide me through some difficult circumstances. Sitting and stewing in my "1-only-ness" just pushed me further into my own head, which was not a very stable place to be. Between my struggles with depression and anxiety and the battle to control my competitive drive to be better than others—to be the best—I had turned further in on myself. I think that's why Whitney Davis's open letter in *Variety* hit me so strongly: it was one of the first times I let someone else's experience breach the walls I put up around me. But I hadn't needed Davis's article to validate my experiences. Any woman of colour could have done that. Any person who has felt marginalized or "alone at the top" could have done that.

So what did I need help with? It wasn't any particular "thing." I was strong, and I was bold, and I could deal with most of the issues that came up. What I really needed to hear from others was some of the ways they navigated the darkness that precedes the unknown. The "unknown" happens every time we are about to do something daring, that moment when the butterflies in our stomachs are telling us that there is something to fear. Even now, each time I am asked to speak in public, the person introducing me finds a way to describe me, or my actions in business or politics, as "fearless." That is so untrue. I am even afraid in the moment before I go on the stage and for another few beats after I get to the microphone. My three-year-old self runs away and leaves me standing there trying to figure out my next move. Serves me right though. I never write my speeches. I either jot notes on a piece of paper a couple hours before the event, or in the car on the way, or I ask people when I get there what they're interested in, and wing it from there. Sounds dangerous, but once I'm over the fright, I thrive on it.

Every leap I took in business or every viral political moment involved some amount of fear—that feeling of standing on the edge of a cliff before you do something daring. Fear is crucial to our survival as human beings. Fear is necessary. I was not fearless, I just didn't allow fear to stop me from doing what needed to be done. Some of the time.

If I am perfectly honest, a combination of my fear and the exhilaration I felt in resisting the status quo has allowed me to accomplish a lot. I've already mentioned *Faces at the Bottom of the Well*, one of my favourite books. In it, Derrick Bell writes of a woman named Mrs. MacDonald who lived in the American Deep South during the Jim Crow era. She knew she could never defeat the racist power structures around her on her own. Engaging in small but persistent acts of resistance against them was her goal. Such acts add up. Whether it was changing the words in a speech to be more provocative or speaking out against racism, I made my own acts of resistance in politics, and I still do. On their own, none of my acts can change systems that have existed for longer than Canada has been a country, but I want to rattle the barriers at every opportunity. Each persistent and sustained act of resistance, each moment of defiance, attacks what Bell describes as the "permanence" of the racism and sexism that permeate our institutions. Understanding this reassured me that my time in politics had been valuable.

In every situation, I was motivated by the responsibility to represent my community—the people who looked like me and the ones who did not. People say that "representation matters." Seeing someone who looks like you in politics, in business, in academia—anywhere—helps you realize it's possible to get there too. However, if representation matters, the representative person sitting at the table needs to be fighting for something that matters to them. If nothing matters to them, why are they there? If they are not going to speak up for issues, why are they there? Especially in public office and public service, they should be vocal on important issues, pushing the powers-that-be to be bolder and advocating for interests that might be outside of their own but promote the greater good. If they don't, they should get out of the way and allow someone who will take their place. If they are only there for the title, the paycheque, the status or the photo op, how does "representation" really matter?

It took me a while to get my feet under me, but I finally realized that if I was going to be at the political table, I had to speak to the subjects that mattered to people in a meaningful way. I needed to be disruptive—in word, in action and in appearance—in order to get through to people and get them thinking differently about privilege, racism or mental health. For change to happen, lots of people need to be prodded out of their comfort zones, and I found I didn't hesitate to raise the uncomfortable topics.

My last act as an MP was to introduce Bill C-468, an act to amend the Employment Equity Act. It was designed to remove the barriers that had stood in the way of Black people rising to the top of the federal public service. In those dying days before the 42nd Parliament was dissolved, so much was deemed urgent that I thought it might not be possible to get the bill on the record. However, with the help of some Conservative colleagues, especially Colin Carrie and Opposition House Leader Candice Bergen, the bill was ready in a matter of weeks.

I rose in the House for the last time on June 20, 2019, and, from my spot beside Jody Wilson-Raybould, who had joined me in my independent corner and who seconded the bill, I thanked all involved. "I came to this place to be a voice for all the people

I represent, to raise awareness on issues, to move the status quo and to remove barriers," I said. "This bill represents the voices of those both past and present in the federal system. It is my hope that it will examine and help remove the barriers that prevent them, especially those from the Black community, from achieving success and promotion within the system. Their voices are reflected in this bill, and it is my honour to bring their voices to this place."

Although the bill did die on the order paper at the end of the term, I was satisfied to have placed the need for change on the record. In February 2020, after the Liberals were re-elected with a minority, both Bill Matthews, the deputy minister of public services and procurement, and Treasury Board President Jean-Yves Duclos announced their commitment to removing barriers and improving opportunities for Black employees.

In addition to growing my village, using my fear for good and representing what matters to me, I have needed to reinforce a couple more truths after I left politics. The first is that life is not a competition. There is no point in comparing myself to those who came before me or those who will come after me. I am my own benchmark. Trying to act like someone else is an exercise in futility if what you want most is to become a better person, to live authentically and to use your voice for good. The goal is to try to be the better version of you.

When young people say that they want to be me some day, I am quick to tell them that it is a terrible goal. "Set better goals," I say. "What is the point of aspiring to be me when I have been so candid about my failings? Create the best version of yourself by learning from your own failures, rather attempting to become a carbon copy of someone who already exists."

Politics had been a painfully beautiful experience—somewhat like childbirth, where you forget how difficult it was to the point of getting lured into doing it again. I appreciate that in a country of 37 million people, only a fraction of a percentage point of us have been members of Parliament; I am grateful for the honour and thankful for the experience.

I appreciate this even more now that I've taken the time to look inward, and to tell the story of my life over the past four-and-a-half decades. Every moment, I realize, was built on the previous one. Every success was built off a previous failure, and every joy heightened from previous pain. There have been times when I've questioned *everything* about myself, every decision I made and every action I took.

This year of self-reflection has been painful, too, but it was what I needed to do to end up here—to appreciate the impact of the awkward and painful moments and to dismiss the noise that resulted when I stood up for what I believed in.

I realize that some of my decisions may not be what others would have made. And that is okay. I stayed silent in the face of assault, just as I stayed silent in my first couple of years of politics, in order to survive.

The last truth I came to is that my journey does not have a destination (well, except the final one). There is no achieving an ultimate state of authenticity, any more than there is a final destination called "becoming a leader." When you define yourself as "the leader," you inevitably begin to defend your positions as if there is no other option, worried that if you respond flexibly to the demands of the day people may call you "inconsistent." The fallacy of believing that you have *arrived* at leadership or authenticity is that you risk turning away from the opportunity to learn in the moment, to change your position or your reaction to a given situation.

Many who have witnessed me trying my best to speak and act from an authentic place have asked me if being authentic "works" in business or in politics. That is a difficult question to answer, because authenticity is a struggle. Don't get me wrong. It is not a struggle because I don't know how to be authentic. That I do know! It is a struggle because authenticity is just as multi-faceted as the idea of leadership. I can't be always singing the one note. I need to take different approaches to the different situations and challenges that arise. So do we all. Some situations require us to be quiet. Sometimes we need to speak audibly and clearly. Other times we are required to shout and take to the streets.

Authenticity is a process of discovering how to use every part of you to make any given situation whole. This includes using your perceived weaknesses and flaws, the parts that embarrass or shame you. We often hide those parts and show the world only a portion of who we really are. That never works out in the end. I could not be anything different, even if I tried. I needed to embrace my anger, and the sound of my own voice, as much as I embraced the desire to do good—*in order* to do good—in the world.

From childhood, I realize, I was never sure if anyone could hear me no matter how noisy I was. Chasing this desire to have my voice heard, I have had ups and downs. That said, I have learned from the experience, and it is my hope that in sharing what I learned I can help transform lives, communities and our world, and strengthen our humanity by sharing our truths.

Before I entered politics at forty-one years of age, I let others or my circumstances define me, much as I wish that wasn't the case. Inside that political bubble in Ottawa, alone at night in my little apartment after daunting, desperate days, I was forced to re-examine everything about myself. To break all the hidden pieces apart and see what made me tick. To have had that long period of reckoning and struggle with my strengths and weaknesses, traumas, secrets and true sources of joy was what allowed me to survive one setback after another, and not just find success, but purpose.

Six years after I took my first train to Ottawa, I not only know who Celina is, but I appreciate her as well. Specifically, I appreciate the "flaws" that have allowed me to grow independent, resilient and authentic. For the first two years in politics, I was so afraid of being labelled an "Angry Black Woman" that I tried to be as polite as possible in order to fit into the "politician" mould. Those days are over. I have embraced all of me. And I won't look back.

On March 21, 2019, I looked out the window at the Ottawa streets and knew I had to leave them behind. But on that day, and every day thereafter, I have had to look in the mirror and face myself. I now see the reflection of someone who is not perfect, but has formed a more perfect union with her self. A woman who is not content with staying quiet, going with the flow and blending in, but who is outspoken, audacious and unique.

Can you hear me now?

ACKNOWLEDGEMENTS

I want to thank, especially, the people who came before me and the people in my lifetime who have given me so much, including the ability to speak confidently and unapologetically. To my ancestors, who had the wildest dreams I now live—thank you. My gratitude, also, to the confident women in my life, who inspire and tell the most wonderful stories, especially Cousin Marie, our family's griot. Thank you for believing in me and sharing my story. I appreciate you.

To those who think their ideas are too small, their voice too soft and who doubt their capacity to run, I will tell you what I tell the moms who approach me thinking they can't take politics on: don't sell yourself short. Think of how your skills in life could transform politics rather than how you need to transform yourself to fit the way politics are done. When you run a campaign, you need to manage different people on your campaign team, and manage the different personalities in your constituency. No one does this better than moms! We give different chores and responsibilities to our children based on their skills and abilities. We know that one child is going to feel like you're asking too much of them, while the other feels like they've been given too little responsibility because you don't believe they're old enough to help. This is the same as managing any team, but particularly a political campaign team of volunteers! Mothers know how to make their children feel included and important, and that their contribution to the family is valued.

Use those skills to run a political campaign. As well, every mother has that one child who likes her and will vote for her no matter what (that's my Johnny), one child who will vote for her, but will require some convincing (that's my Desiray) and one child who will like her, but will vote her off the island so fast her head will spin (that's my Candice). We all have the capacity to use the skills and experience we have to change the world. Let's do that.

I want to acknowledge those who believed in me even when I did not believe that this crazy idea of politics would work. My gratitude goes to the young people who dream of a better world and work towards that goal. To Brianne, Dilara, Jordyn, Onome, Olivia, Heba, Arezoo, Sydnie, Calille, Rhayelle, Raisha, Jaida and Alicia, and others who want to change the world, I will reiterate what I wrote in the first version of my resignation letter: "I also know that I have no right to ask what I am about to ask, but I will do it anyway. I am going to ask women, of all backgrounds to run, and run in packs. Get your girlfriends and their girlfriends and run like we have never run before. My experience in politics has demonstrated to me that there is capacity to change political structures from the inside, but only if we are there in numbers. The treatment I have received from the leadership in my own party is disappointing and regrettable, and I apologize for leaving before I had an opportunity to make any change, but I trust that women, especially women of colour and other Black women, who are way stronger and braver than I am, will finish this job. I know that our country will be better for it."

To those described as "voiceless" or in need of empowerment—often the poorest and most vulnerable among us—you do not need anyone to be your voice. You already have one. It may be a whisper that is ignored, but it exists. You also do not need anyone to *make* you empowered, you already are. You just need the right tools to maximize that empowerment. And most certainly, you do not need a McKinsey report to tell you that when women are given the tools to achieve their maximum potential they can add $12 trillion dollars to the global GDP. Or to tell you that, in the United States alone, the racial wealth gap will cost $1.5 trillion by 2028. This is the economic power of those often described as voiceless and lacking empowerment. Women, people of colour, Indigenous people, LGBTQ2S persons, people with disabilities, poor people and others on the margins of society: can you imagine what your collective strength will achieve when demanding social changes or challenging political will?

To the people of Canada, and beyond, your value is not determined by your title and leadership does not require a title. The power has always belonged to the people. It is time that people realize their power. It is not enough to hear my voice. We need to hear you, too.

INDEX

CELINA CAESAR-CHAVANNES is an equity and inclusion advocate and leadership consultant, and a former Member of Parliament who served as parliamentary secretary to Prime Minister Justin Trudeau and to the Minister of International Development et la Francophonie. During her political career, Celina advocated for people suffering with mental illness and was given the Champion of Mental Health Parliamentarian Award in May 2017 by the Canadian Alliance on Mental Illness and Mental Health. That year she was also named one of the Global 100 Under 40 Most Influential People of African Descent (Politics & Governance category) and Black Parliamentarian of the Year. After she stepped away from the Liberal Party to sit as an independent member in 2019, Celina was picked as one of *Chatelaine*'s Women of the Year. Before entering politics, she was a successful entrepreneur, launching and growing an award-winning research management consulting firm, with a particular focus on neurological conditions. Celina was the recipient of both the Toronto Board of Trade's Business Entrepreneur of the Year for 2012 and the 2007 Black Business and Professional Association's Harry Jerome Young Entrepreneur Award. Celina holds an MBA in Healthcare Management from the University of Phoenix as well as an Executive MBA from the Rotman School of Management. She lives in Whitby, Ontario, with her three children, and her husband, Vidal Chavannes.